ENCOMIUMS

Elio Petri was a great artist, a great director, a very great man of the cinema.
—Dante Ferretti

Through a mixture of expressionism, Brecht, and the bizarre, Petri's films brought together Marx and Gramsci, but also Freud and Reich. He dove into the world of dreams with Kafkian lunges and into the maze that divides being and schizophrenia.
—Jean A. Gili

Elio Petri, a lucid and honest intellectual, profoundly human, a courageous and genial director, a true friend.
—Ennio Morricone

The thing that struck me about *I giorni contati*, in fact, more than one thing. First: it places itself in a strange territory, actually still unexplored in Italy, halfway between realism and existentialism. Second: it risked looking for a cinema that was different from the cinema done in Italy up to that moment. I'm sure that *I giorni contati* influenced me somehow. It influenced me the same way that all the films I loved at that time did. I *wanted* them to influence me, and I wanted to be influenced by Elio's films.
—Bernardo Bertolucci

Elio Petri is the greatest Italian director of the past, the only Italian director who made ten films that were completely different from one another.
—Franco Nero

This book is essential for appreciating Elio Petri's films, & to truly understand the importance of "Italian political cinema" in the context of the bloody and lacerating contradictions of the political struggles in Italy during the 1970s. Inspiring the reader to understand and appreciate the man beyond his work, Petri's text is written by a true author, a polemical and modern moralist who took a stand against the compromising and mediocre mechanisms of Italian culture. This is also a book about solitude and society's incomprehension of an intellectual who strove to be different, along the lines of the worldview of Pier Paolo Pasolini. This text comprises all the eloquent writings of Elio Petri, driven by intelligence, by love, and by his sarcastic view of existence. These writings are, and always will be, a seminal reference for both scholars and cinephiles.
—Alfredo Rossi

WRITINGS ON CINEMA & LIFE

Elio Petri

Selected Other Works by Elio Petri

Roma ore 11

L'assassino. With Tonino Guerra.

Indagine su un cittadino al di sopra ogni sospetto. With Ugo Pirro.

La proprietà non è più un furto. With Ugo Pirro.

Scritti di cinema e di vita. Ed. by Jean A. Gili.

Chi illumina la grande notte

WRITINGS ON CINEMA & LIFE

Elio Petri

Edited by
Jean A. Gili

Translated by
*Camilla Zamboni &
Erika Marina Nadir*

Contra Mundum Press · New York

Writings on Cinema & Life
© 2013 Paola Petri
Translation of *Scritti di cinema e di vita* © 2013 Camilla Zamboni & Erika Marina Nadir
Introduction © 2013 Jean A. Gili

First Contra Mundum Press edition 2013.
This edition of *Scritti di cinema e di vita* is published by arrangement with Paola Petri. Originally published in Italy in 2007 by Bulzoni Editore.
"Brief Encounter" is published courtesy of NUOVI ARGOMENTI.

All Rights Reserved under International & Pan-American Copyright Conventions.
No part of this book may be reproduced in any form or by any electronic means, including information storage and retrieval systems, without permission in writing from the publisher, except by a reviewer who may quote brief passages in a review.

Library of Congress Cataloguing-in-Publication Data
Petri, Elio, 1929–1982

[Scritti di cinema e di vita. English.]
Writings on Cinema & Life /
Elio Petri; translated from the original Italian by Camilla Zamboni & Erika Marina Nadir; Edited by Jean A. Gili

—1st Contra Mundum Press Edition
454 pp., 7 x 10 in.

ISBN 9780983697251

   I. Petri, Elio.
  II. Title.
 III. Gili, Jean A.
 IV. Editor
  V. Introduction.
 VI. Zamboni, Camilla.
VII. Nadir, Erika Marina.
VIII. Translators.

2013930263

This book is dedicated to

Tonino Guerra

poet, screenwriter, artist

16 March 1920 – 21 March 2012

http://toninoguerra.org

Table of Contents

Jean A. Gili, **ELIO PETRI: ARTIST AND INTELLECTUAL** 0

1. "CITTÀ APERTA" (1957–1958)

1.1 The Germ of Hatred and Hope: Letter to Pietro Germi 4
1.2 Henri Beyle Says Thanks 14
1.3 The Lesson of *Calle Mayor* 22
1.4 Two-Hundred Thousand Lire (200,000 Lire) 30
1.5 It's Not a Stereotype 40
1.6 Italian Cinema: A Castrated Elephant 46
1.7 Death of a Writer: Notes for a Cheap Film 58
1.8 Elia Kazan: A "Boomerang" Conscience 66
1.9 "Straw" Intellectuals 86

2. THE DEBATE ABOUT ITALIAN CINEMA (1962–1982)

2.1 Questionaire: The Directors of the 1960s 98
2.2 Team Play and Individual Specialties 106
2.3 Crisis or Vitality? 112
2.4 Elio Petri Trusts Italian Cinema 120
2.5 For Whom Do We Write, for Whom Do We Shoot 124
2.6 You Reproach Us, but You Never Took Our Side 134
2.7 The Left is Indifferent to Our Cinema 144

3. "NUOVA CUCINA" (1980)

3.1 *Apocalypse Now* 154
3.2 *Ogro*: Bread and Omelettes, Hammer & Sickle 162
3.3 *Don Giovanni* or Boiled Meat *à la* Dionysos 168
3.4 Ex-hungry People Now Satiated in *Terrazza* 182
3.5 *La città delle donne* 192
3.6 *Kramer vs. Kramer* 204

IMAGES 214

4. COMMENTS ON HIS OWN FILMS (1976–1979)

4.1 Short Tracts on *A ciascuno il suo* and *Todo Modo* 248

Todo Modo

4.2 Interview with Jean A. Gili 260

4.3 Interview with Simon Mizrahi 276

Le mani sporche

4.4 The Plot of the Three Episodes 288

4.5 Short Notes, Preliminary Observations 296

5. ART CRITIQUE (1979–1982)

5.1 For Him, We Would Fight 326

5.2 The Report of the Onlooker 334

6. BRIEF ENCOUNTER

Brief Encounter 346

FILMOGRAPHY 362

BIBLIOGRAPHY 396

INTRODUCTION

Elio Petri:
Artist & Intellectual

First of all, I would like to explain the reason for this edition of Elio Petri's writings — I want to pay homage to the memory of a man who was very important to me. Petri was the only director with whom I developed a profound — almost fraternal — friendship. He was like a big brother to me, a brother who had a lot to teach and pass down.

Elio Petri (1929–1982) is known as a film director and as an artist, but his social and political engagement in the postwar years up to the beginning of the 1980s also makes him an intellectual. He was a man who reflected on his own work and on its relationship to the socio-political context of the time. In *Elio Petri: appunti su un autore*, a documentary on the director made in 2005,[1] Francesco Maselli defines Petri as a unique intellectual, "a man of culture and intelligence, passionate about the figurative arts," a man ready to question the cultural policy of the Italian Communist Party (PCI). He affirms that "[Petri] was more of an intellectual than any of us."

Petri participated in the debates that were agitating the country, using all the tools of theater — the grotesque, the expressionist form, and indirect discourse. Reading his book *Roma ore 11* (1956), it is immediately clear that he not only collected material to shoot a film, but he also conducted a true sociological investigation of the lower social classes of Italian society in the postwar years. He adopted the same perspective in preparing the screenplay for *Giorni d'amore (Days of Love*, 1954).

1. Federico Bacci, Stefano Leone, and Nicola Guarneri, *Elio Petri: appunti su un autore* (Milan: Feltrinelli Editore, 2006). Throughout the text, we will use [TN] to indicate notes that were added by the translators.

In this collection, I chose to include texts published in magazines that are now difficult to find, such as *Città aperta* or *Nuova Cucina*. I believe that Elio would not have wanted these writings to be lost. I hadn't yet met him when he was writing for *Città aperta*, but when he started to write for *Nuova Cucina* he would regularly send me the magazine. He wanted to be sure that someone would appreciate and save his articles and someday collect them in a volume. He sent me a photocopy of the last installment of *Nuova Cucina* since he could not obtain the original issue for me. I myself had solicited some of the articles that appear in the section dedicated to his own films. For example, I had asked him to write for the magazine *L'Arc*, which was preparing a special issue on Leonardo Sciascia. I still have the original text, typed on yellow paper that Petri used for his correspondence and personal writings. It is a text full of deletions and afterthoughts because he truly cared about formulating a thought as precisely as possible.[2] The interview on *Todo modo* (1976), which was a written reply to a series of questions, is another exceptional document, full of erasures and hand-written comments added to the typed text. Petri was especially passionate about the act of writing. He would add corrections by hand with colored pens in order to clarify his thoughts or to correct some of his statements. For this reason, Petri's manuscripts are particularly moving documents.

Petri wrote numerous critical texts about films made by others as well as his own. He was also passionate about painting, as was fellow filmmaker Valerio Zurlini, and he produced valuable texts on the figurative arts. His aesthetic work was directly inspired by painting: the German Expressionists, especially Otto Dix, but also George Grosz, and then American painters such as Robert Rauschenberg, Jasper Johns, & Jim Dine. Dine was the model for the physical movements of the character of the painter in *Un tranquillo posto di campagna* (*A Quiet Place in the Country*, 1969). It is also important to remember the close friendship between Petri and Renzo Vespignani, a relationship that led the director to participate in the debate on Realism.

2. Jean A. Gili, "Elio Petri / Leonardo Sciascia," *Bianco e Nero* 1–2 (January–February 2006) 167–177.

JEAN A. GILI

In this collection, there are articles on Pablo Picasso & Gianfranco Bonchi. Surely other texts exist that we could not find: for example, it seems that Petri wrote a presentation for an exhibition organized by the Museum of Modern Art in New York.

Petri loved subtle, challenging analysis developed through his confrontation with other intellectuals. It was a pleasure to interview him because of his clear and precise way of speaking. He utilized concrete concepts and comments, cinematographic references, and observations derived from literature, philosophy, and psychoanalysis. Petri was an avid reader. Largely self-taught, he formed his literary background through comprehensive reading, the same way he learned filmmaking: not by attending film school, but by watching films.

In the postwar years, he learned on the job: "At that time, cinema already interested me; I would watch even three films a day. I am part of the first truly cinematographic generation. We did not need any technical school: we already knew the grammar and syntax of cinema instinctively, because of our role as spectators."[3] The same goes for Petri's intellectual background, composed of incisive readings and a keen intelligence, ready to employ the acquired knowledge and new ideas.

Petri was also passionate about politics. After the Second World War, in 1946 — when he was seventeen years old — he joined the Italian Communist Party & was active in the party's Youth Federation. He organized cinema clubs and wrote a few articles for the journal *Gioventù nuova*. He was profoundly affected by films such as *Ossessione* (*Obsession*, 1943) & *Roma, città aperta* (*Rome, Open City*, 1945). He discovered Rossellini's film in 1945 at a festival organized in Rome to highlight the revival of cultural activities in the capital. Petri participated in the screenings and in the debates of the Roman Circle of Cinema founded by Cesare Zavattini. In 1950, he was offered a position at *L'Unità* as an assistant to Tommaso Chiaretti. Unfortunately, although research was conducted in the archives of the newspaper on the advice of former employees such as Ugo Casiraghi & Franco

3. Jean A. Gili, ed., *Elio Petri* (Nice: Université de Nice, 1972) 22.

Giraldi (who succeeded Petri as Chiaretti's assistant), it was impossible to find Petri's texts (also due to the common practice at the time of signing one's article simply with "assistant").

The extraordinary text on the adaptation of Sartre's *Le mani sporche* (1978), which was written for RAI, shows the same attention to maintaining his train of thought.[4] This important text should have been published long ago in a book or a magazine. Instead, it risked being completely forgotten in the RAI archives, or among the papers of the journalists who had received the article but who probably did not keep it. The cover of the printed folder is illustrated with an etching by Renzo Vespignani, who was the artistic advisor for Petri's adaptation; it is an unsettling engraving representing two hands, one gnarled and dark on top, the other smooth and light on the bottom. The gnarled hand — the dirty one — seems to be threatening the smooth hand — the clean one.

Roma ore 11

Petri's critical activity led to his first cinematographic experience with Giuseppe De Santis, whom Petri had met through Gianni Puccini: a preliminary inquiry for De Santis' film *Roma ore 11*.

Here are the facts: on Monday, January 15, 1951, there was an accident at Via Savoia 31. A flight of stairs collapsed under the weight of about a hundred young women responding to a job call. Several girls were wounded and one of them died at the hospital a few days later.

At that time, Elio Petri was twenty-two years old, a young man with much experience as a director of cultural activities for the Italian Communist Party. As mentioned, in 1950 he was Tommaso Chiaretti's assistant at *L'Unità* (Franco Giraldi succeeded him in 1951–52).

In May 1951, four months after the accident on Via Savoia, Petri was asked to conduct an inquiry to better understand the

---

4. RAI, or Radio Televisione Italiana, is the major public national TV broadcasting company in Italy. It was originally composed of three television channels, named "RAI 1," "RAI 2," and "RAI 3," but now includes "RAI 4," and "RAI 5," and it is funded and owned by the Italian government.

JEAN A. GILI

reasons that led so many young women to respond to the job call. It was Cesare Zavattini who commissioned the inquiry to supplement the material available to the screenwriters. Petri was chosen despite his youth: De Santis said that he was "still just a boy." Petri got to work at once and started submitting material. De Santis underlined the important role of Petri's inquiry in the preparation of the film. For this reason, when the final screenplay was written in the following months, Petri was invited to collaborate. His name, however, was not credited in the opening titles. This collaboration was decisive for the later career of the young Petri. For a few years, he would regularly work with De Santis. The shooting of *Roma ore 11* took place in the fall of 1951: Petri was the second assistant director working with Basilio Franchina.

On February 27, 1952, the film was released in theaters and *Roma ore 11* was harshly criticized by the newspaper *Il Tempo*. Several left-wing critics also dismissed the film. In *Cinema* (March 15), Guido Aristarco spoke of "schematicism." Moreover, the film was not a big popular hit. Despite the highly topical issues presented & the high number of famous actors employed (Lucia Bosè, Carla Del Poggio, Elena Varzi, Delia Scala, Lea Padovani, Raf Vallone, Massimo Girotti, and Paolo Stoppa), the film earned only 270 million lire. In contrast, Augusto Genina's *Tre storie proibite* (*Three Forbidden Stories*, 1952), although mediocre, also released in the fall and concerning the same topic, earned 371 million lire. *Roma ore 11* received only one award: a Nastro d'Argento for Mario Nascimbene's soundtrack.[5] Furthermore, for political reasons, it was excluded from the Italian selection at the Cannes Film Festival. That year, the competing films were exceptional: Vittorio De Sica's *Umberto D.* (1952), Alberto Lattuada's *Il cappotto* (*The Overcoat*, 1952), Steno and Monicelli's *Guardie e ladri* (1951), and Renato Castellani's *Due soldi di speranza* (1952). Castellani's film, a great success, won the Grand Prix ex aequo with Orson Welles' *Othello* (1952).[6] Steno and Monicelli's film also received an award for its screenplay by Piero Tellini. Finally, Italy received a special mention by the jury for the best selection of competing films.

5. The Nastro d'Argento (Silver Ribbon) is an Italian film award assigned annually by the association of Italian film critics (Sindacato Nazionale dei Giornalisti Cinematografici Italiani) to exceptional performances and productions. It was first distributed in 1946. It is the oldest film award in Europe and the second oldest in the world. [TN]

6. From 1939 to 1954, the highest prize at the Cannes Film Festival was the Grand Prix du Festival International du Film. The Palme d'Or (Golden Palm) was introduced in 1955 by the organizing committee. It is now the highest prize awarded at the Cannes Film Festival and is presented to the director of the best feature film of the official competition. From 1964 to 1974 it was replaced, once again, by the Grand Prix du Festival. [TN]

A few years later, Petri reworked the material collected for his earlier inquiry into a book, *Roma ore 11*.⁷ The volume contained a preface written by Giuseppe De Santis and a letter sent from Cuba by Cesare Zavattini (this letter was omitted in Sellerio's 2004 reprint). Zavattini underlined the usefulness of the inquiry as a way to investigate reality:

> "Dear Petri, it is great that you, at just twenty years old, are naturally drawn to see inquiry as a basic moral need. It took me a long time, almost fifty years, to come to the same conclusion: that's because my generation was afraid to establish these ties to reality; we felt that it would have resulted in a need to change everything we knew. My generation was afraid that the wings of our fantasy would be burdened by these facts, these numbers, this taking of notes, typing, tailing, asking, and seeking answers. Instead, it is precisely these investigations that push our fantasy in different directions. They force us into different daily routines that alter the practical perspective of our daily life. It is not even called fantasy anymore, but what does it matter? It's not even called art. We shall live this other way and then we shall find the name of the things that will be born."⁸

The volume presented some difficult issues:

— why was the book published five years after the inquiry and four years after the release of the film?
— why was it published by Edizioni Avanti! and not by a communist publishing house, such as Editori Riuniti, which in those years published Carlo Lizzani's book on Italian cinema? Was Petri's independence in the Italian Communist Party already too evident?
— in October 1956, Soviet tanks invaded Hungary. This event provoked a series of reactions in the PCI:* a few members, Petri among them, signed a document called "Manifesto dei 101."⁹ In 1957, Petri participated in the creation of the journal *Città aperta*. In 1958, Petri did not renew his membership in the PCI (according to Paola Petri, it was the PCI that "warmly" encouraged the dissenters to do so).
— how much of the original inquiry was modified to be published as a book?

JEAN A. GILI

---

7. Published in 1956 by Edizioni Avanti! in the series "Il gallo," *Omnibus* 27.

8. Cesare Zavattini, "Prefazione," in Elio Petri, *Roma ore 11* (Milan-Rome: Edizioni Avanti!, 1956) 14. [TN]

9. "Manifesto dei 101" refers to a document expressing strong dissent from the Soviets signed by 101 Italian communist intellectuals, following the Soviet invasion of Hungary in October 1956, the Budapest uprising, and its ruthless repression by the U.S.S.R. Red Army. [TN]

*. The Italian acronym for the Italian Communist Party (Partito Comunista Italiano).

Roma ore 11 is a well-written book. Petri carefully juxtaposes the descriptions of the witnesses and gives them room to speak, including several answers in Roman dialect. One can imagine the interview subjects' reticence toward Petri, who, as he asserts in the book, did not introduce himself as an assistant director preparing a film, but instead as a journalist or a writer looking for material for a book. For example, an elderly father of two young girls who were interviewed told the young Petri: "At least I hope the young sir earns a million with this book that he is writing about you…" In those years, Petri was still a "young sir," and maybe he always was.

A few years later, when Giuseppe De Santis was preparing to shoot *Giorni d'amore*, he called Petri again to conduct an inquiry on the sociological and cultural context of the town of Fondi, in the Campania region. This inquiry was found among De Santis' documents and today is available in a volume dedicated to the film.[10] Petri's report — long and detailed, around fifty pages, enough to constitute a volume of its own — is composed of a series of descriptions of couples forced to run away in order to commit the 'irredeemable' crime of getting married without a proper and expensive ceremony. Davide and Santina, Fortunato and Ida, Francesco and Teresa, Edmondo & Elvira, Alessandro and Immacolata, Onoratino and Egidia, Giovannino and Carmina: the stories of these couples, provided by the protagonists, is the fictional material rich with authentic observations that will constitute the basis for the story of Pasquale (Marcello Mastroianni) and Angela (Marina Vlady). The film is dedicated to all those couples who had to endure those difficulties: "To all those girls and young men who must go through painful and often paradoxical events to achieve their dream of getting married."

Petri's report is an elaborate text. It provides an incredible amount of information on Italian rural society in the beginning of the 1950s, and it even offers a detailed calculation of the money necessary to wed. This was a prohibitive sum for poor people because it included a dowry, a wedding dress, a tailor,

10. Giovanni Spagnoletti, Marco Grossi, eds., *Giorni d'amore. Un film di Gisueppe De Santis tra impegno e commedia* (Turin-Fondi: Lindau-Associazione Giuseppe De Santis, 2004) 103–152.

a religious ceremony, and a nuptial banquet for at least one hundred & fifty people.

"Città Aperta"

In 1957, Petri participated in the creation of a dissident communist journal, *Città aperta*. The journal emerged in the context of the occupation of Hungary by the military forces of the Warsaw Pact and of the XX Congress of the Soviet Communist Party, which marked the beginning of de-Stalinization. It is useful to remember that after the revolt in Hungary on October 23, 1956, and the subsequent intervention of the Soviet army on October 29 of the same year, 101 Italian communist artists & intellectuals — as proof of the uneasiness of numerous members of the party — asked the central committee of the Italian Communist party to have the Communist Parties in Europe lead popular movements for renewal. They also criticized the coercive & narrow-minded methods used by Stalinism and in the relations between States and parties, and they called slanderous the definition of "counterrevolutionary putsch" given by *L'Unità* to the Hungarian revolution. Among these intellectuals were: Carlo Muscetta, Natalino Sapegno, Delio Cantimori, Mario Socrate, Renzo Vespignani, Dario Puccini, Vezio Crisafuli, Giorgio Candeloro, Paolo Spriano, Luciano Cafagna, Lucio Colletti, Renzo De Felice, Elio Petri, Mario Tronti, Alberto Asor Rosa, Alberto Caracciolo, & Antonio Meccanico. These are the signatures of the future collaborators of *Città aperta*.

Petri regularly wrote for *Città aperta* during the two years of the journal's existence (his articles appear in all but one volume). The editor-in-chief was Tommaso Chiaretti and the editorial board was composed of Ugo Attardi, Luca Canali, Piero Moroni, Marcello Muccini, Elio Petri, Dario Puccini, Gianzio Sacripante, Mario Socrate, & Renzo Vespignani (notice the presence of the painters Attardi, Muccini, & Vespignani, who were also members of the 'figurative' painters' circle, and of Dario Puccini).[11]

11. Dario Puccini (1921–1997) was a literary critic and professor of Spanish and Hispanic literature.

JEAN A. GILI

The journal was started under difficult conditions. Callisto Cosulich notes: "After continued denials, Mario Alicata, the cultural director of the PCI, gave permission to publish the journal on the condition that Tommaso Chiaretti — who at the time was the editor-in-chief of *L'Unità*'s cinema section — would be the editor-in-chief. In the end, Chiaretti was fired, while the most involved editors, such as Petri, the painters Attardi and Vespignani, the writers Puccini and Socrate, and the philosopher Luca Canali, would not renew their membership in the PCI."[12]

Città aperta had many foci: literature, painting, architecture, and cinema, not to mention many interviews regarding the intellectual debate over Marxist ideology. There were many allusions to the Hungarian situation and the journal sided with those Communist intellectuals who had already left the party in protest. As an anonymous article from the first issue states: "These men were, and still are, worthy of our respect."[13] In another article from the first page of the first issue collectively signed *Città aperta*, alongside an engraving by Vespignani, who provided many illustrations for the journal, we find:

> "First of all, let's introduce ourselves. We are a group of intellectuals engaged in the social, moral, and cultural renewal of our country. Motivated by socialist ideals untarnished by reformist compromises, we intend to fight against the backward mentality of Italian capitalist society, against the feudal fog of clericalism, and against the many manifestations of conformity. We intend to create a journal with a 'direction.' First of all, 'direction' is the measure and the limit of our intentions and ambitions. We do not claim to represent all of the *engagé* culture, nor a whole generation. We do not claim to bridge the gap between the old and the young. But 'direction' also means a particular way of confronting and discussing the themes and problems of our time. We believe that we belong to the movement for the moral and cultural renewal of our country. [...] We want to exert a constant and militant criticism in order to develop & defend our poetics. We support realism in the arts, in film, & in literature, but we also seek to guard

12. Callisto Cosulich, "Germi, Petri e l'impero del male," *Bianco e Nero* 1 (January–March 1998) 73. The article is a reply to Petri's article "I germi dell'odio e della speranza," previously published in *Città aperta*. [TN]

13. Citation missing in the original. [TN]

against its populist and folkloristic degeneration. We hold to the ideal of civil and technical progress found in industrial civilizations, but we renounce mechanical idolatry & all its obsessions."[14]

Although *Città aperta* was originally conceived as biweekly, it came out irregularly. From May to July 1957, the journal was published every 2 weeks, then its frequency decreased to every two months, and eventually its publication ended in July 1958. There were seven issues in total, but there would have been thirty had the journal been published regularly. Petri authored nine articles in *Città aperta*. Some of them are about a director (Germi, Bardem, Kazan), but the majority are reflections on cinema and on political engagement. There is also a (possibly autobiographical) short story, "Two-Hundred Thousand Lire," about the difficulties that a screenwriter encounters when trying to get paid by his producer. Roberto Giangrande evaluates Petri's overall contribution to the journal in his dissertation: "This experience, born amid the strong tension between intellectuals and the Italian Communist Party, represented the explicit desire of some intellectuals to promote a free debate, although not aligned with Togliatti's thought. Petri experienced this division in the party and remembered it as the disappearance of (youthful) illusions. This loss made him understand the necessity for a free debate that was independent from ideological schemes. The journal did not side against the party, but soon the situation became unbearable and in 1958, Petri, along with other colleagues, and due to Alicata's opposition, did not renew his party membership."[15]

In those years, and after his work on *Roma ore 11*, Petri became a screenwriter & assistant director. He was steadily working with Giuseppe De Santis. Mario Socrate, one of the editors of *Città aperta*, was also credited next to Petri's name in the screenplays of De Santis' *La strada lunga un anno* (*The Year Long Road*, 1958) and Carlo Lizzani's *Il gobbo* (1960). The editor-in-chief Tommaso Chiaretti also appeared in the opening titles of Gianni Puccini's *L'impiegato* (1960) and Leopoldo Savona's *Le notti dei Teddy Boys* (1959). Needless to say,

14. Citation missing in the original. [TN]

15. Roberto Giangrande, *Il cinema politico di Elio Petri* (Rome: Università "La Sapienza," 2002) 105. [TN]

JEAN A. GILI

Petri had developed a network in the cinema industry: Gianni Puccini, Tonino Guerra, Cesare Zavattini, and Marcello Mastroianni. Later on, Petri chose Mastroianni's younger brother, Ruggero, as the editor of all his films.

The Debate on Italian Cinema

1960 was a pivotal year in Petri's career: he became a film director. After two short films, Petri shot his first feature film, *L'assassino* (*The Assassin*, 1961), in part due to the support and trust of his friend Marcello Mastroianni, who had become an international star with the success of Fellini's *La dolce vita* (1960).

Alongside his predominant work as a filmmaker, Petri often contributed to the debate on the state of Italian cinema. The texts and his responses to interviews evidence his defense of a certain idea of cinema. In 1962, he responded to a questionnaire published in *Film 1962* edited by Vittorio Spinazzola, and in 1964 he commented on the development of Italian cinema in the pages of the journal *Cinema 60*.

In 1968, busy with the filming of *Indagine su un cittadino al di sopra di ogni sospetto* (*Investigation of a Citizen above Suspicion*, 1969), Petri did not attend the International Venice Film Festival. This was the year of violent protests of Italian film directors against the Festival, spearheaded by Pier Paolo Pasolini — who was opposed to the screening of *Teorema* (1968) — and the boisterous Cesare Zavattini, who had to be physically expelled from the Palazzo del Cinema.[16] After stalling as much as he could, the director of the Film Festival, Luigi Chiarini, eventually capitulated and resigned. That same year, numerous Italian cinema unions gathered in Rome. The Centro Sperimentale di Cinematografia was occupied, and this was reported in the press as a "political" event.[17] Passionate discussions were held in the Centro's lecture halls. The participants not only included directors Pier Paolo Pasolini, Bernardo Bertolucci, Marco Bellocchio, and the screenwriters Sergio Amidei and Ugo Pirro, but also Petri — who appeared speaking vibrantly in historical footage by Istituto Luce.[18]

16. The Palazzo del Cinema is the main screening theater of the Venice International Film Festival. [TN]

17. The Centro Sperimentale di Cinematografia (Italian National Film School) was established in 1935 with the aim of promoting the art and technique of cinematography and film. Citation missing in the original. [TN]

18. The Istituto Luce (L'Unione Cinematografica Educativa) is the oldest public institution in Italy dedicated to the distribution of Italian cinema for educational purposes. It was founded in Rome in 1924. [TN]

In 1971, Petri presented his film *La classe operaia va in Paradiso* (*The Working Class Goes to Heaven*, 1971) at the film festival "Il cinema libero" in Porretta Terme. After the screening, there were many young protestors who reproached Petri for adopting a reformist and passive position, and French director Jean Marie Straub went so far as to propose burning the reels of the film.[19] Pio Baldelli — one of the few film critics who spoke out — considered the film reactionary and fascist, a counterrevolutionary film that should have been immediately destroyed. In France, the debate continued in *Les Cahiers de la Cinémathèque*; a militant of Lotta Continua[20] wrote:

> "I would like to cite two concrete facts to give a global perspective on the reactionary aspect of the film. In the years 1968–69, some factory workers began militant activity in the Pirelli and Fiat factories. These movements (and it is precisely for this aspect that I criticize the film) did not develop from a single individual crisis, but rather they were produced by the contradictions intrinsic to the industry and fomented by independently organized groups. The film totally negates everything that happened in the factories and denies the potential of the working classes. In Europe, we are considered on the forefront. The film should express this, and except for the final 20 minutes, it does. I would have liked for these last 20 minutes to show the existing polemic between the workers' movements and the unions. This is what is missing from the film, and why it is deeply reactionary. [...] This film is the product of a reformist politics &, what is worse, produces a Fascist ideology."[21]

Petri complained that the film critics who attended the screening of *La classe operaia va in Paradiso* did not defend him, and abandoned him to confront an audience that had preconceived ideas and was blinded by political prejudices that characterized the extreme political left in those years.

Returning to Venice, the International Film Festival in 1969 and 1970, under the direction of Ernesto G. Laura, was more tranquil. But the protests were only temporarily stamped down: in 1972, the authors' associations ANAC and AACI organized

19. See the booklet included with the DVD for *La classe operaia va in paradiso* (Cinema Italiano, La cineteca Repubblica-L'Espresso, 2009). Straub's name and citation are missing from the original. [TN]

20. Lotta Continua was a far left extra-parliamentary organization in Italy, founded in autumn 1969 by a split in the student-worker movement of Turin, which had started militant activity at the universities and factories such as Fiat. [TN]

21. *Les Cahiers de la Cinémathèque* 5 (winter 1972) 65–66. [TN]

JEAN A. GILI

an alternative to the official Film Festival, which had been directed by Gian Luigi Rondi since 1971.[22] This alternative festival was called "Giornate del cinema italiano" (Days of Italian Cinema) and it took place, not in the Lido area of Venice, but rather in the city, precisely in Piazza Santa Margherita, and in various cinema halls. The films presented included Marco Bellocchio's *Nel nome del padre* (*In the Name of the Father*, 1971), Marco Ferreri's *La cagna* (*Liza*, 1972), Fabio Carpi's *Corpo d'amore* (*Body of Love*, 1972), and Ettore Scola's *Trevico-Torino* (1973). In 1973, the "Giornate del cinema italiano" achieved a more prominent role because the late adoption of the new statute of the Venice Biennale caused the Venice Film festival to be cancelled. It was reinstituted in 1974, under the direction of Giacomo Gambetti. The outdoor screenings in Piazza Santa Margherita were packed every night; in fact, the theaters in the city were too small to hold all the potential attendees. Among the numerous films presented (from at least a hundred different countries) were: Vittorio De Sica's *Una breve vacanza* (*A Brief Vacation*, 1973), Florestano Vancini's *Il delitto Matteotti* (*The Assassination of Matteotti*, 1973), Marco Leto's *La villeggiatura* (*Black Holiday*, 1973), the Taviani brothers' *San Michele aveva un gallo* (*St. Michael had a Rooster*, 1972), Ugo Gregoretti's *Omicron* (1964), Gianni Amelio's *La città del sole* (1974), Gianfranco Mingozzi's *La vita in gioco* (1972), a selection of "dailies" from Pier Paolo Pasolini's *Mille e una notte* (*Arabian Nights*, 1974), and Elio Petri's *La proprietà non è più un furto* (*Property is No Longer Theft*, 1973).

Petri's film was not well received by the press. A scathing review, published before the screening of the films by a journalist that had seen it months prior in Berlin, caused a veritable scandal. Petri commented:

> "Francesco Savio was behind the original polemic at the Berlin Film Festival. After viewing *La proprietà non è più un furto* he said, 'I hope that this is never screened in Italy.' Do you understand? 'I hope that this disastrous film will never be shown to the Italian public.' He is crazy — even though he is a good person, an enlight-

22. ANAC, or Associazione Nazionale Autori Cinematografici (National Film Writers' Association), brought together directors and screenwriters with the aim of promoting cinema as a means of cultural expression. It was founded in Rome in 1950 and its first president was Cesare Zavattini. AACI, or Associazione Autori Cinematografici Italiani, was a subset association of ANAC, which was created in 1968 by members who wanted to transform ANAC into a trade union to better protect the rights of its members. [TN]

ened bourgeois —, but is also monomaniacal and a snob. I, on the contrary, believe in mainstream culture. My film should be seen with people who laugh, who cry, & who will talk about the film."[23]

In Venice, a spirited discussion followed the screening of the film. Andrée Tournes noticed: "During the discussions, it was always a matter of excluding, condemning, or initiating an 'inquisition' the way that do-gooder spoke about Tinto Brass' film. Sectist mentality was not dead; first and foremost, free speech served to judge and to condemn."[24] Petri was shocked by the aggressive reactions of the audience. He heatedly commented on and justified his aesthetic choices:

> "Maybe the time has come to simply stop making movies. For someone like me, who makes mainstream films, the traditional dramatic structure is the simplest, and therefore easiest, formula. Concessions to the audience? Frankly, I don't think I make concessions; I, myself, am part of this audience. [...] I love spectacle. I read Guy Debord & his book *La société du spectacle*. But if you attack everything that is spectacle, you ultimately destroy everything around you. Everything is spectacle: a way of displaying, a way of walking, a way of looking, and a way of dressing. Man loves spectacle, so accepting spectacle means to accept the human condition."[25]

Petri expressed this aggressive point of view in an interview with journalist Lietta Tornabuoni. A few weeks later, at a conference with critics and directors, no consensus was reached over the polemic. These events would anticipate Petri's hostile relationship with Italian critics; he felt that the ones who should have understood the sense of his work did not comprehend or defend him. A few years later, during the shooting of *Todo modo* in February 1976, Petri refused to prescreen the film for the critics:

> "The critical reception of *La proprietà non è più un furto* made me angry. But in the end, I am not the only one in this situation. From time to time I read film reviews in newspapers or trade magazines and I see that critics say very stupid things. Their criticism is not constructive. They defend elitist positions engendering a discon-

23. Jean A. Gili, "Interview," *Elio Petri et le cinéma italien* (Annecy, 1996) 15. [TN]

24. *Jeune Cinéma* 74 (November 1973) 8. [TN]

25. *Jeune Cinéma* 74 (November 1973) 22. [TN]

nection with directors. The critical reception of Pasolini's *Salò* convinced me that Italian critics had no reason to exist anymore. For instance, to give an example of the sensationalism of some critics, just a few hours after Pasolini died, they immediately ran to see *Salò*. Then, they all rushed to write. And they dissected both the film and the author. They confused Pasolini's life with his film, a truly vile act. *Salò* is a wonderful film, which nobody understood — and nobody wanted to understand. The critics clearly did not intend to accept a film so pure in its provocation, and so un-provocative in its purity. Pasolini thought he was making a provocative film, but really he made an extremely poetic film — and this film is provocative only because it is poetic. It couldn't have been understood by people with such low morality, who moralize, and who are so tightly bound to bourgeois morality."[26]

In February 1975, Petri was invited to Perpignan to present a retrospective on his films by the Institute Jean Vigo — in fact, the director has often been better understood in France rather than in Italy. In the event's guestbook, he wrote two short texts for Marcel Oms, the director of the Institute, which display all of his sensibility, modesty, and attention to human relationships:

> "Your Perpignan has only one big flaw: you talk too much about me, which makes me uncomfortable. And it is a little distressing to come all the way from Rome to here, to your Perpignan, only to hear you talking about me. This shows my own weakness, as well as the strong weakness (if I may say so) of the cinematic profession and its protagonists; or, more generally, the weakness of those who create ideas, and images, and idea-images. Little by little, they become door-to-door salesmen of themselves, of their ideas and images. This feeling of becoming someone who advertises himself and what he most jealously guards surely generates shame and bitterness. As much as I have done and do, even with the help of your friendship, intelligence, and warmth, I cannot avoid this feeling of exploiting you for my own goals. Will we ever be able to free cinema and human relationships from this blackmail, from this cold shadow? Thanks for who you are and what you do."[27]

26. Jean A. Gili, *Elio Petri et le cinéma italien*, 13–14. [TN]

27. February 9, 1975. Citation missing in the original. [TN]

"Nothing else is left but to add my gratitude for having given me the chance to get to know Perpignan. This name comes from the deep reaches, from the penumbra of childish memories, and it is synonymous with: stages. Perpignan is an important 'stage' of the Tour de France, before getting to the Pyrenees. Then, it is a stage on the streets of Spain. It was a stage for the volunteers of the International Brigades. It was also the first safe stop for those who were running from Fascist terror. I have the feeling that it will be a stage for me, too. The analysis of my old films with all of you already has great value in my personal history during these last few years, and in my future. So, thanks. I hope, after this warm stay in 'your' Perpignan, to get better."[28]

"Nuova Cucina"

In 1980, Ugo Tognazzi reactivates the culinary magazine *Nuova Cucina*. The author asked his friend Petri (who directed him in *La proprietà non è più un furto* in 1973) to take over the column on film criticism initially titled "Cinefagia"[29] then "Cinema on the plate." Petri clearly enjoyed himself — he often alludes to the 'director' of the magazine in these articles. He wrote the film reviews in a culinary vein. From February to July 1980, he wrote three reviews on Italian cinema — Gillo Pontecorvo's *Ogro* (1979), Ettore Scolas' *La terrazza* (1980), and Federico Fellini's *La città delle donne* (*City of Women*, 1980); and three on international cinema — Francis Ford Coppola's *Apocalypse Now* (1979), Joseph Losey's *Don Giovanni* (1979), and Robert Benton's *Kramer vs. Kramer* (1979). A light-hearted rubric next to the first review, that of *Apocalypse Now*, showed the symbols that explained the evaluations: "inedible" (upside-down plate), "indigestible" (broken plate), "insipid" (one plate), "satisfactory" (two plates), & "good" (three plates), "delicious" (three plates topped with the chef's toque). *Apocalypse Now* was declared "inedible," *Ogro* "satisfactory," *Don Giovanni* "inedible," and then the evaluations disappeared.

28. February 10, 1975. Citation missing in the original. [TN]

29. "Cinefagia" is a neologism in the original Italian, meaning "the act of eating/consuming film." [TN]

JEAN A. GILI

With regard to *Don Giovanni*, the editorial board pointed out:

> "This is a great cinematographic happening; it is a marriage between the lyric art of Mozart's *Don Giovanni* and the skillful scenic interpretation of a director like Joseph Losey. Therefore, a close observer of cinema like Petri couldn't help but notice it. However, in his astute analysis of the film, Petri maintains a purely gastronomic tone, in line with the original perspective that distinguishes his column on cinema and that is suited to our journal *Nuova Cucina*."[30]

Petri, Sciascia, Sartre

In his screenwriting, Petri at times came in contact with the work of many writers: Lucio Mastronardi for *Il maestro di Vigevano* (*The Teacher of Vigevano*, 1963), Robert Sheckley for *La decima vittima* (*The Tenth Victim*, 1965), and above all, Leonardo Sciascia for *A ciascuno il suo* (*They Still Kill the Old Way*, 1967) and *Todo modo*. Furthermore, we should not forget Jean-Paul Sartre for the adaptation of *Le mani sporche*.

Petri wrote many texts dealing with the adaptations of Sciascia and Sartre. The question of his relationship with the Sicilian writer passed unnoticed at the time of *A ciascuno il suo*. However, *Todo modo* provoked much reaction. Initially, the film risked being prohibited from screening given that it was during a political campaign, so it was released on April 30, 1976. The Christian Democratic Party was enraged: even though he only saw a short clip of the film on television, politician Bartolo Ciccardini furiously stated:

> "Petri is like Goebbels, this film is like *Süss l'ebreo*. It is an uneducated and partisan contortion, and an incitement to civil war. Let's be clear: there may be ten thieves among us Christian Democrats, and it is ok, in the play of democracy. That is, in the alternating of the parties in power, it is licit to send the Christian Democrats to the opposition in parliament, but this hate, this mendacity, the logic of this film, is terrible. If you follow this logic, you arrive at lagers. You should realize that this film takes you to the ghetto."[31]

30. Citation missing in the original. [TN]

31. *La Repubblica*, 8 May 1976. Complete citation missing in the original. [TN]

Even Sciascia enters the debate to calm the parties:

> "Two years ago, in my book, I was joking (while saying very serious things). Petri doesn't joke. And Rosi wasn't joking either when he adapted my novel *Il contesto* into his film *Cadaveri eccellenti*. Why? This question invites many different answers. Some answers have to do with the times in which we are living. We leave them to the readers and the spectators."[32]

In 1979, at the request of Jacques Bonnet, who was coordinating a special issue on Leonardo Sciascia for the magazine *L'Arc*, I asked Francesco Rosi and Elio Petri to take part in the section "Sciascia and Cinema" for which I had written an ample introduction. I asked the two directors to talk about their relationship to Sciascia's work. Though Rosi's text on *Cadaveri eccellenti* (*Illustrious Corpses*, 1976) is relatively short, Petri, speaking of *A ciascuno il suo* & *Todo modo*, wrote an in-depth essay ironically titled "Short Tracts." He wrote it during a stay in Sardinia. A few days after sending me the essay consisting of many typewritten pages filled with erasures and corrections, he sent me no less than eighteen new corrections and additions, proof of the assiduous — bordering on neurotic — precision of his thoughts.

As for *Le mani sporche*, Petri was involved in the preparation of the press release from RAI. He wrote a summary to illustrate the foundation of the work, offered a long analysis of Sartre's political thought, and also added his own thoughts on the Italian political situation. The text, with the ever-ironic title of "Short Notes, Preliminary Observations," contains seventeen well-developed points. It is shocking to think that this fascinating document was relegated solely to promote the film on television.

Writings on Painting

Painting was really important to Elio Petri. Francesco Maselli called him a "painting buff." Petri's long-lasting friendship with Renzo Vespignani proves this: Petri asked him to collaborate on

32. *Paese Sera*, 9 May 1976. Complete citation missing in the original. [TN]

the set design for *L'assassino*, and used the artist's engravings for the opening titles of *I giorni contati* (1962). He also used Vespignani's paintings in the opening sequence of *La proprietà non è più un furto* (the images were also used for the film poster). Finally, Petri sought Vespignani's advice for the visual aspects of *Le mani sporche*; the artist is credited as "artistic advisor." Vespignani also illustrated the screenplay of Petri's last film, *Chi illumina la grande notte*, which was never shot.[33] In the foreword, Vespignani wrote:

> "Ours is not a mysterious symbiosis: we grew up together, with the same passions and the same anxieties. Together we breathed hope like oxygen in the still air of post-war Rome and stench of what was dying around and inside us, year after year. Why depict your night if it is the same as my characters'? To be sure, a painting is not a film frame; and we constantly spoke about this, laughing about cinema that looks like painting, & painting that imitates cinema. And yet, reading your screenplays, I always 'saw' them already photographed and composed, already 'painted.' I saw your colors because they were also mine. Ours."[34]

Petri was a refined art collector and decorated his apartment with well-chosen artwork: for example, I remember seeing Ugo Attardi's painting *Piazza Navona* in his apartment. Petri also closely followed American painters and particularly pop art, which greatly influenced him in *La decima vittima*. In this film, Petri, with the help of cinematographer Gianni Di Venanzo (who demonstrated here to be as good as he was in his black and white masterpieces), employs a groundbreaking use of color. In an essay on *La decima vittima*, Lucia Cardone stated that the protagonist's sets (as designed by Piero Poletto) show the influence of Andy Warhol, Joe Tilson, George Segal, Jasper Johns, Richard Smith, Claes Oldenburg, and Roy Lichtenstein's comics. Also, Giulio Coltellacci's costumes were inspired by Courrèges' 'space' models. Cardone continued:

33. This screenplay was published by the Biennale di Venezia in 1983.

34. Citation missing in the original. [TN]

"Petri demonstrates a deep and focused understanding of the complex panorama of American painting during those years. Due to his disparate interests, which lead him to divest himself of his 'provinciality,' the Roman director well understands the development of American art and is well-informed on pop and the other trends of the avant-garde, particularly with regard to visual explorations."[35]

After Petri met American painter Jim Dine (who had shown his work at the Venice Biennale in 1964 with Rauschenberg, Johns, and Oldenburg), he decided to utilize him as a model for the protagonist of his film *Un tranquillo posto di campagna*. Petri went to London to meet the artist and invited him to Cinecittà to paint around fifteen large canvases, all of which would appear in the film. Jim Dine was filmed while working so that actor Franco Nero could later replicate his gestures when portraying the film's protagonist. Petri wanted Dine to stay in Italy to advise Nero and perhaps weigh in on some visual aspects of the film. However, the painter had to return to London for other commitments.

On a related note, in *La proprietà non è più un furto*, the depiction of the butcher was directly based on Otto Dix's engravings.

Conclusion

I would like to conclude this introduction with a personal postscript. I will never forget the walks I took through the Roman streets with Elio on Sunday mornings in the 1970s. Before stopping for a coffee at the St. Eustachio bar in the piazza, we would navigate the tiny streets of the historic center with our dogs, Snoopy (the cocker spaniel who appears in *Un tranquillo posto di campagna*) and Magoo, a fox-terrier. These Sunday walks, full of long chats, are tied to a sad memory. On November 2, 1975, we were returning to Elio's house. After crossing the Tiber, we met Dante Ferretti, Petri's friend, and collaborator on *La classe operaia va in paradiso*, who a few months later created the extraordinary sets for the underground hotel of *Todo modo*.

JEAN A. GILI

35. Lucia Cardone, *Elio Petri, impolitico. La decima vittima* (1965) (Pisa: ETS, 2005) 49. [TN]

Together we went to the Ruschena bar, in Lungotevere dei Mellini. At one point, Ferretti walked away from the counter to make a telephone call. Ferretti rushed back to us. He was red-faced: he had just heard of Pasolini's death. We quickly parted ways; each man went home to get more information. I think that Petri and Ferretti wanted to go to the morgue to see the body of the deceased poet.

When I heard of Petri's death in November 1982, I was at the Luxembourg Cinematheque where I was presenting *Maria Zef* (*Maria Zeff*, 1981) with Vittorio Cottafavi in a hall full of people from the Friuli region: a member of the audience had heard the news on the radio. He told me after the screening.

The memories of Petri and Pasolini will always be with me.

WRITINGS ON CINEMA AND LIFE

Elio Petri

1.
"CITTÀ APERTA"
(1957–1958)

§ 1.1 The Germ of Hatred and Hope: Letter to Pietro Germi[1]

Dear Germi, some time ago we had a heated political discussion at a film studio. More than a real discussion, it was a kind of explosion where you were the bomb and I was the unwary detonator.

You told me that I, along with those like me, would have fifty thousand deaths on my conscience (the dead people from the Hungarian revolution). That I, like many Communists, would be like those people who pretend to be something that they're not; and that Togliatti was an anti-Christ dressed up as Christ. You told me that the Communists were like Jesuits: in order to make political gains, they praise the Pope in the pages of *Unità*, and that they paralyze the socialist and democratic conscience of ten million Italians.

I wondered during that discussion: is this the man who made *Il ferroviere* (*The Railroad Man*, 1956)? Initially I didn't think so. There was such hatred (almost pathological) in his words that at first sight had nothing to do with the humanity of that film.

Then I gave it more thought and I understood that the man who spoke to me in such a way was, in fact, the director of *Il ferroviere*. Further, I realized that, in the end, the director and his protagonist have so much in common that it would be difficult to tell where Germi ends and where Andrea begins, and vice versa. This is not only due to the fact that Germi and Andrea look the same (since Germi himself played Andrea in the film), but also

[1]. Published in *Città aperta* 1 (May 25, 1957). In the original Italian, director Pietro Germi's last name and the word "germs" (*germi* in Italian) are the same. The title and the article play on the double meaning of the word "Germi."

due to the fact that the two men share the same contradictions: they both are hung up on the sentimental world, on the common sense and the prejudices of 'old-fashioned' men, while they are fascinated by the tangled pile of moral and social problems that characterize modern life. They both aspire to a status of individualist, bourgeois calm, while at the same time they lean toward the laws of collective solidarity that are the most basic elements of a true socialist conscience. One could say that *Il ferroviere* represents a sort of 'poetic' autobiography of Germi. Therefore, it is not by chance that the film depicts an important character of our times: a socialist-democrat worker.

The hatred in your words, Germi, sounded to me like the product of these contradictions (as is the particular tone of your personal humanity, and the sour and unpleasant accent that Andrea brings to the screen). In your words, one could find a trace of the evil that has been corrupting Italian society for the last thirty years: anti-communism. (This is a human and intellectual attitude that is inconsistent because of its religious and irrational aspects while simultaneously wanting to fight the same religious and irrational aspects of communism).

Anti-communism is an evil that takes rather contradictory forms, and you, Germi, demonstrate this, since you, as an artist, are more immune to it than your behavior shows. However, even in men like you this evil can cause damage if it is indeed true that you refused to direct a film based on the life of the Cervi brothers in order not to side with the Communists. In so doing you only favored those that Zavattini calls the "enemies of Italian cinema," and you lost one of the best opportunities of your artistic career.

I wonder if we can continue like this, or if there will ever be a moment where we can set aside all our factious prejudices to focus on those matters that are dearest to us.

Many avenues are now shut to Italian cinema. We are at a crucial point of its artistic and industrial development. All the issues that have plagued our cinema in the confusing past ten years are now laid out in front of us: political corruption, artists' arrogance, narrow-mindedness and the unhealthy entrepreneurial spirit of producers, the selfishness of a whole social class, and film critics who were detached from the real problems of the cinema industry (including aesthetic ones). This is what we inherited from the past ten years, a burden weighed down by a financial loss that became more acute after popular interest for cinema decreased.

Ten years marked by political divisions and petty distrust of one another, by a splitting into factions that rarely have looked beyond their own contingent interest, and by personal envy and hatred, have made it extremely difficult to find a solution to the problem of the freedom of expression, where we find our chance to survive and keep up with the times.

First of all, one thing needs to be understood: the problem of the freedom of expression concerns all those who face reality in a non-conformist way. This issue is not an excuse for political struggle devised by the Left, behind which Leftist politicians hide other goals. And if there are some among the Socialists or the Communists who still think that way, that is unfortunate for them, since they are no better than the censors on Via Veneto. To mistake the problem of freedom of expression — regardless of where that mistake comes from (although so far it has come only from a very specific area of the political spectrum: the government) as a purely or essentially political matter, is to yield to a view of culture and cinema where we accuse each other with ever-increasing bitterness (while the freedom we have progressively decreases). Our freedom of expression must be defended for what it fundamentally represents: the artists' right to express themselves and to critically investigate the reality in which they live, whatever the kind of society might be. Within these societies then, everyone will draw their political consequences and their class decisions.

I know that you will remind me of the Soviet experience and the restrictions in which Soviet artists and intellectuals had to work. I believe that the contribution of Soviet thought, literature, and cinema to the history of modern art and culture cannot be denied, and your best films, dear Germi, bear witness to that. With this being said, there is no doubt that the problem of freedom of expression exists also in dramatic form — with a socialist class content — for Soviet artists, and I am not among those who would deny it. But it is up to Soviet culture itself to find a creative solution to that problem, and the more progressive artists and writers in the country such as Nekrasov, Tendriakov, and Dudinzev, certainly went ahead with their struggle against vacuity and conformism. We can collaborate in only one way: by affirming the right of artists and other intellectuals to express themselves freely here in Italy. The history of culture does not move forward in separate blocks, and the new frontiers reached by art in Italy will be valuable also for Soviet art, just like the advancements in Soviet art became milestones in our experience.

You will probably reply that the freedom of expression is consolidated and enlivened through works of art. However, when the problem is to defend this very freedom, artists and intellectuals are faced with only one path: that of unity and solidarity (words that should not have not been made completely worthless by political wear).

This is the point to which I wanted to bring my discourse.

Above all, the solution to our fundamental questions requires a profound unity between film directors and screenwriters, young and old, who have contributed to the affirmation of realism as a method and as an environment in Italian cinema. Without such unity, the moral and artistic crisis that plagues our cinema will never be resolved. This does not mean that you or others cannot make good films, or even masterpieces, but that there won't be an environment conducive to good cinema, that is, an environment engaged in all its parts and not only in its most advanced exponents.

ELIO PETRI · "CITTÀ APERTA" (1957–1958)

Good films alone don't make for good cinema, as the past five years have shown. If artists remain shut in their shell — even if is to produce such great works as *Il ferroviere* — it will become impossible to produce such works in Italy, and there will no longer be any artistic loose cannons. The manner and measure in which an environment polluted by ideological confusion and by moral disintegration weighs on everyone's work is unsettling; the stifling of a collective engagement can be fatal even on the work of a single, isolated artist.

We can say that this is only a matter of custom. But we are at a point in which custom, morality, and culture are tied together in one knot, the same knot in which Italian cinema is bound up.

There are directors and screenwriters in Italy who don't even enjoy the limited freedom granted to their colleagues abroad (and some of them are ready to deny this fact): yet nobody ever examined their conscience and manifested, in any way, a bit of solidarity. There are directors in Italy who see their films tampered with; some of them suffer in silence in order to keep the fact secret, some others prefer to turn to the protection of a cardinal, rather than seek solidarity among their colleagues, directors, screenwriters, and intellectuals of their country. (We should also ask ourselves, however, how much solidarity such directors would have found if they hadn't gone to a religious man).

There is, fundamentally, a profound ignorance, for which everyone is partly responsible: men, the government, and the media that have let things go awry. This is how the current situation presents itself.

And it is in this perspective that we should also place the development of a new generation that is becoming, at this point, a "generation in the middle," to which I belong. Young people will be able to further the work of their predecessors only if they have the chance to pursue the themes that concern them the most, in a more serene environment: the rethinking of the Fascist experience, the moral issues born in the postwar years, the social contradictions through which they have had their first human experiences, the dramatic fluctuations of custom that characterize our time. Young people who are, in light of their education, sensitive to the theme of realism, started to work in an already declining time and they were the first to be affected by the crisis that was beginning. Now they risk not knowing or not being able to find their own path, and only a groundswell towards renovation in the community of Italian cinema will make a difference.

Do artists like Germi and those of his generation feel the responsibility of this arrested development, of having behind them many young filmmakers who know the technique, but are lifeless and deprived of their ideas?

Just like among the workers that Germi loves so frankly — and nobody can deny this, unless they have a mind wronged by strict ideology —, among the intellectuals, there are also problems of solidarity and of collective responsibilities. This is the worker's lesson that Italian intellectuals were not able to learn in the past ten years, to great disadvantage for their work.

I have asked some frank questions, dear Germi, because after the discussion that I mentioned in the beginning, I understood that you were a man "wearing his heart on his sleeve." You should know that I was educated to be wary of those who speak "wearing their hearts on their sleeves." Now I am wary of those who treat so-called sentimental reactions with arrogance and contempt, as if the sentiment were not part of our being human. For a person like you the words "unity" and "solidarity" cannot have lost their true meaning. I believe that on these words we will come to an agreement. (Some of us should should stop to see in every Communist a new Beria, and others to see even in men like you the shadow of Guy Mollet, if we want democracy and socialism to triumph in our country: but this does not concern all the people of cinema, for now. But it does concern you.)

ELIO PETRI · "CITTÀ APERTA" (1957–1958)

§ 1.2 Henri Beyle says Thanks

*T*he "Taking Stock of *The Thaw*" outlined by Ilya Ehrenburg in the *Literaturnaya Gazeta* no. 18 and 19 (a large excerpt was also published in *Il contemporaneo* of March 2),[1] responds only marginally to the numerous questions that arise when confronted by a document like this, written by someone who was in the forefront of Soviet cultural life.[2]

In this premature attempt at 'taking stock,' Ehrenburg exhibits a somewhat simplistic attitude with respect to the crisis of groups of Western 'leftist' intellectuals. There is a clear distinction between Sartre's position, which acts critically from within forces aligned with socialism, and Fast's revolt, which lines up with an uninterrupted democratic vision of cultural and political problems, as opposed to the confusion caused by a group of Italian intellectuals who returned their membership cards to the party.

Unifying the disparate 'crises' of so many progressive Western intellectuals could turn the analysis into a shortsighted & ambiguous vision with insular generalizations.

Ehrenburg writes: "And yet the Western literati that now call into doubt all the indisputable successes of Soviet culture, so admired everything five years ago that came from our country, including novels and the most mediocre films, that today these literati seem like delusional adolescents fixated on their love-object. Soviet culture has given the world many magnificent works

1. *Literaturnaya Gazeta* is a weekly cultural & political newspaper published in Russia and the Soviet Union. In 1932, *Literaturnaya Gazeta* became the official organ of the Union of Soviet Writers, the government-controlled organization responsible for most literary publications and the employment of writers in the USSR. The first issue was published in 1830 and it continues to be published today. http://www.lgz.ru

2. Ilya Grigoryevich Ehrenburg (1891–1967) was a Soviet writer, journalist, translator, and cultural figure. His most famous novel is *The Thaw* (1954).

of art. But when I read an article full of enthusiastic praise for a second-rate novel, for the gigantic canvases of a mediocre painter, or for the film *The Fall of Berlin* (1945), I often ask myself how could men who love and understand art admire these works?"

It is not difficult to spot the danger in this kind of thinking: the risk of the discussion is in getting bogged down in the boring game of complaining, blaming, and scolding.

However, the discussion can, and must be, more worthwhile. To contribute to this discussion, Ehrenburg should also turn to those who, far from putting things in doubt, fossilize the merits of Soviet culture through turning them into monuments and mummies, demanding, on the contrary, that the culture must be renewed, and contrast its "indisputable successes" with others, no less indisputable, of Western culture.

Not everyone involved in Italian film on the Left can easily admit that *The Fall of Berlin* — which Ehrenburg wants to summarily dismiss — is a terrible film, all wrong, to be trashed. Instead, there are many of us who believe that in its roughness, Caureli's film remains an important work. Behind our enthusiasm for a film like *The Fall of Berlin* hide political reflections that stem from the environment in which the socialist forces in the Western countries found themselves: to advertise the results of culture and art in the USSR. The protective attitude toward Soviet culture came out of a strict concept of the political-cultural relationship, and from a sincere, undeniable, & profound love for the USSR. But also the weight and impact of Soviet cinema of the great decade on the formation of Western artists and critics 'on the left' and not 'on the left,' cannot be underestimated when reviewing our opinions at the time. That is why we can now say that we must be wary of the myth of men but also of the myth of a great culture, which is what is also happening with Italian 'neorealism.'

For many of us therefore, the problem is not so much to review the criticism of *The Fall of Berlin*, because a part of this is dedicated to the mythologization of the mythical personage of

Stalin, as much as understanding what is the amount to which we feel that Soviet cinema is mutilated, and identifying the reasons for which it did not properly express all of Soviet life, or at least its peculiar aspects. And this 'rethinking' will be crucial for our work.

We believe that the fundamental responsibility of films like *The Fall of Berlin* (besides the specific reason of contributing to the lionization of Stalin) consists of imposing on Soviet artists, regardless of their artistic integrity, the task of getting inspiration from a model of life still to come, and not from Soviet life as it was. This responsibility consists of channeling artistic productions towards laudatory goals, as if Soviet society were perfect and Soviet man a kind of abstract hero: that is, outside of modernity and not subject to the natural contradictions that characterize human life within a capitalist society. But, on the other hand, these films cannot also have a totally different nature, because men in general, and eras in general, despite the different social orders that come into play, cannot be stopped, and a single social order does not represent the universal.

What is missing from Soviet cinema of the past fifteen years is a critical understanding of men and the world that can only be found in rare works of art, such as in the deeply melancholic *Vozvrashcheniye Vasiliya Bortnikova* (*Vasili's Return*, 1953), a film in which Soviet man appears not only as a 'comrade' but also as a 'brother.'

For these reasons Ehrenberg's reflections on bourgeois ideology in the course of his 'taking stock' seem dated. How can bourgeois ideology be such a monster if Hemingway is translated into Russian only now and it is a big deal, and Soviet youngsters of our generation only saw *Tarzan* of all the Hollywood films (and which Ehrenburg complains of their showing in the USSR because "they had nothing to do with art and negatively influenced our children and adolescents"). For many Soviet citizens, it must truly be a monster if as Ehrenburg's article has to aggressively declare: "as far as Shakespeare, Rembrandt, or Stendahl are concerned, we can proudly bow before them and these bows would not humiliate anyone." (We seem to hear the heartfelt 'thanks' of Henri Beyle.) How could such a thing be put in doubt? We don't understand.

Ehrenburg writes: "Whatever their idea about communism, since Caldwell, Mauriac, and Moravia are true writers, they do not vaunt the idea of the capitalist world but rather they point out its flaws and errors…"

Ehrenburg could have used less paradoxical, but better, examples. In any case, it seems to us that by this definition, he is behind the times. The criticism that many 'true' Western writers rail against the capitalist world is not as direct as Ehrenburg seems to believe. It is what many readers of the *Literaturnaya Gazeta* will end up believing, but their view is mitigated by their way of being, by the criticism filtered through the lens of spokespersons of the problems of their times, and of the contradictions that have always existed for 'true' writers.

This is the dimension that Soviet art and cinema have not yet discovered and which their most talented exponents are seeking. It is the conscious criticism of living in their socialist society, which is imperfect (as are all the creations of man from time immemorial) and that Soviet artists have not yet achieved and the most brilliant — from Pudovkin to Solochov — have never abandoned. Even from the point of view of the social function of art with regard to the men living in their times, or in other words, a guidance or an illumination, these artists have not been able to move their society along.

We go on knowing that this is not year zero. But the truth must be told. The state of being "deluded adolescents" is a stop. On the other hand, so is "betrayed lovers."

§ 1.3
The Lesson of Calle Mayor (The Lovemaker)[1]

The Spanish film Calle Mayor, directed by Juan Antonio Bardem,[2] was recently shown in Rome at the "Circolo romano del cinema" before its general distribution.

Many people were impressed with the fact that such a courageous film could be produced & distributed in Franco's Fascist Spain. It must certainly be shocking today to those who have been reduced to fear in proposing, let's say, the subject of adultery to a film producer. Shocking that *Calle Mayor* contained ideas and images that could have never been portrayed in an Italian film.

Actually, films like *Calle Mayor* clearly evidence how decisive courage and initiative on the part of the artists can be in modifying the conservative political conditions under which they must work.

There is no doubt: without Bardem's initiative and courage, there would be no *Calle Mayor*. Without the initiative and courage of Michael Wilson and Herbert Biberman, there would be no *Il sale della terra* (*Salt of the Earth*, 1953). Without the initiative and courage of Luchino Visconti, of Giuseppe De Santis, of Gianni Puccini, of Mario Alicata, in 1942 there never would have been an *Ossessione*.

That this is the essential lesson of *Calle Mayor* is clearly stated by Bardem himself: isn't the theme of moral engagement at the center of his film? Isn't the problem of courage what Bardem

1. Published in *Città aperta* 2 (June 10, 1957).

2. Juan Antonio Bardem (1922–2002) was a Spanish screenwriter and film director. His most well known films include *Muerte de un ciclista* (*Death of a Cyclist*, 1955), which won the FIPRESCI Prize at the 1955 Cannes Film Festival, and *Calle Mayor* (*The Lovemaker*, 1956). He was the uncle of Javier Bardem.

places dialectically in front of the conscience of his protagonist in *Calle Mayor*? Isn't it also a problem of choice that the young writer from Madrid, the 'ideological' character of the film, throws in the face of the other writer who has just arrived to sequester himself in the country to work on a collection of his writings and who wallows in the agnosticism of a life far from worldly conflicts?

There is a dilemma that confronts the young protagonist of *Calle Mayor*: whether to tell the truth to a young woman that he stupidly betrayed or to continue his human compromises. There is a dilemma that confronts the old writer: return to telling the truth in his books or consider his career over.

Even in Venice, where Bardem's film received an award, no one really considered these issues. Some critics immediately looked at the historical antecedents for *Calle Mayor*. They found a direct link to Fellini. One image among many in the film, four unhappy youths kicking a can, is not enough to establish a strict lineage. The clear engagement that underlies *Calle Mayor* and renders it a modern work that strains against the suffocating confines of a provincial culture is enough to differentiate this film from *I Vitelloni* (1953). The essential limit of Fellini's film lies precisely in the total absence of any commitment that is not just words on a page or in the form of a draft: and today no one can deny that besides inspiration and talent, what determines artistry (even in a film) are thoughts, idealistic impulses, and moral and philosophical values.

To go beyond the idea of kicking cans to a more important discourse, we can say that *Calle Mayor* harkens back to some American films of recent years, such as Robert Aldrich's *The Big Knife* (1955). It is not a matter of establishing stylistic kinship among these artists: Bardem and Aldrich have opposite styles. Bardem works with lyric images and follows a logical discourse with an elaborate and strictly European and literary sensibility. Aldrich employs an angry narrative, more modern in certain aspects, relying on a cinematic environment fraught with anxiety and tension that derives from the American theater. These two directors employ traces of their respective national artistic traditions and therefore use completely opposite cinematic language. It is not important to determine if they belong to the same school or if they have common poetic influences; what the films of Bardem and Aldrich (especially in *The Big Knife* (1955) and *Attack!* (1956)) have in common is the way in which they delve deeply into the modern conscience and its confrontation with moral dilemmas.

The protagonist in *The Big Knife* must choose: either sign a new contract that would keep him tied for many more years to corruption, to soulless jobs, and to money, and would keep him far from his artistic aspirations, or return to starving in provincial theaters.

The young man in *Calle Mayor* must also choose: between becoming a man, achieving complete morality, and finding the strength to accept responsibility for a mistake; or staying the way he is, a smarmy whoremonger and a degraded billiards player.

We don't know if there is poetry or art in these films. We don't know if they will remain in the history of cinema. For sure they are forgettable. However, they certainly present their own rigorously bitter path. They are realistic because they take place among the people, not only because the camera is placed in the middle of the street or focused on real faces, but also because it goes deep into the peoples' consciousness. It is not so much verisimilitude as it is truth. The poetry is not just for art's sake but comes out of real situations.

The moral choices are the psychological center out of which come the daily actions of the millions of individuals who constitute modern humanity. Existence (and perhaps it was always this way) is nothing but an accelerated succession of choices, always more important, between truth and *non*-truth. The key to many contemporary characters is inherent in the quotidian choices that confront them and the way in which they make their decisions.

During the Second World War, for every individual, decisions were total and dramatic. Afterwards, little by little, as the world was re-establishing an era of peace and bourgeois order (although a false peace and a fictional order), choices were more subtle, more nuanced, although no less dramatic. It was a time of choosing a social class for the workers, and a morality — and it wasn't necessarily their own — for the bourgeois, a time which was metered out by the explosions of atomic bombs.

Moral choices: chosen in the face of bosses, the government, love, oneself. The choices of the worker who votes for the bosses' trade union to guarantee his own peace; of the professor who decides to strike for the first time in his life; of the politician who must admit all of his mistakes; of the politician who betrays his own platform just to stay politically active; of the journalist who knows he is reporting lies; of the priest who has to defend the interests of a particular social class; of the soccer player who can choose to fix a game or not; of the wife who may or may not cheat on her husband; of the scientist who works for the military in developing life-threatening arms; of the senator who could start a war; of the industrialist who fires workers to increase his profits; of the lawyer who knowingly defends criminals; of the firing squad that knowingly kills an innocent man.

Many men, many choices.

It is no accident that the most aware directors — especially those of a 'mature' American generation, from Aldrich to Brooks, to Robson to Wise — tend (when not compromising) towards defining themes that evoke these problems.

It seems that in this sense, Italian cinema is one of the least engaged in the world. Aside from a few isolated examples, Italian film has practically ignored the dramatic conflicts that arise out of modern society between individuals and their consciences. Italian film directors and screenwriters are now moving toward different themes from what inspired them in the past and are searching in the reality of today's problems. We are not saying that it is enough just to look around to find great ideas:

this is the old neo-realistic order that was at one time new but now has engendered controversy. Great ideas are great ideas: you don't find them on street corners. They must be looked for and found deep in the consciousness of thinking men and not in the gaze of a newborn baby.

It is up to the courage of artists to create work conditions so that this research can be effectuated with the maximum daring and liberty.

These artists are also confronted with the problem of a choice: they must choose: it is about time.

§ 1.4
Two-Hundred Thousand Lire (200,000 Lire)[1]

Mario never felt comfortable in producers' waiting rooms. An acute sense of inadequacy would overwhelm him. That morning there was only an old man, whose face was vaguely familiar, waiting for Corbucci.[2] He was composed, sitting on a sofa and reading a magazine from above his *pince-nez* glasses.

Mario sat down, grabbed a magazine, and started to look furtively at the old man, trying to remember who he was. He must have been about sixty. Two trapezius-shaped pits imprinted his face from his jaws to his cheekbones, giving him a hungry look. Suddenly Mario recognized him.

The old man snorted and threw the magazine on the sofa.

"It feels like the Pope's waiting room," he said, smiling at Mario. "I've been waiting for an hour and forty-five minutes."

"You get used to it," replied Mario.

"I was born without illusions, but I get beaten down just the same," he said, mitigating his grave verdict with another smile.

He shook his head. "People forget about you, young man."

"I remember you very well," said Mario.

The old man took off his glasses and looked at him more closely.

"You are too young."

"You are not so old that I don't remember you," replied Mario, respectfully. "You were with Eduardo, with Taranto. You also

1. From *Città aperta* 3 (June 25, 1957).

2. Corbucci is a film producer. [TN]

had your own acting company. I used to come to see you at the Principe Theater."

The old man looked at him, baffled.

"You must have been a child."

"The postwar variety shows were good."

"Variety shows have really declined lately."

"If it were only the variety shows…"

"Not only because I was younger, those years were good," said the old man.

"Wasn't it then that you worked on *Rome, Open City?*" asked Mario.

"That movie ruined my career," replied the old man. "They typecast me in the role of the policeman for the rest of my life. They say: he's Neapolitan, in *Rome, Open City* he played the role well; let's have him play a policeman again. And even in that role, I never advanced in the ranks. At most, I was a sergeant. I never went beyond that."[3]

Mario laughed.

"Oh, Rossellini is a nice man. A bit crazy," continued the old man. "Who would have thought that he would create that masterpiece? We worked so quickly, without fixed hours, and they never paid us. I remember one day, when we were shooting scenes with the Germans, some extras went to lunch with their uniforms on and they were almost arrested. It was a low-budget film. We used to shoot in a small theater that is now gone, on Via Avignonesi, almost in front of the casino."

Corbucci's secretary poked his head in: "Mr. Zecchi."

Mario stood up and leaned over the old man, shaking his hand. "I am sorry, you were here first."

"Don't worry. Don't worry," whispered the old man. Then he pulled Mario's sleeve and added: "I know that they are working on a film set in Naples. If you could recommend me…"

Corbucci was ensconced behind the enormous mahogany desk, on which lay untouched books and screenplays bound in red Moroccan leather.

---

3. This text alludes to Neapolitan actor Eduardo Passarelli.

"Do you want the money or not?" he said, as soon as Mario entered the room.

"It wouldn't hurt," replied Mario. He couldn't add anything else, although he had other words on the tip of his tongue.

"You're all as greedy as whores," said the producer. "One hundred thousand lire."

"You owe me four hundred thousand."

"Listen, I have no money. I'll give you one hundred thousand." He took out his checkbook.

"I finished ten days ago. I was on time," said Mario.

"Why do you always have to bust my balls?"

Mario looked at that jovial man, leaning on the desk, with his pen poised to write the check. He hated him profoundly.

"You shouldn't subsidize the MIS and instead save money for the screenwriters," he managed to say jokingly.[4]

"I'm not involved with the MIS anymore. They're a bunch of jerks," replied Corbucci. He was about to write the amount on the check when the phone rang.

"This is Corbucci," said the producer nervously into the receiver. "Oh, right. That tune is awful, *maestro*. I want something catchier, more moving. Don't you understand that everybody should whistle it on the streets after the movie comes out?"

Mario observed his gestures, his angry look, his big mouth, his flaccid round chin. Every time he looked at him, he couldn't help but picture him in a Fascist uniform. Few people knew the origin of his fortune; Mario was one of them.

Corbucci ended the phone call. He hung up snorting.

"You don't understand anything. Useless intellectuals. You should thank us because we give you work."

"*You* should thank us," said Mario, but it was just a servile joke.

"And then you go to Rosati and complain."

"True," replied Mario, smiling falsely.

"But you want the money."

"From the way you talk, it sounds like we don't do our jobs."

4. The Movement for the Independence of Sicily (*Movimento per l'Indipendenza della Sicilia*, MIS) is a separatist movement; its goal is to obtain independence of the island from Italy. [TN]

§ 1.4 · TWO-HUNDRED THOUSAND LIRE (200,000 LIRE)

34

"The real communist of us all — that's me," said Corbucci. The phone started ringing again and he picked it up.

"Yes, it's me," he said, almost screaming. "No, no, I want the red one. If it's not the red one, I'm not going to pay you, and I won't change my mind."

After the armistice of September 8th, Corbucci sided with the Fascists of the RSI.[5] During a bombing in Livorno, he found a PAI officer with a bag full of gold rummaging among the rubble.[6] Corbucci eventually had him killed. The money disappeared. The PAI officer had thought it was all a joke and he screamed: "Comrades, that's enough," and he laughed hysterically, but he was shot and the money was never found.

"See?" said Corbucci hanging up. "I'm even getting a red car. Could I be any more communist?"

He scribbled something quickly, then he added: "Come on, how much do you want?"

"At least half of the total," replied Mario.

"One hundred."

"Two hundred now, at least, and the rest in fifteen days."

Finally, Corbucci gave in. He wrote the amount on the check and he waved it to dry the ink. Then he handed it to Mario, who grabbed it, looked at it, and continued to wave it.

"What terrible friends I have," said Corbucci. "Look how you all treat me. I give you money to eat all year long and you can't even wait two days." There was a sincere note in his voice.

"How am I supposed to pay the baker?" said Mario, putting the check in his wallet.

"Don't start again with the baker. Everybody talks about the baker. Better to use the mechanic as an excuse, not the baker. You have a car — 'the baker' is what the construction workers without cars say."

The producer grabbed a screenplay and showed it to Mario. "You know how much this costs me? Four million lire, and even then they complain. When they write a book, though, they don't get paid. All this money for a name. A name that at most thirty thousand people know. Look what happens when you go to fa-

---

5. The Italian Social Republic (*Repubblica Sociale Italiana* or RSI) was a puppet state of Nazi Germany led by Benito Mussolini, largely dependent on the German military to maintain control. [TN]

6. The Italian African Police (*Polizia dell'Africa Italiana*, or PAI) was the police corps of the Fascist colonies in Africa from June 1, 1936 to December 1, 1941. [TN]

mous writers. They write such awful stories that I, who am almost illiterate, feel ashamed for them."

At this point, Mario almost felt at peace with the big man in front of him and almost ready to share his opinions. The short slip of paper in his wallet gave him a sense of safety.

Corbucci was waving the screenplay. "Here's four million! And not one good line. Dialogue is supposed to be their forte. They write huge novels that nobody reads, except some intellectual snobs like you, and they deliver crap to the cinema."

"This is a true cultural problem," said Mario. "The relationship between cinema and literature."

"Who cares about the relationship between cinema and literature," replied Corbucci. "The problem is that with these boring screenplays, nobody goes to the movies, and the sponsors don't want to pay anymore."

Corbucci was shaking his big blond and pink head. His jaw slacked and his mouth hung half-open while he leaned on the desk to scribble another note in his notebook. At times he looked like Mussolini, Mario thought. Mussolini would have been perfect as a producer for these types of film. He chose the wrong job. If industrial cinema had existed in 1905, maybe Mussolini would have been attracted more by cinema than by journalism, and Italy would have had a few more *Cabirias* (*Cabiria*, 1914) and no Fascism.

"Well, now you can leave," said Corbucci, raising his head from his notes.

"I'm off then," replied Mario, getting up.

"Remember what I'm going to tell you," continued Corbucci. "In this country, cinema cannot survive. In a year, all this will be over and we'll all go to work in the fields."

"That's what I'm saying, too."

"Stick around. Come back in fifteen days. Maybe there'll be more work for you."

"Don't worry, I have to come back for the other two hundred thousand lire."

§ 1.4 · TWO-HUNDRED THOUSAND LIRE (200,000 LIRE)

"Go away," said Corbucci. "Or I'll throw this inkwell at your head."

In the waiting room, next to the old man, were sitting a woman in her forties dressed in bright colors and a young girl with a grotesquely developed body. Mario tiptoed out so that the old man wouldn't notice him.

In the street, he took out of his wallet the slip of paper on which "two hundred thousand" was written. Two hundred thousand lire. Two more months to live. Another breath of air. All the vulgarity that he had inhaled during the previous thirty minutes remained in his lungs like toxic air. After all, what could he expect? Wasn't it money that he wanted, behind all his talk of ideas that supposedly had nothing to do with it? Here was the money. Not much, he thought bitterly.

He went to De Santis' shop on Via Corso Umberto and bought two quartets by Beethoven, the only two that he was missing. He felt like a dog wandering in the fields, rummaging through trash and gnawing a broken shoe.

§ 1.5
It's Not a Stereotype[1]

Defensively viewing every invitation to unity to be a tactic is itself an obsessive use of tactics. Or rather maybe the meaning of such a simple concept has been lost. Those who work in Italian cinema have some well-known enemies in common (besides they themselves, and their personal drives). What is more natural, then, than a call for unity?

Even Filippo M. De Sanctis admits that in these past few years, a united front within Italian cinema has been lost. I am not proposing that it should be 'rebuilt' as if we were a sort of CLN.[2] The time for generic and pre-constituted alliance is over. Unity now arises out of specific situations. The issue of the censorship cuts to Antonioni's *Il grido* (*The Outcry*, 1957) was an event around which directors and writers of Italian cinema could have found unity and solidarity.

However, personal hatreds and a clannish spirit brought such divisions among us that nowadays it is difficult to even find unity on such a basic principle as defending a colleague's work from censorship.

Further, the diffidence with which every invitation to unity is greeted everywhere, even by some communist intellectuals, surely does not help to create a collaborative atmosphere.

It is true: "The crisis of these years is also one of delusion."[3] However, such moods can be overcome through willpower working against instinct, instinct which in Italy manifests in attacking everyone.

1. Published in *Città aperta* 3 (June 25, 1957).

2. CLN, or Comitato di Liberazione Nazionale (National Liberation Committee), was the underground political entity of the Italian Partisans during the German occupation of Italy in the last years of WWII. It was a multi-party entity, whose members were united by their anti-fascism. It was created by the Italian Communist Party, the Italian Socialist Party, the Partito d'Azione (a Republican liberal socialist party), Christian Democratic Party (the Catholic party), and other minor parties. The Committee was allowed by the United States to take control of the local administrations of Central and Northern Italy as they were freed from the Nazis, and it formed the governments of Italy from the liberation of Rome in 1944 until the proclamation of the Republic in 1946. [TN]

3. Citation missing in the original. [TN]

Unity and solidarity: let us place these concepts in a more modern vision of the work of the people in a modern art such as cinema. Twenty film directors today, or even two (the example of Bardem and Berlanga, who formed a company in Madrid, is a lesson for us) cannot keep working while stubbornly ignoring what differentiates their works; especially since we live in a time in which every personal crisis comes from the same matrix.

Therefore it is a matter of finding, dialectically, a unity that is cultural and not corporate, in which the poetic tendencies, instead of excluding each other a priori, can complement each other and create a composed picture of our cinema. The greatest obstacle we have encountered on the path to unity in these past few years is anti-communism, which causes a hardening of opinions on all sides, serves as a façade for obsequious acts toward the government, and casts suspicion on everyone.

A singular aspect of many radical or social-democratic intellectuals' attitude consists in their stubborn requests for "an examination of conscience" on the part of Communists. Their own reasoning, however, is likewise lacking a personal "examination of conscience."

It is pointless if the "examination of conscience" comes from only one side.

I might be falling again into a stereotype (according to Filippo M. De Sanctis), but I don't know a more hackneyed stereotype than anti-communism, and nothing more damaging for an intellectual who wants to face Italian reality from an autonomous position.

In my letter to Germi I was referring to a kind of current anti-communism that I believe he suffers from and not to personal controversies that everyone has the right to have against Communists. I will not mistake Calamandrei for Saragat, nor Gide or Sartre for Panfilo Gentile (and, turning the argument around, I will also not mistake Lukács for Rakosi).

But the current anti-communism takes away from an 'engaged' intellectual the possibility of understanding, as in the case of

Pietro Germi, that the Cervi brothers were seven Italian farmers before becoming Communists.

It is very rare to find a kind of anti-communism that is not *pro forma*, even in the attitude of those who left the party as a consequence of the dramatic perplexities caused by the twentieth congress[4] and the Hungarian revolution.

Città aperta represents our personal 'act of will,' and people will call us visionaries: better to be visionary than to stagnate in conformism.

In recent years, the ideological debate in Italy resembles a conversation among deaf people. The different positions are impervious to any new ideas. Everyone needs to get rid of their qualms. *Città aperta* was started as an autonomous journal because we wanted to extricate ourselves from our own hesitations, and not those of our political direction, or of the intellectuals from *Contemporaneo*. Rather, those intellectuals have always pushed for cultural action that moved freely within the limits of their field of interest, and outside any ideological confines and dogmas. It suffices to read the archival material as well as the new issues of *Contemporaneo* to see that this is true.

Città aperta was started spontaneously and thus autonomously. Other opinions, whether they come from Cassola or other party members, are not objective.

We were — and we continue to be — critical of the "cultural" direction of our party, and thus of ourselves. But it is not the Communists, with all their mistakes and schemes, who bear the most responsibility for the crisis in which Italian cinema, like many other aspects of national life, finds itself: it would be paradoxical to affirm that.

In order not to be *pro forma*, anti-communism can only proceed in one way: by ceasing to be anti-communism. De Sanctis should instead speak of "a communism" since it is a more broad-minded viewpoint and thus completely different from what I was criticizing about men like Germi.

4. The 20TH Congress of the Communist Party of the Soviet Union was held during February 14–25, 1956.

§ 1.6
Italian Cinema: A Castrated Elephant[1]

In the fall of 1945, *Roma, città aperta* (*Rome, Open City*) was screened for the first time at an international film festival at the Quirino Theater in Rome.[2] It was a critical date for those of our generation, who — sooner or later — ended up working in the film industry. Some of the best European films made between 1943 and 1945 were shown along with *Roma, città aperta*, such as *Les enfants du Paradis* (*Children of Paradise*, 1945), *Alessandro Nevski* (*Alexander Nevsky*, 1938), *Les visiteurs du soir* (*The Devil's Envoys*, 1942), *Arcobaleno* (*Raduga*, 1944), and *Enrico V* (*Henry V*, 1944). Seeing those works in direct contrast with one another was stunning, and *Roma, città aperta* stood out in a way that dramatically showed the two main paths that cinema throughout the world could then take — and could still take today: on the one hand, a cinema deeply engaged with reality; on the other, a profound and deeply intellectual cultural free-association. A communist critic argued that there could be a "third way" for cinema, which was not the one established by *Roma, città aperta*, but rather that of *Les enfants du Paradis* and *Enrico V*.

Now, twelve years later (after all the disappointments, the bitterness, and the defeats that still weigh on us), the new opening in cinema's goals, poetics, and formulas — even production formulas — caused by Rossellini's film appears to us in all its revolutionary power. Some people say that *Roma, città aperta* was born by accident, and there is much to be said about this

1. From *Città aperta* 4–5 (July 25, 1957)

2. Here and later in the text, we listed the international release titles of every film in parentheses. IMDb.com was used for reference. We used the original Italian titles throughout the text. [TN]

misconception. Many critics keep repeating this claim aimlessly, although it lacks foundation, even from the simple point of view of 'language' — and here, there would be even more to discuss. In any case, the film exuded the deep and unsettling energy of Italian revolution.

We will never forget the confrontation of that autumn which excited us and moved us to tears. It was also at this time that the distributors were trying to circulate, without any advertisement, a second run of *Ossessione* (*Obsession*, 1943), which had been banned by Fascist and Catholic censorship. They were the first to discredit our national cinema because of their ignorance and because of a *miscalculation* that would later be fatal.

Many of us watched *Ossessione* right before or after seeing *Roma, città aperta*. We realized that there were two passionate faces to Italian cinema: on the one hand, that of an investigation of social norms and of denunciation; on the other, that of a rigorous historical novel about morality and about those underworlds vulnerable to every crisis.

Italian cinema should have started from those foundations: from *Roma, città aperta* and *Ossessione*. Instead, it followed the fate of the national society.

Italian cinema had only five years of real and rich activity. It was just enough time to gain a national audience that had been 'historically' averse to Italian production. This distaste was exacerbated by the wretched Fascist film production, a fact that is never taken into consideration when one speaks or writes about the traditional 'hostility' of Italians of all classes toward Italian films. Only five years: from 1946 to 1951, and already in the last two years, the life of Italian cinema had become difficult.

The conservative nucleus of the ruling class, which little by little was increasing its power, immediately started to tighten the financial reins. Active censorship occurred from the very beginning. *Il sole sorge ancora* (*Outcry*, 1946), which more than any other seemed to follow the direction taken by *Roma, città aperta* (and not only because it tackled the theme of the Resistance) risked being banned — and it was only 1946. Even Rossellini's *Paisà (Paisan)* bore the mark of the PWB,[3] even though it maintained a significant humanistic quality.

From the idealistic foundations of *Roma, città aperta* and *Ossessione*, our cinema started to go backward instead of forward. During the last twelve years, its history has consisted of partial victories, some strategic and conscious retreats, others not, leading to the present bitter defeat both on an artistic & industrial level.

Every realistic film produced in the past twelve years can be considered a real victory in the daily struggle between artists and the philistine conservative authorities and producers who, for the most part, side with the government. A realistic film can also be considered the result of a generally unknown struggle, unknown even to intellectuals. Now that everyone is criticizing realism and those who represent it — often starting from a justifiably critical position that we share — it is necessary to touch upon this battle, fought film by film, from *Il sole sorge ancora* to *Caccia Tragica (The Tragic Hunt*, 1947), from *La terra trema (The Earth Trembles*, 1948) (which Visconti financed with his own money) to those films produced by official studios. These last films were more tolerated than protected and they managed to elude government censorship thanks only to the international status gained by Italian cinema and its best representatives.

People only ever talk about these twelve years with an apologetic or sensationalist tone, or to blame Communists & crypto-Communists. Nobody ever searches through ostensible reality to find the hidden truth. Even the most liberal of liberals, even the third parties that purport to be independent in their research and critical judgment, and even the fiercest men fighting for the sophistication of our country, avoid the real problem of Italian cinema. And not only in their words — like Moravia, for example, who is the author of shoddy screenplays and has made a lot of money by selling the rights for *Racconti romani (Roman Tales*, 1954), but did not contribute to the defense either of neorealism

3. The "Psychological Warfare Branch" (PWB) was an organization created by the Anglo-American Military Government in 1943. Its purpose was to control the Italian media, specifically press, radio, and cinema. [TN]

or of good cinema. The central issue from which everything else derives began with the elephantine bloating of industrial structures, and then continued with the castration of ideals conceived and effected by Giulio Andreotti, who surely could not ignore the fact that castration leads to sterility, to aging, and eventually to death.

It is not by chance that the core issue is mostly ignored because the majority of critics and intellectuals still demonstrate a tendency to consider cinema as an artistic or at most an industrial phenomenon. On the contrary, in reality, cinema is a huge phenomenon that is not only artistic, but also political and public. It involves vast political & economic interests to a degree that is disproportionate to what its ideal dimensions should be in a more advanced — even capitalistic — society.

Political power — at times even that belonging to progressive forces — does not like super-structural renovation of any kind that can directly or indirectly effect a change in mass values.

(Symptomatic of this is the absence in Italy of a 'problematic' cinema specific to the Church. In a Catholic country governed by political forces that identify themselves with Catholicism, such an absence would be inexplicable if one did not consider the government's distrust of any form of 'problemicity,' even a mystical one. This is true even for ideas that have little in common with Marxism or idealism — as is the case with Fellini's last film).[4]

Along with the constant and increasingly explicit strangling of national cinema carried out by the government, the most qualified artists have retreated over the past twelve years essentially for transitory reasons: fame, money, the approval of international critics, the great success of their films (and success usually leads to arrogance). All of these factors drove artists away from their natural sources of inspiration, regardless of the government's pressure.

The theorization of 'poetics,' the failed attempt to raise poetics to the status of a veritable artistic conception, is the clearest symptom of this decadence: neorealism is like this, it's made

4. Federico Fellini's *Le notti di Cabiria* (*Nights of Cabiria*), released on May 27, 1957. [TN]

like this: non-professional actors, 'real' stories, camera out in the street, etc. Abstract theorization leads to an uncritical view of the results obtained, and this doesn't only happen in cinema. It crystallizes these results, prevents forward movement, and produces stagnation in artistic research and invention. An example of this can be found in *Il tetto* (*The Roof*, 1956), a film that, as soon as it came out already looked eight years old because while it perfectly followed the classical models and theoretical 'canons' of Zavattini's neorealism, it no longer corresponded to our need to confront the new reality of the country, nor to our most recent cultural experiences.

Reality usually moves faster than theories rooted in current events — such as those created by neorealist artists — or rooted in social norms, and theory becomes official only if it has the force and depth of historical perspective. In this regard, *Il tetto* clarified many of the issues. If neorealism is not understood as an overarching need for research and investigation, but rather as an outright poetic tendency, it no longer appeals to us. This is not because, as some have argued, we only care for the usual 'quality leap' (from 'neo' to 'realism,' from impression to reflection, from 'fragment' to 'novel'); that is only one aspect of the neorealist impasse, included in the wider issues of theme, of the ideal attitude of neorealism, or of the choice of 'content.' This troubled Italy, born from post-war compromises, cannot be represented with the implicitly Christian innocence of neorealism; there is a need for stories and images that are more relevant to the moral lacerations inflicted on the mind by the return of capitalism. We need to face up to modern myths and incoherencies, corruption, great examples of worthless heroism, and fluctuations in morality; we must *be able* — and know how — to represent all of that.

If one considers the history of our cinema over the past twelve years, it is clear that the Italian progressive forces that identify themselves with Marxist principles have had a hegemonic influence on said cinema, which was purely cultural. The battle for new content was at the core of the Marxist critique; this was the correct center, the only axis around which cinema could renew itself.

Little by little, however, the goal (or as people too often say: the buzz word) of 'new content' became crystallized and restricted to themes that came from a partial vision of national reality. 'New content' became a blueprint, even for the most qualified Marxist artists and critics, and thus turned neorealism into a formula for all of us, including the youngest of our generation. To take inspiration from reality meant to see in that reality only those events most overtly connected with class struggle and only the facts that directly originated from great political and union battles. Class struggle in the form of politics and trade unions did not seem to continuously produce conscious and subconscious qualitative changes in men's consciences, and these changes did not generate new facts, characters, and feelings, or problems of life, morality, and relations among men. We Marxist artists and critics saw only the *strike* and never *after the strike*.

All this was worsened by the local battle against so-called 'cosmopolitanism,' which prevented us from fully understanding the value of many foreign experiences and made us embark on pointless 're-discoveries' in a passive acceptance of the Italian tradition. The 'struggle' against 'naturalism' exacerbated this pettiness, led to 'optimistic' and 'collectivist' visions of life, and did not allow us to overcome the 'philosophical' distress of the realistic experience, which would have opened up said experience to the problems of modern humanity as a whole.

This overly mechanical tie to the most evident aspects of class struggle was clearly exposed by a widespread tendency among communist painters and filmmakers to focus their investigations on the South of Italy with distinct folkloristic accents. This was due to the misunderstanding of the concept of a national-popular art, which in Gramsci's conception had little to do with folkloristic attitudes. Gramsci spoke of an art that could express national unity, and this, in his opinion, was the core of the working classes cultural politics.

With Gramsci we can say: "The lives of peasants occupy a significant place in literature, but here, too, not as hard work and fatigue" — and this last sentence doesn't fit with our argument — "but rather, farmers as 'folklore,' as picturesque representatives of curious and bizarre customs and feelings."

Thus, many communist artists, even though they dealt with farmers' lives "as hard work and fatigue," bore the mark of those communist artists whom Gramsci mentioned.

Nobody really cared about correcting this attitude. Due to ideological conflicts aimed at making artists aware of the cultural problems of national unity and of the working class, nobody tried to compare the communist artists' work with the new themes originating in the life of the working class, in the fact that the working class was part of the government, in the profound crisis of morality and mores that the fall of Fascism, the Liberation, the Resistance, and the revolution caused in every stratum of the Italian people and in the core of Italian *humanity*.

The goal of the cultural direction through which the Italian progressive forces exert their hegemony on cinema is correct — and we need to start from there again, from 'new content.' Instead, however, the form this direction took was schematic and restricted.

Turning again to Gramsci we recognize that: "We surely cannot impose the task of addressing this or that aspect of life on one or more generations of writers, but the fact that one or more generations of writers share certain intellectual and moral interests is, in itself, significant, and it indicates that some specific cultural direction is predominant among intellectuals."

The dominant direction among communist artists cannot be imposed: yet a group that intends to revolutionize society, to build a new society and a new civilization, *must* wage a battle of principles, through dialectics, that develops into a 'cultural direction.'

In our opinion, at several important moments, a true 'cultural direction' was missing, or it manifested itself too many times through purely opportunistic motivations. While a certain theoretical, schematic, and abstract rigor was visible, there was no concrete development of a battle for the principles of an engaged and realistic cinema and art. There was, to use a language typical of party members, "opportunism in the practice."

There is no doubt, for example, that the majority of deficiencies in the cultural direction of the Communist Party were the product of merely political and often stifling motivations.

Sometimes it was even the fear of antagonizing the most iconic men in Italian cinema, who were becoming very popular in Italy and the whole world. The cultural direction of the communist party 'played nice'; it did not go beyond friendly and diplomatic — at times even personal — relationships with the artists and failed to promote a national and unitary art that could express, with its works, broader needs and more audacious & revolutionary research.

One of the principal leaders of the communist party told a communist director who was almost exiled for his very socially engaged film (probably the best of his still short career) that more was "not allowed" and that it would have been better for him and for the working class to deal with topics less controversial than unemployment. It was the end of 1953, right before one of the biggest defeats of Italian conservatives. Why did that politician not secure his and the party's endorsement so that in cinema, political conditions favorable to progress, not regression, could have been created?

To fail to understand that defending freedom of expression — for all intellectuals — means to defend the constitutional principles of democracy, is a symptom of grave blindness. This compromised the fate of Italian cinema, and it is one of the faults that Italian progressives must bear on their shoulders.

The problems of Italian cinema have become particularly acute today, especially in the tragic situation of the national film industry. The reasons for the crisis are the much-discussed changes in collective habits caused by technological progress, by the spread of television, by the extraordinary increase of private transportation. But such a phenomenon, in a field of cultural activities, cannot be dependent only on quantitative causes. Today the film audience, with all its conscious or unconscious contradictions — depending on the social stratum — assigns to cinema a function that goes beyond mere entertainment. Television has become the new 'nickelodeon.' In the historical perspective of show business, cinema assumes a new role in which its noble character as modern art is exalted. The success of films like *La strada* (*The Road*, 1954), inasmuch as one can discuss all the other causes, affirms this conviction. Film artists cannot be idle with respect to the new possibilities opening up for cinema as a creative instrument. In order to be loyal to their means of expression, they will have to be more courageous and more consistent than before.

We cannot wait for a new revolution — as strong as the one that produced the neorealist films — to appear and show the new directions.

To start again from *Roma, città aperta* and *Ossessione* is impossible. After all, despite the abuses, the oppression, and everything else, Italian cinema has gained new protagonists and experiences, as well as precise attitudes and personalities. We must start from these results and from the most recent experiences in world cinema (from Japanese films to *Limelight* [1952], from *Il ritorno di Vassili Bortnikov* [*The Return of Vassili Bortnikov*, 1953] to *On the Waterfront* [1954]).[5]

The essential condition for a strong and coherent investigation is for artists to have the greatest freedom possible. This is the reason that we still talk about 'unity,' despite the risk of looking like old-fashioned 'tacticians.'

---

5. In the Italian version, *On the Waterfront* was listed as *Fronte del porto*, but we decided to use the original English title. [TN]

§ 1.7
Death of a Writer: Notes for a cheap film[1]

Anybody looking for ideas for a cheap film? Here's one: only one 'set,' a clinic in Rome. Three protagonists: a dying man, a priest, and a Communist. The story should be brief, tense, and take place during the dying man's last three days. A door opens: a Jesuit priest enters with his swirling black robes, which make him look like a crow and that stand out against the blinding whiteness of the room. There is a pale man in the bed. The priest approaches the bed, points his finger at the sick man and utters: "You don't know it, but you have cancer: you should think about settling matters with your conscience." This is the beginning of the film we propose.

The sick man is an intelligent, refined, and outgoing writer who has always loved to show off. He employs harmlessly imaginative and bizarre gestures. He has a sense of being 'protected' and tolerated (in a way that is typical of Italian culture) in his opposition to the establishment. He feels he is 'in the forefront,' but his own forefront, from which he attacks everything and everyone. In reality, the 'enemy' he should be attacking is watching, applauding, and probably even charging for the show. In other words, the sick man is an *enfant terrible*: he is a Fascist and an anti-fascist, a dictator's spokesperson and an exiled man; an anti-Communist, but he has written articles, under a Tuscan nickname, for a communist newspaper, right after the liberation of Rome. The writer is a man of the world (and I truly like this man,

1. From *Città aperta* 4–5 (July 25, 1957)

because I still retain a great admiration — again, a very Italian characteristic — for all great adventurers — I am still fascinated by the likes of Cagliostro and Al Capone).

Now facing death, the writer fears that his life was a big mistake. Maybe he feels the weight of his cynicism and the cruelty and uselessness of his actions. He is now truly alone, as he had always preposterously claimed before. He is completely, absolutely, irreparably alone; he has no children, or woman, or person who truly loves him.

Remorse torments him, and I believe this is true, deep remorse: I don't want this character, right before dying, to devise his last twist to the story, one last journalistic scoop that would make the echo of his death last more than one day. (This would also be a realistic character, but then the style of the film should change: it should be grotesque and satiric. This could also be possible, but it would have to be discussed).

The dying man cries often; he is afraid to die. He is a young man, and his outlook has always been life affirming rather than decadent. His body is also not ready to die: it is still strong, young, and alive.

The writer's obsession is that, in a moment of supreme terror and weakness, he would accept last rites before dying. He is not a true atheist: but he is neither a believer nor a Catholic, and he did not go through any spiritual crisis like Papini, despite the many affinities between the two men. This is probably the only consistent element in his life. He doesn't trust himself anymore, so he asks that someone guard the door of his conscience for him. But who, if he has no friends, and he has never had any?

In the clinic there are politicians from all political factions, even the government, because the writer's popularity was great.

To whom should he turn, in this anonymous crowd of strangers? He needs people he can trust, who have no interest in common with priests. How could he trust, for example, that leftist Republican deputy, or that liberal journalist, knowing full well that they collude with the priests and Christian Democrats all day long? He thus turns to the Communists, his old 'enemies' and his 'loyal' adversaries. "Be careful," he says. "In a moment of weakness I could give in to the priests' moral pressure, and I don't want to."

The writer knows himself: he knows that his conscience has already indulged in these repentances and in these sudden and enlightening conversions.

A sort of defense perimeter is set up around the writer's tormented body. Cancer is corroding his desiccated and yellowed flesh from the inside, lacerating it piece by piece, and devouring it tissue by tissue, cell by cell.

The steady stream of priests is thus controlled and diminished little by little. At sunset of the second day, it even seems that the priests have decided to call a truce with the dying man, or maybe they are thinking about what to do. They did not expect the Communists' opposition: maybe they fear throwing their spells and their excommunications in front of witnesses.

In the meantime, the writer and the Communists learn to know each other better and they become friends. (In truth, the writer has always shown a penchant for the Communist party, though its founder left a scathing judgment about him in his Prison Notebooks). They don't even reproach each other about their past acts of enmity; rather they remember them with nostalgia. The dying man confesses with tears in his eyes that his greatest torment, in his last moments of life, is knowing that he will be remembered as a man who opposed progress, a literate in collusion with tyrants and men of power.

An idea pops up in the alert mind of one of the Communists who most painstakingly attended the writer. Why not boldly propose to the dying man to convert to communism? Why not help him to appease his ideological torment? A signature, a 'yes' and all his moral suffering would be at least alleviated. (He forgets that he is the representative of hundreds of farmers: he's only propelled by the delight of having a good idea).

He communicates his idea to his comrades. Some are outraged and reject it: "That man was a Fascist, he changed political allegiances many times, this is not possible." Others calculate the political weight of the act, and conclude that it would be counterproductive. The more naïve members are ecstatic that they can collect the last will of such an important man, of such an important and influential bourgeois.

They proceed to test the sick man's intentions. He only has weak objections. By now, he can barely talk. He communicates with few words, more with his big, black, expressive eyes, which become even more deep and humane in these last few days of intense suffering. Soon the writer accepts.

The Communists run to get a party ID, surreptitiously, so that neither the priests nor the politicians or the journalists in the room will notice.

In the afternoon of the third day, right when the end is nearing, the writer is presented with a party ID accompanied by a few simple words.

Right after that, the body succumbs completely to the illness and that's when the priests come back. They arrogantly push aside the Communists, they push them away, and they take hold of the writer, who, upon seeing them, bursts into desperate tears because in their presence he sees the end of his life. The fear of the afterlife grips him and the priests don't help him, they don't even talk to him: they kneel around the bed and they pray under their breath.

The dying man starts to scream and asks to confess. He is left alone with a priest, he confesses, and then, already in anguish, he takes communion. He is done. Everyone can come back inside the room. He is calm, serene. He gestures to the Communists to come and join him. He asks them, with gestures, to hold his hand. On the other side of his deathbed is a priest, and the writer gestures to him to hold his hand, too. And so he dies. He wanted to be coherent, for once in his life, but he is overcome by his nature, by his temperament, by his long acquaintance with compromise.

It wouldn't be difficult to pick names for the screenwriter, or for the director or the actors for this kind of film: from Jean-Paul Sartre to Budd Schulberg, from Elia Kazan to Fredric March.

It would be difficult to find a producer, especially because no country in the world exists where a government is ready to tolerate the production of such a film. Maybe in a few centuries. But cinema won't exist anymore.

§ 1.8
Elia Kazan: A "Boomerang" Conscience

How many consciences the cold war has constrained, corrupted, blinded on both sides in the whole world cannot yet be established.

The years between 1948 and 1956 comprised a brief but dark time in which people rushed in fear to take refuge on islands of indifference. A form of modern barbarism was at work, disguised as severe and repugnant intolerance, a good long way from being defeated, difficult to define, and technically and ideologically advanced. This barbarism — if we push away the principle of "the ends justify the means," which is one of the most over-used clichés — brought together conservatives and progressives, reactionaries and revolutionaries. It made use of the authority — under whatever social system at the time — and of many idealized myths to obtain from everyone the highest degree of acquiescence.

The people, the little or the 'important' people — the intellectuals and the artists — were afraid of everything, in the West as well as in the East: of imminent and final catastrophes, of hunger, of persecution, of blatant payback, of retaliation.

In the United States, this barbarism found a fertile ground in Puritanism and in American nationalism. Puritanism and the *American Legion* became allies, sustained by industry and followed on by Catholic prayers. They armed themselves with the *Smith Act* and in the name of the Cold War they launched their crusade. They presented themselves to all the Democrats, from one day to the next, as a hysterically reactionary America, a far cry from the liberal and optimistic image that the Democrats loved.

To this new America, cinema was too important as a means of communication to the general public, so Hollywood couldn't be forgiven its liberal past.

"In the last months of 1947," wrote one of the Hollywood Ten, Adrian Scott, "the 'House Committee on Un-American Activities' sent their first spies to Hollywood."

"Under the pretext of denouncing a handful of alleged Communists, the objective of the Committee was to discourage the liberal left and its cultural lineage, to have it join in the pursuit of the Cold War."

"At the end of 1947," continued Scott, "the reactionary offensive found its way to Hollywood and that necessary offensive instrument, a blacklist, was established. A confluence of extremely rigid conditions was devised to enforce it. A *charnel house* existed in every film studio. Here the liberals were invited to sign *affidavits* and explain their past political positions, which were not in line with the new allegiances."

The blacklist was comprised of 214 names: 106 writers, 36 actors, 3 dancers, 11 directors, 4 producers, 6 musicians, 4 cartoonists, and 44 other show business types.

Hollywood was gripped by a hysterical fear. Many people caved in front of the Committee. The top Hollywood group started to come apart: who went to jail, who left the country, who in the *charnel houses* lost their self-respect. Maltz, after his incarceration, went to Mexico. In 1950, to escape persecution, Dassin, John Berry, Losey and Barzman went to Europe. Dmytryk, after making *Give Us This Day* in the United Kingdom, inexplicably returned to California and confessed to having been a member of the American Communist Party and turned in some of his colleagues.

Some lukewarm non-conformists like Huston buried themselves in their work and got involved in big productions, never realizing their full talent. Someone like Brooks was able to maintain the party line through prodigious acrobatics. Others cockily drag along the anguishing weight of their surrender but do not succeed in hiding the marks impressed upon their consciences during the wakes in the *charnel houses* and the questionings by the 'House Committee on Un-American Activities.'

From the Theater to the Cinema

The phenomenon that is Kazan came from this poisoned atmosphere.

Kazan arrived to Hollywood as an *enfant terrible* of Broadway after becoming one of the most important directors of the Group Theatre.

He made his mark immediately, imposing hot and modern themes: racism, intolerance, fanaticism. Between 1945 and 1949 he directed: *A Tree Grows in Brooklyn, Boomerang, Gentlemen's Agreement,* and *Pinky*, not to mention the commercial interruption represented by *The Sea of Grass*.

His filmic language was still rough and basic, but clear. His ideas were also elementary but passionate. *Boomerang* and *Gentleman's Agreement* were militant manifestos. *A Tree Grows in Brooklyn* — the first film he made in Hollywood after a brief New York documentary experience — allowed him to express his nostalgic memory; it was a deeply-affecting work regarding family affections and childhood, a sentimental journey in historic Brooklyn that in long-ago 1913 housed the family of Armenian emigrants named the Kazanjoglous.

Pinky was a conventional film in which an anti-racist theme was not able to cover the fundamental conformism of the setting and the psychology of the film.

In *Panic in the Streets*, we saw a new Kazan: more ambiguous than murky, in spite of his newly affirmed focus towards murkiness and the irrational. Having already mastered a great technique and formally tied to the Italian neo-realist school, Kazan was out of ideas and seemed totally tied into the rhythm of *thrilling*: a turn to emptiness, a great Grand-Guignol spectacle.

Panic in the Streets was made in 1950. From 1945 to 1950, Kazan was on Broadway directing Arthur Miller's *All My Sons* and *Death of a Salesman* and then Tennessee Williams' *A Streetcar Named Desire*.

In 1951, Kazan made *A Streetcar Named Desire* for 20th Century Fox. His new focus was clear: the film was truly murky. A schizophrenic and humid American South in the middle of buckets of molten iron and copper beds. The psychology of Kazan's characters, previously fairly one-dimensional, became tortured and loony. The sweaty torpor in which Stanley Kowalski and his women languish is shaken up by the animalistic violence of sexual instincts. The artistic maturity of the director is manifested through the medium of a perfect and almost nauseating naturalism. But besides the anxious stressing of characters trapped by their mental illness, in the film there is a decadent theme where sociology and Freud are mixed together. The aesthetics and morals of the film expand from this intersection. The idea of existence is closed within the sociological naturalism of sin and fatal necessity to a sin that emerges from the dehumanized souls of miserable human beings.

An America of losers and impotent *refoulés* (sic) obsessed with sexual totems as the only creative impulse: this was Kazan's new America.

The siege of 20th Century Fox's *charnel house* was oppressive and agonizing. McCarthy's sinister power was at its peak. The blacklist was ready to engulf even the innocuous conscientious objectors.

In 1952, Kazan made *Viva Zapata!*, written in collaboration with John Steinbeck. This film deals with alleged historical premises now known to be false. The character of Zapata is grossly misrepresented. The pivotal points of the action are completely historically inaccurate. If *Viva Zapata!* was conceived as a politically aware western, or an allegorical literary text regarding the workers' revolution, then the discussion could have been otherwise: in that case, how could we not recognize Kazan's devotion to the homeless Mexicans, even if shown with picturesque scenery, and how could we not be affected by the bitter atmosphere of the civil war and not appreciate the intelligence of the costume drama? And we wouldn't be able to deny a certain appeal and adherence to the theme that seems to follow Kazan (no less decadent and historic than that in *A Streetcar Named Desire*). The director distorted psychology, he bent historically true events to show that power corrupts the leaders and extinguishes their revolutionary fervor; it separates them from their people, and consigns them to history as conservators of their own thinking and actions.

Although politically aware, *Viva Zapata!* is not however only a western (even though in spite of Kazan's intentions it cannot be called anything but a western); it wants to be a film about the history of Mexico, by the explicit declarations of its authors, and as such it calls for a clearly political discussion.

The fear of McCarthyism, which had a neutral effect on some people, pushed Kazan to zeal and put him in conflict with his own instinct and his own realistic education. It distorted him and caused a split in his own conscience. Kazan feverishly wanted to prove his 'new' loyalty because he was to soon testify in front of the HUAC. What better proof than a film? He and Steinbeck invented a character-chorus to accompany Zapata almost as if to limit the emblematic power of the protagonist: a revolutionary leader, even a false one, is always dangerous, the figure of an intellectual revolutionary that, as Kazan wrote: "impersonates those that take advantage of the demands of the people and are prone to betray everything to take and keep power."

This character, so dear to the director, is really only a naïve and grotesque little puppet, the caricature of a paranoid completely separate from the narrative arc and setting of *Viva Zapata!* Without a doubt, this gives an idea of the demons that tortured Kazan's sleep; Kazan, the star of 20th Century Fox, close to being grilled by McCarthy's men. Almost as if Kazan wanted to transfer to his para-communist professional revolutionary character all his disdain for himself and the action he was about to take.

The Trial

April 1952: Kazan was called to speak in front of the HUAC. Imagine the setting: the long interviews with 20th Century Fox executives, the endless discussions with lawyers, the blackmailing, and the last-minute indecision. All around Kazan there is a desert. Over Hollywood flies the yellow flag of intolerance.[1] Whoever resisted was struck down. He lost his income and his freedom. He was isolated from friends who didn't want to compromise themselves. Let's imagine races of powerful automobiles towards gigantic mansions, a completely different world from the one that welcomed little Elia Kazanjoglous in 1913, for insincere meetings with cold magnates of the business world, or perhaps nervous telephone calls and unrequested and unsolicited advice. A dark future weighed upon the talented and hypersensitive Kazan. He must have asked for support and the solidarity of producers and of political leaders, those in both America and other countries who never offered neither support nor solidarity. In his colleagues' eyes and in the eyes of the employees at 20th Century Fox, he must have seen pity and sympathy.

The night before the trial he must have looked at the film studios, the cameras, all the other instruments of his work as if for the last time. He may have remembered his difficult childhood: "I was twenty-four and a second-rate theater director and actor, and when I worked I earned $40 a week. [...] At that time, almost all of us felt threatened by two things: the economic depression and the ever-increasing power of Hitler. The streets were filled with the unemployed and the poor." Maybe he was afraid of poverty and returning to his sad roots.

Or perhaps a sharp Washington lawyer who was a specialist in McCarthy-esque inquisitions had already written his

---

1. *Bandiera gialla* is the Italian title of Kazan's 1950 film, *Panic in the Streets*. A yellow flag was an international maritime signal once used to indicate contagion. Now the yellow flag ("Quebec" or Q in international maritime signal flags) is employed to request boarding and routine port inspection. The "Lima" flag or "yellow jack," which is comprised of four alternating black and yellow squares, now denotes a quarantined ship.

ELIO PETRI · "CITTÀ APERTA" (1957–1958)

part. Perhaps he had already styled the dialogue of the accused Kazan, the *red* Kazan, the subversive Armenian immigrant who had unexpectedly arrived at the top of the social ladder and was the pride of the Kazanjoglous family, formerly at the edge of an abyss. Maybe Kazan had to learn this script in front of the mirror before his inquisition, just like one of his students at the Actor's Studio. Who can say whether, other than political blackmail, perhaps the gangster cabal was working on Kazan by planting bugs, or like the detectives in the famous trial of the film *Confidential* that screamed: "In Hollywood, everyone is a pederast or a Communist!"

"Elia Kazan [...] swore [...] that he and Clifford Odets, the playwright, were former members of the Communist Party [...]. He added that Mr. Odets had *assured* him that he, too, had done the same thing (quit the party 'permanently' in 1936) at about the same time."[2]

"Mr. Kazan [...] declined to identify party associates. Then he reconsidered: 'I have come to the conclusion [...] that I did wrong to withhold these names before, because secrecy serves the Communists and is exactly what they want.'"[3]

"The members of the communist unit to which he was assigned, Mr. Kazan said, all were associated with the Group Theatre [...]."[4]

Kazan named Lewis Leverett, J. Edward Bromberg, Phoebe Brand, Morris Carnowski, Tony Kraber, and Paula Miller.

"Two party 'functionaries,' he said, were assigned to 'hand the party line' to the unit. He listed them as V.J. Jerome [...] and Andrew Overgaard [...]."[5]

Written in the affidavit that he consigned to the Commission to exonerate himself apropos of *Viva Zapata!* was: "This is an anti-communist film. I recommend that you read my article regarding its political aspects in the *Saturday Review* of April 5, which I have already sent to one of the members of the investigatory committee, Mr. Nixon."

In his declaration, after his testifying, he wrote: "I was also

2. *New York Times*, April 12, 1952.
3. Ibid.
4. Ibid.
5. Ibid.

constrained by a typically specious reasoning that silenced many liberals. It goes like this: You may hate the Communists but you don't have to fight them or expose yourself because if you do, you fight against the right to have an unpopular opinion and you unite with those that fight civil liberties. I thought about this quite seriously. It is simply a lie. Secrecy helps the Communists [... ;] liberals must speak out."

Therefore, at first Kazan held himself back. After a few hours, he decided to "speak without reserve." Who can say whether even his hesitancy was not pre-scripted by the talented Washington lawyer? To save his face and simultaneously dramatize his actions?

"The last straw," declared Kazan, "was when I was invited to undergo the typical communist scenario of squirming in the chair and admitting my wrongs. I had a taste of living in a police state and I didn't like it [...]."

No doubt the "typical communist scenario" must have occurred during the brief time that Kazan was a member of the American Communist Party. How to explain then the ceremonial McCarthyism that he enthusiastically embraced?

Kazan returned to Broadway where the news reported a highly charged dialogue with Arthur Miller. It seems as though Miller, who had gone to Kazan's house for an explanation of Kazan's behavior, left the house saying that he couldn't be in the same house as an informer. Kazan followed him in his car all over New York, yelling at him at the stoplights, asking for understanding. Understanding which evaded Miller, who never forgave Kazan, not then and not later, when he wrote the polemic play *A View from the Bridge* (1955).

At that time, the importance of earning $4,000 a week seemed inconsequential to Kazan. Arthur Miller represented the America that he loved and then betrayed, perhaps all the while still loving. Although he experienced a sense of relief in having lifted such a weight from his shoulders, it was quickly followed by the anguish of isolation and solitude.

Furthermore, his job wasn't finished yet. The Smith Act required more evidence and more testimony. Kazan agreed to make a second-rate anti-communist film, *Man on a Tightrope* (1953), in which the actor Fredric March, after his success in *The Best Years of Our Life* (1946), had a difficult past that needed to be forgiven: he was a member of the Hollywood Anti-Nazi League and the Committee to Assist Spanish Refugees, he did the voiceover for the documentary *400 Millions* by the communist Joris Ivens on the war in China, and he was one of the most active propagandists against Germany, his birth country, and they say that the Nazis condemned him to death during the war *in absentia*: therefore, a typical subject for the HUAC.

Where Are You Running To, Kazan?

To further confirm his weakness, Kazan could have retracted his actions. Instead, he faced all of the consequences. He wrote newspaper articles defending the anti-communist contents of *Viva Zapata!*, he invited "all good liberals" who "had seen their livelihood threatened" to follow his example. He tried to be coherent. And yet, in 1954, he couldn't take the accusations anymore and publically denied filming *On the Waterfront* (1954) on the suggestion or the order of the McCarthyites. In a noted article criticizing the film, John Howard Lawson[6] wrote: "The denial is equal to a confession. Kazan or the screenwriter Schulberg, and Lee J. Cobb, who had the part of Johnny Friendly, officially promised to only pursue projects that conform to the ideas of the most reactionary in the Congress."[7]

Kazan filmed *On the Waterfront* at the end of 1953. It was the first film with a screenplay by Budd Schulberg, at least according to Kazan's official filmography.

Budd Schulberg also actively participated in the democratic pre-war climate in Hollywood. Just read his novels from that period: *What Makes Sammy Run?* (1941) and *The Disenchanted* (1950).

6. John Howard Lawson (1894–1977) was an American writer. He was for several years head of the Hollywood division of the Communist Party, USA.

7. John Howard Lawson, "Hollywood On the Waterfront: Union Leaders Are Gangsters, Workers Are Helpless," *Hollywood Review* 1.6 (1954) 3–4.

The first is the story of a newspaper office boy who becomes a famous film producer, infamous for his iron fist, beating down whomever he can, tricking, corrupting, and betraying before he is betrayed. His 'antagonist' is a screenwriter of a liberal bent who watches with objective disdain Sammy's rise to power, clinically writing about the different phases of his life.

The Disenchanted (literarily more interesting) came out of Schulberg's life. In his later years, F. Scott Fitzgerald returned to Hollywood to look for work. While he was successful, he disdained the cinema (his antipathy for the cinema became 'classic' in brief polemics such as *The Beautiful and Damned*, 1922, and *The Great Gatsby*, 1925). In 1937, alcoholic, diabetic, after a decade of obscurity and full of debt, Fitzgerald was compelled to accept Hollywood's handouts. He was offered a mediocre screenwriting job. During this project, his assistant was the twenty-something and enthusiastic Budd Schulberg, who was full of radical and Marxist ideas. *The Disenchanted* recounts the last months of the life of Fitzgerald and the beginning of a polemical friendship between the young man in politically active times and the disenchanted literary lion.

Among these novels, *On the Waterfront* is without a doubt of lesser quality. *Waterfront* is verbose and declamatory even though it is purportedly neorealistic (and the neorealism springs only from ill-used formal Farrellian formats). The description in the novel is separated from the general frame of American life: as if the laborers of the Bohegan port were the unhappiest American workers, or even the only unhappy people in America.

Budd Schulberg, too, a little while before, thought it appropriate to "speak without reserve."

Clinging to an Idea

That the port of New York was dominated by the teamsters' union is a fact. That blackmail & crime were used as administrative measures by the powers-that-be outside the union is also a fact. But as Lawson pointed out in the previously-mentioned article, the focus of the governmental inquiry was not to clean up an intolerable union situation in which worker's rights were ignored but rather to "introduce direct political control on New York's *Waterfront*: the first step towards the supervision and control of the unions on the national scale."[8] No wonder then if *On the Waterfront* was suggested to 20th Century Fox directly by Wall Street (which controlled the entire great American cinema) or by governmental authority.

Whatever the idea that got *On the Waterfront* produced, it is not a stretch to surmise that Kazan stubbornly took on this project to show coherence with his actions in April 1952 and to vent his inferiority complex with respect to progressives and Communists. In his 'Declarations' left for the McCarthyites, he said: "We cannot leave to the Communists the pretense of defending and wanting the same things that they kill in their countries. I speak of freedom of speech, freedom of the press, property rights, the rights of the worker, of equality, and above all, the rights of the individual. [...] The films I made or the comedies that I have chosen for directing represent my convictions."

Kazan clung to Schulberg's social ideas. He tried to shake them from inside his characters, refilling them with his restlessness, imbuing the story with a style that expresses social outrage, yet conserving, and worsening in some cases, Schulberg's storied conformism. In this way, the film seems like an insoluble knot of oppositions, stylistic as well. The Grand-Guignol aspect of the gangster scenes is superimposed over the limpid delicacy of the love story between Terry Malloy and Katie Doyle. The conventional figure of Father Barry dominates the sharp denouncing of the intolerable conditions of the dockworkers, and in the film the polemic against the ecclesiastical hierarchy that Schulberg originally put in his novel is tamped down. Decadent poisons and surprising emotions, vague and realistic intentions don't mix together. They remain inert and contradictory elements even if we are speaking of pure propaganda. On another level, there

8. Ibid.

are the same ideological incongruities in *On the Waterfront* as in *Viva Zapata!* Kazan's conscience, not an abstract conscience suspended in an historical emptiness, but an artist's conscience that was formed in a concrete period of time in a culture between the most modern and illuminated, shows its degradation once again.

Kazan declared himself against gangsterish blackmail and against the bestial exploitation of the workers, but the only action he proposes in the film to stop the ordinary course of events is to inform on the gangsters to the authorities. A crime is a crime and as such it must be denounced, and the port of New York is dominated by the criminals: but is the simple choice proposed in the film, to go from the docks to the police station, really able to change the relationships between the dock workers and their idea of solidarity? Or is it able to persuade them towards other & more profound individual responsibilities, which are themes that Kazan considers central to his film? We don't think so.

Without considering the probable political origins of the film, we think that Kazan was primarily interested in recounting *that* action of Terry Malloy, his informing, of the state of his soul *before* and *after* and of his finding himself in the middle of people that do not understand the scope of his action. One man is accusing his brother's murderers: this is a simple action. Malloy-Kazan instead takes his action knowing that he is more a mere informant than a man taking full advantage of all his rights. Once he has made his objectively brave decision, he is still anguished by the isolation that his colleagues impose upon him through their disdain. This notwithstanding, his solitude is more interior than social. Not only because the character Malloy-Kazan's morality, steeped in honor, is addressed, but because the director Kazan-Malloy essentially agrees with those who have isolated him in disdain, almost as if the director's subconscious blurred his vision.

If, in fact, presenting Terry Malloy's 'understanding' Kazan wanted to once again invite people to "speak without reservation" in the sense that images convey facts, he unconsciously renders the brave act of his protagonist as his own. There is no doubt that Kazan and Schulberg, whatever their intentions may have been, gave On the Waterfront a testimony of their will to work on a modern and engaged problem. Their incapacity to go beyond the analysis of a partial reality merits further study.

Kazan seemed to exhaust his 'social' interest in On the Waterfront as if the character Terry Malloy had appeased him and helped him free himself from his inhibitions.

In 1955 and 1956, years in which McCarthyism was beginning to wane, Kazan made two very different films: East of Eden and Baby Doll, working once again with John Steinbeck and Tennessee Williams. The first film turns on the restlessness of a southern boy who is affected by the artifice of family relationships created by patriarchal and religious hypocrisy, confusedly manifesting his tension towards the truth.

In Baby Doll, a girl is reduced to a neurotic state because of her impotent husband. Another man helps her with her emotional needs. Moravia states that, literarily speaking, the story is Boccaccio-esque but filtered through the sensibility of two modern and decadent Americans who are incapable of a real immoral joke.

The American South dominates both films: with the irrationality of moral scruples in the first, and the corruption of the psychological and social fabric in Baby Doll. Even though they are stylistically different, given the commercial constraints set by 20th Century Fox and the personalities of the writers employed by Kazan, the social environment is forcefully underlined in both, almost to suppose that from Kazan's original intellectual exchanges with American Marxists, he inherited a pronounced sociological sense (which in Baby Doll coincides with the psychological).

Only in 1957 with A Face in the Crowd did Kazan return to confronting the most explicit problems of the country. In the four years between On the Waterfront and his latest film, much had transpired in the world. McCarthyism was on the wane due to unforeseen changes in the international climate. The cold war was turning into a thaw. The Hollywood political climate also lightened up for commercial reasons, in order not to be isolated from the rest of the world. New directions were coming from official production offices. New men appeared on the scene, less cerebral and less able, but more courageous: from Aldrich to Ray to Delbert Mann. Odets wrote for Aldrich a violent and anti-Hollywood (and indirectly, anti-McCarthyism) film, *The Big Knife* (1955), which is almost self-critical. Then he wrote a film for Hetch Hill Lancaster Production Company on the scandal sheets: *Sweet Smell of Success* (1957), which was directed by Fred Zinneman (who in those years had made *From Here to Eternity*, 1953). In 1955-1956, in this thick group of problematic films in Hollywood, *Baby Doll* seems to fall from another planet.

A Face in the Crowd however, is part of the new atmosphere of American cinema. Kazan's new *engagé* film after the highest point of McCarthyism is against the alienation of mass habits and the mytho-maniacal cruelty of the Americans.

As Schulberg had written for Robson a fiery manifesto on the world of boxing, *The Harder They Fall* (1956), he wrote for Kazan a no-less intense manifesto against television. Here and there we see the classic Kazanian themes: a morbid view of sex and self-betrayal and betrayal of those who believe in him. It takes on whoever has power (even a television show and therefore, the direction of a film). But *A Face in the Crowd* expresses American impotence in the face of its myths. The style is rough, the characters' psychologies revert to the basic ones of the early films, but they all express a bitter and courageous pessimism. The narrative line is Schulberg's traditional one: a corrupt environment (Hollywood in *What Makes Sammy Run?*, boxing in *The Harder They Fall*, television in *A Face in the Crowd*), a negative character who embodies it (Sammy, the boxing organizer, Lonesome Rhodes), a positive character struggling to resist the corruption (a screenwriter, a sports journalist, a writer): a narrative technique imbued with dialectical and Marxist outlines and that reminds us of the theories of John Howard Lawson. Schulberg and Kazan's old radical passions arise in the film. Maybe the *boomerang* of their conscience had finished the parabola of its journey. Their love for Roosevelt's old anti-trust America turned into disdain for the frenzied form of American alienation after McCarthy: theirs seemed like disdain for a situation that constrained them to act against their conscience, to go against themselves. Isn't the protagonist of *A Face in the Crowd*, Lonesome Rhodes, a victim of political stupidity, thirsty for myths and lies? To satisfy his admirers' tendencies and internally pressed by egotism, Lonesome Rhodes transforms his provincial personality into an American demagogue: when the public realizes that Rhodes is lying to them, they smash the myth, helped by the powers that now know that the myth is unsupportable.

Like in *The Harder They Fall*, Kazan's film's intellectual figure is put in contrast with the negative character and the environment, and has written or is about to write a book where he *tells the truth*. So for Schulberg and Kazan, the intellectual is the only traditional custodian of dignity and civility. And this is the only dubious element of this recent Kazan film. There is nothing to disagree with in the polemic against inertia and the credulity of the masses in the film, since to shake people up, not only one but many shocks are necessary, in film, in literature, in politics, and with every means possible to go bravely on, at the cost of being unpopular.

Precisely on the basis of their film, it would be right to ask Kazan and Schulberg how much they have contributed to bringing Americans to the point that they are describing them. "Conserve that way of liberty, open and healthy, that gives us self-esteem," wrote Kazan speaking of the American way of life and no one, not even he, can forget those words.

Ours are hard times for he who wants to keep his self-respect. We would like (and we suppose that Kazan would as well) that the working conditions for artists and intellectuals be different than they are, that the future writers could write their books without having to re-write them for political inquisitions, that authors and directors would be free to express their dramas and tend to their opinions without answering to the FBI. If the way intolerance is used by political power is horrible and criminal, then so much more culpable are those that cede to the oppression, since they make it more difficult for the people to not have fear.

§ 1.9
"Straw" Intellectuals [1]

Dear Lucentini,[2] if you arrived at the letter "p" in your questionnaire of those who replied to the "Questions for a program" proposed by *Città aperta*, you wouldn't be disappointed. I would honestly reply that "I am not a Christian," as undoubtedly the other "p's" in the list would as well.

You could extend your poll beyond our 26 not-so-revered names and you would still be quite satisfied, since many others would respond the same way.

But in your brief article, even you implicitly admit that to stop at the result of this poll, although important, is not really productive except for, "clarifying [...] the exact amount of Christians in Europe, which is 475 million people according to the De Agostini atlas."

This is where the most important part of your work would start: that is, to establish the value that everyone places on their words: "I am not a Christian," and to which Christian daily practice this simple sentence corresponds.

We would discover that for many people it derives more from their desire not to be Christian than from truly not being Christian. I see in many people, including myself, a continuous struggle to divest our consciences of the tedious remnants of a Christian education that many of us could not avoid (since we were not old enough to assert our will). The religious prejudices affect us deeply. Just as André Gide sighed: "Gospel! Gospel! Such

1. Published in *Città aperta* 9-10 (June-July 1958).

2. Franco Lucentini (1920-2002) was an Italian writer, journalist, translator, and editor of anthologies.

peace you promised to the world...," there are still too many "leftist intellectuals" who believe (perhaps dragging these opinions around like lazy prejudices) in the social value of Christianity.

Elio Vittorini,[3] who always has a distinctly dramatic and charming way to demonstrate his contradictions, wrote in the *Politecnico*: "In my childhood, I also believed in His divinity. I went to Mass, I went to confession, I took communion. I was twenty years old when I last went to confession and took communion. Then I stopped believing in His divinity, and I started to believe in His humanity. Now I believe that He was the greatest Man who ever existed, and that everything that men have said since Him, whether more modern, concrete, or useful, is always in contrast with what He said."[4]

It is admirable that an intellectual can profess an honest disbelief in Christian Divinity. Yet such a position is undermined when an obscure mysticism is intimated — as is happening — in the author's use of capitalization and when controversial claims about the nature of man, who becomes a new sort of god, exist in the text.

However, the most pernicious aspects of Christianity that remain in the consciences of non-Christians are not of a moral nature.

I saw and heard this first-hand, when many of my friends who were for the most part Communists and atheists were confronted in crucial moments of their existence with a choice between a Christian morality (which they found automatically ready, just like a maternal breast), and a non-Christian morality that had to be constructed within their own conscience, reflection by reflection, renunciation by renunciation, choice by choice: whether to baptize their children or not, whether to divorce or not (when divorce became necessary as the only way to salvage familiar situations which were irreparably deteriorated), whether to redefine the stale Italian idea of family, or surrender to the status quo.

Moment by moment, along their whole existence and in their solitude, non-Christians find themselves in need of constructing

3. Elio Vittorini (1908–1966) was an Italian writer and novelist. He was an influential voice in the modernist school of novel writing. His best-known work is the anti-fascist novel *Conversazione in Sicilia* (*Conversations in Sicily*), for which he was jailed when it was published in 1941.

4. Elio Vittorini, "Lettera a Carlo Bo," in *Diario in pubblico* (Milan: Bompiani, 1976) 193.

a morality that is different from the current Christian morality, because in order to live it, it is not enough to just deny the Christian one. And everyone's existence is too short for our consciences to be able, on our deathbed, to remain non-Christian: we have too many fears and our Christian ancestry weighs too heavily on us.

Anatole France's cold-blooded & non-Christian Professor Bergeret, after catching his wife prone on a couch with his prize student, first experiences the instinct of a "simple and violent man and of a wild animal." Then he "stopped being purely instinctual, primitive and destructive, without ceasing to be jealous and irritated"; and in this second stage, "his thoughts went from rudimental to social; remnants of old theologies would pile up confusedly with Decalogue's fragments, shreds of ethics, Greek, Scottish, German, and French mottos, and pieces of moral legislation that, like a flint stone, hammered on his head and set it on fire."[5]

The influence of our Christian ancestry is so similar to that of Professor Bergeret's — except for his occasional deplorable family disgraces — that before even the tiniest 'ethical' dilemma in our life, for example, making a private decision; giving to charity; tipping; deciding whether or not to look at and subsequently desire and seduce someone else's wife; in every moment when we are faced with a decision among different moral alternatives, the religious foundation of our 'morality' shakes us up, pushed by even more retrograde and remote instincts. (It is enough to think about the tremendous individualistic yet sometimes irrational drive in many people's ambitions, and to the sad picture of the relations among those who constitute the cultural *milieu* of our country: looked at analytically, our cultural and artistic life may seem more like a breathless race toward success rather than a peaceful competition of ideas. And for the most part it is not the ideas that create the contrast, but this irrational individualistic emulation).

5. Petri is referring to *Monsieur Bergeret à Paris* (Monsieur Bergeret in Paris) (1901), part four of Anatole France's *L'Histoire contemporaine* (A Chronicle of Our Own Times). The first three parts are: *L'Orme du mail* (The Elm-Tree on the Mall) (1897), *Le Mannequin d'osier* (The Wicker-Work Woman) (1897), and *L'Anneau d'améthyste* (The Amethyst Ring) (1899). [TN]

Some leftist intellectuals, even militant Communists, are a bit like Pietro Germi's *L'uomo di paglia* (*A Man of Straw*, 1958) in the way in which they face specific problems of their moral life. (Aren't all the obstacles in Germi's film tied to the moral confusion of its protagonist, in his refusal to know and clearly analyze the terms of his moral issues? The poetic reason of the film could have been the protagonist's incoherence, if the director's own attitude weren't also confused and contradictory and even expressing a conclusive religious position. And even this final element could have been, if not a poetic inspiration, at least a new psychological and social aspect in the protagonist's portrait if it had contained a critical foundation, or any recognition of impotence, and if the author's own inspiration hadn't fallen to the expressive level of a dime store novel).

Many non-Christian intellectuals (straw men) get married in a church and they secretly let their wives baptize their children: do they do that, I wonder, to avoid 'painful' discussions, as a justification of the unconscious fear to act outside the dominant religious doctrine?

We are accustomed to justifying many things in this context: a modern, tolerant spirit yearns to find a reason for everything. The understandable fear of fanaticism transforms indignation into silent comprehension. We don't talk about some of our friends' weaknesses because they belong to the realm of private feelings. It is difficult to judge, criticize, and accuse others when it is about such intimate matters. A friend comes to you, Lucentini. He has been with this girl for a long time and they have now come to the inevitable discussions: she, maybe even just to not 'break' from her family, requests that they have a religious wedding ceremony. Your friend believes that since this is a pure formality and he is not a 'believer,' it is not a big issue.

He is a refined intellectual, he reads Baudelaire and Valery, or maybe he is a nuclear physicist: but he is in love with this girl and the very thought of losing her drives him crazy. What would you do, Lucentini? Would you start to explain to him that that way of loving is irrational, that love in itself is not an eternal feeling? Would you send him back to Seneca & Lucretius? Would you remind him of the immensity of the universe and of the sputniks that revolve around us like children gone mad? What would you do, Lucentini? Tell me. Whatever you say to him, he won't get it: in order to marry the girl, he will go to church &, if needed, he will confess, take communion, go back to church two or three times. He will tolerate the priest paternally patting him on the shoulder and he will listen to the priest's pretentious and empty sermons. He thinks: "It doesn't matter, I am not a believer." (And even you, when thinking of the infinite vastness of the universe, to the sputniks and to Seneca, and seeing everything as brief & vain, maybe you agree with him).

It is also through these innumerable acts of weakness that the Christian ritual multiplies and survives the rhythm of modern times.

From the hodgepodge and the dismissal of 'moral' questions, considered by everyone to be of secondary importance, we can move to the observation of true political and ideological distortions.

Just take a look, dear Lucentini, at some titles in *L'Unità*, like the one cited by Chiaretti in the latest editorial of *Città aperta* in which the author complained that the Pope did not support the Soviet antinuclear initiatives. And I could cite, in the same newspaper, an article whose title triumphantly announced that in Poland, since the Communists took power, the number of believers has risen. From this we can deduct: A) that the Marxist-Leninist ideology, with support from Stalinism, pushes toward Christianity; and B) that under communism, people seek refuge in churches.

Recently, a well-known communist journalist commented in *L'Unità* on the issue of the seventy bishops who declared themselves against the Republican constitution. He particularly underlined the political direction of these rebellious clerics, while overlooking the absolutely arrogant illegitimacy of their gesture.

It was only later that Togliatti stressed this aspect. While suggesting how to respond to the bishops' action, he opined that, "first of all, one must consider the illegitimacy of the act, and then the political view that the bishops shamelessly embraced." If the bishops had sided with a political view opposite to that of the Christian Democrats (what the journalist from *L'Unità* seemed to secretly hope) their action would not have been less unconstitutional.

The journalist wrote: "There is no hope that the cardinals and bishops would unite and pronounce themselves for peace [...]." Should a communist journalist really end up hoping that religious men get interested in politics? (The journalist in his article addressed not only the issue of peace, but also that of the 'social question'). In our daily life, priests already act like psychoanalysts and the majority of 'believers' consider religion a totally private matter. Why would we regress? In the illusion of achieving a socialist revolution with Catholic priests?

Political compromises and ideological distortions allow some Marxists to call the worker-priest movement 'progressive.' They confuse the thirst for knowledge that pushed pastor Vincent van Gogh to go to the miners of Borinage (and even the painter's religious fever was controversial), with the mystic missionary drive that leads pale intellectual priests to preach God's word to the proletarian non-practitioners. And this is not to alleviate the proletarian's misery, but to madly and egotistically teach them religion and metaphysically repeat Christ's sacrifice. To this end, we should reconsider some judgments (except those on his own judicial issues) on the ideas of Danilo Dolci,[6] whose late Protestantism can provide vast sociological documentation but not any modern ideological enlightenment. It is disconcerting that different currents of Marxist thought seek a dialogue with social Christianity and calculatedly ignore Existentialism.)

Therefore we are not Christian, and like you and I, many others are not as well, ranging from Attardi to Vespignani and Zigaina.[7] But is it enough to say that?

6. Danilo Dolci (1924–1997) was an Italian social activist, sociologist, popular educator, and poet. He is best known for his opposition to poverty, social exclusion, and the mafia in Sicily. He is considered to be one of the protagonists of the non-violence movement in Italy.

7. Ugo Attardi (1923- 2006) was an Italian painter, sculptor, and writer. Renzo Vespignani (1924-2001) was an Italian painter, printmaker, and illustrator; in 1956, he also co-founded the magazine *Città aperta*. Giuseppe Zigaina (b. 1924) is an Italian painter.

ELIO PETRI · "CITTÀ APERTA" (1957–1958)

Just like Christians are required to comport with the principles of their religion, so the non-Christians should be asked to be more consistent with their own consciences and that they start with small gestures (big gestures).

Is that a request for fanaticism? No, but we should pay increased attention to these delicate and fundamental problems, knowing that we won't be able to completely eradicate our internal irrationality. In two hundred years, another Professor Bergeret, after seeing his wife prone on a couch with one of his best robots, will conjure lines from the gospels and the scriptures, fragments of encyclical letters, and obscure previously unheard-of voices will pile up in his thoughts. And it will be difficult for him to say he is not Christian, if he won't know how to act with his wife, his favorite robot, and within himself.

Dear Lucentini, when you compare us with those that you call Christian 'comrades,' we should draw a clear line of distinction. I don't want us to end up being their 'non-Christian comrades.' I would also like to see someone else to join this debate with more coherence and not jump all over the place like I did here.

2.
THE DEBATE ABOUT ITALIAN CINEMA
(1962–1982)

§ 2.1 Questionaire: The Directors of the 1960s[1]

We dedicated the following questionnaire to 'new' Italian and foreign filmmakers. Many of those we have addressed so far directed only one or two films. All of them, regardless of their age, have revealed themselves to the general public in the past few months. We didn't receive all the answers we expected: however, we feel that those that we have collected can offer an important overview of the intentions and the goals of the filmmakers who will shape the cinema of the 1960s.

Elio Petri's Answers

In what ways do you feel different from the film directors of the previous generation?

I won't deny that I still look up to some of these directors: the impact of the revolution they brought about in Italian and international cinema is still difficult to evaluate today. *Ossessione* might recall *Toni* (1935), but it is through *Ossessione* that many understood how to proceed in filmmaking. Ten years after their first release, *Roma, città aperta* and *Paisà* (*Paisan*, 1946) directly influenced the French *Nouvelle Vague*. If in Italy we cannot talk of a current *Nouvelle Vague*, it is because we already had one with those directors of the past, and that was more than a *Nouvelle Vague*. It was not only a linguistic or a cerebral revolt but

1. First published in Vittorio Spinazzola (ed.), *Film 1962* (Milan: Feltrinelli, 1962). The other interviewed directors were Giuseppe Bennati, Peter Brook, Henri Colpi, Damiano Damiani, Vittorio De Seta, Nicolò Ferrari, Edgar Morin, Ermanno Olmi, Gillo Pontecorvo, Lionel Rogosin, Franco Rossi, & Jiří Weiss.

also a rebellion against Fascism, and against the provincialism of Italian culture and the very structure of Italian society. Many of these directors still now have interesting ideas and worldviews. If we think of the artists from the postwar years until now who contributed to the formation of the Italians' self-awareness, these are the filmmakers that would first come to mind, followed by a few writers and painters. Other filmmakers couldn't or didn't want to adapt to the 'restoration': their work would have been very different if their freedom of expression hadn't been constantly impeded by political power. In this light, we should reconsider the filmographies of many directors. What are the differences between them and us? At a fundamental level, it is a matter of talent: I feel ten times less talented. Then there are differences of interests, but then we should also talk about our different backgrounds and the different periods in which we took our first fundamental steps. After the cinema revolution came a restoration, and the atmosphere during a counter-reformation is always suffocating and obstructionist. Therefore, the themes that come to our attention today are all 'internal': the protagonist of *Ladri di biciclette* (*The Bicycle Thief*, 1948), today, must face not only the society in which he lives, but also his own conscience.

Besides the specifically cinematographic, what cultural and intellectual traditions do you intend to connect with in your work?

For those, like me, who want to tell stories about individuals and about the mental encumbrances they find within themselves without ever losing sight of social and historical phenomena and their social class direction (as an external imposition but not a deterministic one), Sartre's is a necessary lesson. Sartre's continuous effort to bring Existentialism back to earth and his attention (I would say tension) toward Marxist research, and his open-mindedness (which allows him to find the new and lively aspects in techniques shunned by others, for example, his interest in psychoanalysis), all of this is very important material to study.

With regard to cinema, I believe that the neorealist tradition is still very valuable as a window into people, sentiments, and reality. The neorealists must be absorbed for the spirit that animated neorealism & not for the problems it exposed.

What elements of filmic storytelling attract your interest?

For me, the basic magic of filmic storytelling resides in its essentially objective nature. The psychology and physical appearance of actors, the concreteness of objects and sets, the materiality of light, the power of a realistic atmosphere, the theme and the screenplay: each of these elements has an autonomous objective presence and when they combine, under the energetic direction of a filmmaker, they produce a human event, unique in its appearance and even in its substance. It is great fun to unleash these elements, and it is very difficult to master them. The struggle is consciously inserting one's own subjective view within these objective elements.

Which aspects of the society in which you live and of the contemporary world in general directly or indirectly capture your attention?

Some powerful forces tend to alienate man from himself, to extinguish every thought in him, and to roil his conscience. Life can oppress us under the weight of a pile of social relationships and can reduce itself to the monotony of mere survival and to the obsessive ticking of fixed hours that rotate around our physiological centers. There exists an apparently contradictory link between the uncertainty in which we live today (which in theory should push us toward a continuous renewal) and the stagnation of consciences, that is, the fear of thinking and living: many things stem from the unraveling of this knot. All that is human is also fascinating, but nothing is more valuable to us than our conscience and our integrity. The worst act of arrogance that cinema could do is to penetrate men's consciences and to invent a 'special' camera. Images have the great advantage of being more objective than words. The foundation of modern art is all in the will to stubbornly keep or give man back to himself, even in his suffering, and in the desire to be an alert witness to events, a witness not in the service of alienating forces. To have an idea, then, is different from fully representing it: here begins my personal situation.

Besides official censorship, what kind of prejudices, misunderstandings, & obstacles did you encounter while developing your work?

A fundamental incomprehension is that still today many people mistake cinema for simple distraction, and this opinion is shared even by people of the so-called educated classes. (I am not saying that some films, or many films, shouldn't be commercial. As a spectator, I would be sad if adventure films or Totò films didn't exist, but I wouldn't want every film reduced to that level.) Audiences can be an obstacle in developing a cinema focused on ideas or at least on issues. Since cinema is fundamentally a spectacle (and nobody, not even the most Calvinist of us, can deny that), its natural destination is the audience. If this relationship is not understood dialectically, then cinema, instead of exercising an active cultural function, places itself behind the last row of the audience. Among the duties of our cinema are to goad, animate, and provoke the critical spirit of the viewers, and to expose the problems of our times. This often sets cinema to go against the tide and to isolate itself from the audience, as has already happened (with Stroheim, Visconti, and Antonioni). Producers don't like this, although it is a fact that films that go against the tide eventually penetrate the viewers' consciences until the films become profitable (and I would cite the same names here). These films, in short, constitute a sort of investment that only few people dare to make. As we know, cinema is an industry (this also can't be denied), even at the level of thirty million films.[2] As such, it follows market regulations, so that production 'flirts'

2. Petri here means thirty million lire, the old Italian currency. It corresponds to roughly $20,000 USD.

with the audience's apathy and predilection for distraction (market regulations explain the massive presence of comedy and of erotic, even soft-porn films in Italy). Producers easily give in to the possibility of exerting some influence on the audience so that they can direct their taste.

So, a serious impediment in the development of a film is its expected cost, but this can be resolved by being alert. Political censorship, on the contrary, is an almost insurmountable obstacle, since it reaches deep into the subconscious of the cinema community. An extreme example of the combination of uncertainty, stagnation, and fear comes from the events of our political life: I would gladly make a portrait-film of a young political man (such as Mario Alicata, or Giulio Andreotti, or both in the same film), in which the names and the positions of political life are true, but is there a producer available to face such a challenge in Italy? Politics, which takes up such a great part of the life of Italians, even in the consciences of those who think they can avoid its decisions, has no right to appear in our cinema (the only example remains Francesco Rosi's great *Salvatore Giuliano*, but that should be discussed separately). Cinema's contribution to the development of a real democracy in our country was only minimally influenced by politics, and it could have been much greater. But some of 'them' didn't want that. Very few people, in our country, truly love democracy.

§ 2.2
Team Play & Individual Specialties[1]

Art and culture have always had the function of saving man from himself.

Art is and was a voluntary and involuntary witness of the de-humanization of human relationships, the reification of man and alienation. These are ancient phenomena that have taken different forms over time. For the first time in modern society, art has acknowledged the value of its testimony by acquiring a freedom of expression that strives to be absolute, and by venturing into the heart of the human condition. At the same time, we are making artworks into commodities.

Cinema has always been part of this commercialization. Even before being accepted as an art, it was established as an industry, and that's what it has been and it continues to be: a means of persuasion, a tale for illiterates, and a giant clown.

A relationship of victim-perpetrator has developed between films and viewers, and the two take turns playing each role. As the middle-class spectator experiences a film, his need to see everything at the same level of his private existence rises: he is accustomed to looking down and he refuses to raise his gaze.

In Italy, among middle-class viewers (from the bourgeois to the factory worker), vulgarity has increased, which demonstrates an unconscious desire to be scoundrels, and a masochistic desire to see themselves mirrored, yet mocked, on the screen. So the relationship between cinema and audience is set on a dynamic

1. Originally published in *Cinema 60*, 44 (August 1964).

that begins to have an obsessive tendency to infinity: cause and effect, the effect becomes the cause and vice versa. The audience demands vulgarity, cinema offers more than double of the requested vulgarity, the audience asks for three times the vulgarity, and cinema gives out eight times the vulgarity.

The viewers are seen by authors like whimsical children, who must be praised and led into the direction of their weaknesses, like ignorant masses waiting to be urged towards their most base instincts.

I don't believe that a filmmaker should work only for himself. I believe in cinema as a spectacle, as a mean of communication for general ideas. I think that without its natural and only interlocutor — which is its contemporary audience —, cinema loses a great part of its vitality. Departing from this idea, I think that the future perspectives for free cinema — or, in other words, the future perspectives for the liberation of cinema — are connected with those of the birth of a free audience — that is, for the liberation of the audience from its mental conditioning.

The history of free cinema in Italy corresponds to the history of our best cinema. If ever there were a *Nouvelle Vague* in Italy, it didn't represent a generational or linguistic revolt. Rather, it was born under the push of a revolution; it was the result of a critical movement of renewal. From the new developments of the *Nouvelle Vague* came a method that was used in the restoration phase to depict its effects. We can say that from *Roma, città aperta* to De Sica and Zavattini's films, to Visconti and up to Fellini's last film, all this has developed unbeknownst to the producers, against the rules of supply and demand, and even against the desires of the middle-class audience, by taking advantage of the lack of organization and the wild entrepreneurial spirit of film production. Today things are different. The structural crisis of cinema caused the disappearance of small film producers & led to the formation of a monopolistic market, in which there is no room for producing films that differ from those which already make money on paper.

Probably, for a while, the cinema of ideas will have to exist outside the industry, without its support.

Today, films of ideas can count on the same audience that appreciates a successful book; this is already something. We must address this audience, and start from this economic fact. In other European countries this kind of audience has already gone past the pre-natal stage; and, in fact, we should aim to create an international market for the cinema of ideas. There are forces in Italy that may be interested in limiting the alienating power of cinema: we should turn to them. But first of all, I believe that the initiative should be the author's. Among the lessons we can learn from the French *Nouvelle Vague*, or from the English *Free Cinema*, or from the avant-garde American groups, is a moral and cultural one that concerns the research conducted by the authors to find a common ideological and economic base. They immediately looked at broader interests, while sacrificing their own individual interests. They were team players from the start. Here, instead, we prefer quick and individual specialties. Perhaps, thanks to the intelligence and perseverance of one author, good films of ideas will still be produced. But if the cinema of ideas will be able to survive in Italy thanks only to the initiative of groups of authors, I can't say.

§ 2.3
Crisis Or Vitality?[1]

"*Crisis or Vitality?*" Those of us who have been working in Italian cinema for twenty years and have witnessed so many defeats, still retain the stubbornness to keep working and believing in it. Yet, from the outside, it might even seem a form of regression, a monomania. We know that dealing with cinema means dealing with the problems of society. Even in moments of confusion and ideological panic, our effort has always been to reconcile the discourse on film with the discourse on society. I maintain that one of the few concrete results of Marxist activity in Italy is having imposed on their adversaries some elements of their analytical method: so that many Catholic film critics today unconsciously speak *en marxiste*.

It is not impossible — and not only for the love of paradox — that the best Marxist economists are now in the research offices of Confindustria.[2]

If you say: "Crisis or vitality?" you must mean the crisis or vitality of Italian society, since we know that films, and the crisis or vitality of who makes them, are consciously or unconsciously a testimony to larger phenomena that not only involve taste, but also qualitative changes in people's feelings and thoughts.

Witnesses can also be reticent: and in the current reticence of Italian cinema, in fact, we can see the whole history of Italian society of the last twenty years, a history made of frustration and repression of the best cultural instincts; of the triumph of petty bourgeois rationalism; and of the great attempt on the part

1. Originally published in *Cinema 60* (April–June 1967) 62–63.

2. Confindustria is the Italian employers' federation, founded in 1910. It groups together more than 113,000 voluntary member companies, accounting for nearly 4,200,000 individuals. It aims to help Italy's economic growth and thereby benefit its members. [TN]

of the bourgeoisie to make every news official, whether coming from intellectual research or from a mere journalistic scoop, so that often the first would be equal to the second.

The great moral breadth of postwar Italian cinema that we call neorealism allowed our cinema, and along with it a part of our culture, to become less provincial. After twenty years, we are experiencing a reverse phenomenon: the return to the basest of provincialisms, that which speaks the language of television and tends to make cinema a futile and petty escape.

In Italian society, blind egoism, which is the most miserly of the drives that originate in man's unconscious, has won. The power of this instinct lies in the exploited man's hope that he will one day be able to take the place of the exploiter, so that he takes the exploiter as his role model. The joys of the exploiter become the joys of the exploited. For example, the sight of Gianni Agnelli on his giant yacht makes his employees feel proud.[3]

In these past twenty years, the very concept of class has changed. I cannot tell you the scientific terms of this problem, but I believe that it would be easy enough to find them if a courageous attempt were made to research them. Surely the bourgeoisie doesn't have an opponent class that can contest its *whole* way of living, its *whole* morality anymore. The goals of a bourgeois and of a proletarian are the same: they both are of an exclusively material nature and they are concerned just with their own wellbeing. There is a sentence by Marx quoted by Engels in *Origin of the Family* that perfectly describes the situation in which we've lived for the past twenty years: "Innate human casuistry to seek to change things by changing their names! And to find loopholes for breaking through tradition within tradition itself, wherever a direct interest provided a sufficient motive."[4]

So we have abstract paintings in a bourgeois living room, Socialists that support the Atlantic pact, Soviet presidents who meet the Pope, psychoanalysis employed in market research, and I am going to spare you any more of the endless "human casuistry" that since Marx's time hasn't gotten any better.

3. Giovanni or "Gianni" Agnelli (12 March 1921–24 January 2003) was an Italian industrialist and principal shareholder of Fiat. He was one of the richest men of the 20th century. [TN]

4. Frederick Engels, *The Origin of the Family, Private Property and the State* (Chippendale: Resistance Books, 2004) 66. [TN]

The bourgeoisie found a way to break their tradition compelled by historical development while remaining "within tradition itself." The bourgeoisie sedated its main adversary by providing it with symbols of wealth that fill its house and empty its heart and mind. We haven't yet found an agreement on the salary to assign to class collaboration. But as you will see, the argument is of an economic nature.

Europe is sedated, and in this Europe, Italy was "the easiest to sedate" because of the low level of education, the far-stretching misery, and the supremacy of the Church, which make it easy to corrupt everything and to take control of the symbols of wealth.

Our society is rooted in old principles that were badly or never applied. Now we don't even have those principles anymore, and maybe the only advantage is that soon we will reach a point in which there will be no principle at all.

In this situation, intellectuals found that the only instruments to (influence and) organize culture were in the hands of those in command, so each of them found the 'loophole' that Marx mentions. A great number of literary prizes, consulting, study centers, festivals, and retrospectives flourished along with technological innovations, such as motorized cars & the automated laundry machine. Today an intellectual, whether 'integrated' or 'apocalyptic' (the first is worried about not being integrated enough, and the second about not being apocalyptic enough), is ready for any book introduction, presentation, conference, and roundtable; he is available for any questionnaire, survey, and prize jury. Now intellectuals even appear on television; so Montale will be on after Bobby Solo,[5] and even the mystery of existence hidden in a few of his verses offered in the daily televised programs becomes a petty bourgeois least common denominator. Today one could even be afraid to sign a manifesto against the Vietnam War, since in all this confusion it looks & sounds like a sinister advertisement.

It is thus an etheric society that found in cinema a very reliable witness, since an etheric quality has always been predominant in cinema.

5. Bobby Solo (1945) is a popular Italian singer and musician.

§ 2.3 · CRISIS OR VITALITY?

The harshly fought protest of the first postwar years, including the direct and brutal intervention of politicians (do you remember Giulio Andreotti's battles against *Umberto D.?*), is today protected by those who protested. There is more: while Marco Bellocchio's first film[6] — which is an extreme attempt at revolt — might not have pleased some old Communists, it was enthusiastically praised by *Il Popolo*; this is to say that the confusion has become embarrassing even on a purely human level.

Up to now I have tried to suggest some ideas for discussion, but above all this one: let's try to understand how it could happen that in Italy, the films of ideas — even those most clearly engaged in a battle for renewal — can only find the support of the bourgeois spectator who is theoretically against them since they completely lack the empathy and support of the proletarian audience.

What did the authors of those films do wrong? Was there ever a guide in Italy who educated a conscientious audience? When and until what year? And why did this guide lose our support and trust? And how can we recreate that previous situation? Is it even possible? The contradictions are many and obvious: some of the most courageous films that appeared in these past few years in Italy, in France, and in Great Britain, were produced with American money. Moreover, they were successful only thanks to the European and American bourgeois audiences.

Do these contradictions mean something that, once discerned, can help to better understand what needs to be done?

---

6. *I pugni in tasca* (*Fists in the Pocket*, 1965), is an excoriating attack on Catholic morality and the institution of the bourgeois family and its value system.

§ 2.4 Elio Petri Trusts Italian Cinema[1]

There is a group of authors that every year produce interesting and original work that is alive, full of character, and intuitive: and this group isn't small. With this I don't mean to say that the reality of cinema is without worries, uncertainties, and annoyances. Today's cinema faces a most dangerous enemy: the industry that tends to commercialize it, to divest it of interest, to take the energy and the character out of it.

According to many producers, the audience is tied to cinema in a simplistic relationship of cause and effect: instead of worrying about raising the quality of the audience by providing viewers with innovative films and by presenting them with gradually more ambitious films, producers propose poor-quality and naïve products that contribute to deaden the audience's intelligence and imagination. The break that exists with the avant-garde has widened: avant-garde cinema proposes more sophisticated expressive means while the audience prefers an amorphous and conventional language because of laziness and lack of curiosity. For this reason, the industry exploits the trends: yesterday it was James Bond and its spin-offs, today it is westerns, tomorrow it will be dark-themed comics such as *Diabolik, Satanik, & Batman*.

The greatest enemy, however, is inside the authors' conscience and it consists of their fear of not being successful, and therefore their acquiescing to the producers' requests, even the most humiliating.

I have noticed that when the top group of Italian film authors is alive and ready to fight, the so-called commercial cinema also tends to work at a higher level.

1. Originally published in *Cineforum* 62 (February 1967).

2.5 For Whom Do We Write? For Whom Do We Shoot?

Questionnaire of the journal *Bianco & Nero*[1]

We would pose the problem in another way, with a slightly provocative intention.

More than twenty years ago, at the end of an interview, writer Cesare Pavese said: "The greatest contemporary narrator is [...], among Italians, Vittorio De Sica." His statement was then understood mostly as an explicit reference to a narrative 'national-popular' ideal and audience, common in books and films; but an ideal and an audience that only postwar cinema eventually really and fully reached.

Today, however, many people would even consider that result a generous neorealistic illusion that flourished in the 'unitarian' atmosphere of storicism. And maybe they will sarcastically compare it to the success of *Love Story* — as a novel, film, a confection — as the concrete reality of a relationship finally established between a narrative ideal and a large 'audience' in the 'unitarian' atmosphere of consumerism.

Between the two extreme poles of a polemical scheme, that is, the ambitions of the 1940s and the regression that ensued, are valid alternatives possible? Alternatives that won't exhaust themselves within the context of an elite? In other words, is it possible to imagine any authentic relationship (analogous or different, and even opposite) between a common ideal for books and films, and its collective audience? And where would we put the problem of the televised 'original' or 'drama'?

[1]. Originally published in *Bianco e Nero* 5–6 (May–June 1972).

If instead we deem it impossible to have a common ideal, then how do the different forms of communication place themselves before their specific mass audience? And how have the socio-economic transformations of the past twenty years, and particularly the industry, influenced the process of differentiation between film and novel: were they relevant on a technical-structural level (that is to say, within the very structures of language), on a communicative level (the different forms of fruition), or in terms of the psycho-physical mechanisms of perception and knowledge (images and words)?

On a general level then, we can now speak about the existence of a collective audience, a vast group of readers or viewers (similar or different among themselves) that is relatively homogenous from a sociological, ideological, and cultural point of view. If that is the case, what function does it have: purely receptive, passive, consumerist, or consciously active and critical? Does it remain conservative and motionless, or can it become a real interlocutor? If that is not the case, if the 'audience' is only a misunderstanding, then for whom do we write or make a film?

Elio Petri's Answer

In order to tackle the themes that emerge in every part of the questionnaire, analysis that compares the 'audience' of a novel and the 'audience' of a film would be needed. Without an analytical study of this particular sociological situation, we can only list a series of questions and perhaps we will have an approximate idea of how to proceed. What is the value for the individual and also for the social context, of the human experience of purchasing a novel and consuming its pages in one's own home, or in a train, in a waiting room, in the bathroom, or before sleeping at night? Are there novels that are suitable to any kind of situation? Can Proust be read on a train?

Can a detective novel be read at a table? Is there an age at which Proust can be read anytime and anywhere, and other moments in life when reading his work requires a ritual? Is it a ritual to read Proust? Is it a ritual to read Dumas? Flaubert's *Sentimental Education* is a quick read. Tolstoy's *War and Peace* is also a quick read, but can we say the same about Beckett? Is the act of reading a ritual in itself? And if it is a ritual, which social classes are involved in its social content? Is *being able to* read a sort of social promotion? Is reading itself a sort of social promotion? Is *being able to* write a sort of social promotion? Are writing and publishing a sort of social promotion? And in what measure does the goal of social promotion affect these two choices? And, going back to the beginning, what is a 'reader' and what is a 'novelist'? Beyond the merely social reasons, are there reasons that bring people to read or to write, that concern communication, or the rigorous desire to communicate with other people? Is the isolation of a person who reads or writes an escape from oneself? And if it is an escape from self, is it just that, or is it an attempt to come together with 'others' in the act of reading and writing?

We could turn all of these questions into cinematographic terms, along with the other hundreds or thousands that one could ask on the same topic.

What is the value, for the individual, but also for the social context, of the human experience of withdrawing from one's work and life and entering in a movie theater, sitting in the dark and watching a film? Are there films that are suitable to any kind of situation? Can Bergman be watched in between train rides? Does it make sense to go out at night in winter, alone or with friends, to 'go watch' an escapist film? Is there an age at which Bergman can be 'watched' anytime and anywhere, and other moments in life when watching his work requires a ritual? Is it a ritual to watch Bergman? Is it a ritual to 'watch' Groupe Vertov's *Lotte in Italia* (*Struggle in Italy*, 1971)? Is it a ritual to watch Ford's *Stagecoach* (1939)? Chaplin's *Modern Times* (1936) is a quick watch. De Palma's *Scarface* (1983) is also a quick watch, but can we say the same about Bergman's *Persona* (1966), or *Lotte in Italia*? Is the act of going to watch a film a ritual in itself? And if it is a ritual, which social classes are involved in its social content? Is *being able to* (that is to say, having the time and money to) go and watch a film a sort of social promotion? Is the very act of going to watch a film a sort of social promotion? Is making a film a sort of social promotion? And in what measure does the goal of social promotion affect these two choices? And, going back to the beginning, what is a 'viewer' and what is a 'filmmaker'? Beyond the merely social reasons, are there reasons that motivate people to go and watch a film or to make a film, that concern communication or the rigorous desire to communicate with other people? Is the act of gathering with others in a public setting considered communicative? Is the act of entering in a room for a public spectacle, and immersing oneself in darkness next to a mass of unknown 'others' the same as isolating oneself? And does the act of shooting a film with the creative support of dozens of technicians, actors, and stage workers equal an escape from self? Instead, doesn't this act of making public one's own perspective as a spectator and of 'working' together with many people mean that in a film the moment of 'identification' is privileged over the moment of 'meditation,' which instead is at the basis of a reader or a writer's isolation? Doesn't this mean, perhaps, that the drive to directly communicate is stronger in a film, or even that it tends to provide the very structure of a film?

Another series of questions could bring together these two fields of inquiry in an attempt to establish what the common data are in the experience of a reader and that of a viewer (while remaining within a purely sociological context), or in the experience of a writer and that of a filmmaker.

Is 'reading' a book the same as 'watching' a film? What kind of perceptual commitment do the acts of reading and watching require? In his meditation, does a writer think of a reader as an 'other' in the act of reading? Does he think about the senses that the reader is employing while reading? Does the writer factor in that reading might include pauses, going back, and even a decision to reserve the reading for more objective moments & more favorable mental dispositions? Similarly, in his meditation, does a filmmaker think of a viewer as an 'other' sitting in the dark and in the act of watching, so does he think about the senses that the viewer is employing while watching? Does the filmmaker factor in that screening a film is traditionally an irreversible act and that communication often relies more on the viewer's subsequent memory of what he saw rather than on the momentary perception? Is the relationship between 'senses' & 'conscience' for a reader and for a viewer based on the same structure? Can a reader of detective novels also read Proust? Can a reader of Proust also go and watch a film with Franco Franchi and Ciccio Ingrassia? Can a viewer of Franchi and Ingrassia also read Proust? And can a viewer of Franchi and Ingrassia also appreciate Bergman? Did Proust think of one of his readers as a possible spectator of De Funes' films? Or, in other words, did Proust think that a Grand-Guignol spectator could draw 'spiritual' enjoyment from his books? Did he *see* his reader, in his twenty-five years of writing, always in the same way, with the same face, and with the same clothing? And Bergman, who took five weeks to shoot his film, what did he *see* in the viewers that will leave their house to go watch his film? *How* does he see them, what are their faces, what are they wearing, what language do they speak? Does the writer also think about posterity? What kind of posterity? Can we say the same about the filmmaker?

In sum, why 'narrative'?

I believe that a sociological survey has yet to be done on the topic that the questionnaire proposes. However, I also think that at the end of the research, after obtaining important results, we would return to the starting point. In fact, a sociological point of view may set the topic for discussion, describe it, circumscribe it, but it is socio-political analysis that will find the fundamental answers.

The act of 'reading' and 'watching' clearly reflect the situation of social classes in our society because reading and watching films is a privilege, just as writing a book or making a film. The protagonists of the *petit* intellectual bourgeoisie are mostly involved in these dialectically integrated acts in a self-gratifying process that become true rituals. Novels and films are gratifying both for the authors and for their readers or viewers, according to their cultural level. The verticality of the social structure is reflected in the vertical hierarchy that divides high, medium, and low culture. So, just as the social structure is based on the exclusion of workers and farmers from ownership by the means of production and power, so the system of communication and culture relies on the conscious exclusion of the majority of the population. But even within this high cultural level there are further exclusions because the literary 'height' of a product excludes from fruition the level immediately culturally and socially lower. This leads to the creation of a semi-divine cultural staff that 'enlightens,' while excluding all the other social strata, the 'century,' or the historical period: within the same century, the different 'centuries' of different staffs from different social strata pile up. They coexist but ignore each other, in a fixed temporality that ends up looking back to the past. In this way, culture is produced in vertical ghettos and feeds on the lack of communication among the social strata in a continuous process of dehumanization.

The discrimination of the working classes from the 'making' of culture (which cuts off great chunks of human energy and intelligence from the creative process) is already at work in the schools and then it spreads everywhere thanks to the complicity of the *petit* intellectual bourgeoisie that drives the whole discriminating system. Within the scheme that separates culture into 'high' and 'low,' isn't the act of 'writing' and 'shooting' for the lower social classes just as non-communicative as the 'writing' and 'shooting' for the higher social classes? It is the system of communication, and thus the vertical social structure mirrored in it and also their psychic content, that must be revolutionized by separating them from social discrimination.

Facing the great mass of unsolved, unexploded, or imploded problems that limit our view, the relationship between 'my' films and 'your' audience is irrelevant, unless it is understood as a symptom, though minuscule, of a universal imbalance and irrationality.

No audience, then, and no film? No, because films will continue to be made and an audience will always be present.

I must then answer your question directly since I, too, continue to make films, though I am aware that I am an accomplice of a colossal discrimination.

For whom do I shoot? For my 'friends,' whether they belong to the high, medium, or low level of culture. By 'friends' I mean those who share your opinions and your desire for change, with whom it is right and necessary to have a real exchange and a productive discussion, within the ghetto-like boundaries imposed by the irrationality of the system. These 'friends' represent a true point of reference in the darkness of movie theaters, which tends to transfigure and erase any human presence. They can be few or many, even tens of thousands: that depends on your opinions and on your hopes.

The 'for whom' in your questionnaire, in the context of a more and more programmed dehumanization of social relations, should perhaps be included in another question, even more simple & fearsome: 'why' write a book or make a film today?

§ 2.6 You Reproach Us, but You Never Took Our Side

Interview by Umberto Rossi[1]

With the help of the Theater of Genoa, you made your debut as a stage director with The American Clock *by Arthur Miller. Why this choice after so many years dedicated exclusively to film?*

In my most recent films, beginning with *La proprietà non è più un furto* (Property is no Longer Theft, 1973), there is a certain theatrical thrust: for example, the critics criticized my use of monologues in *La proprietà non è più un furto*. But even now I still defend that choice, even though is it a theatrical conceit. In the same vein, *Todo Modo* represents a kind of political and theatrical 'mystery.' The film faithfully respects what is at the basis of a theatrical performance: a certain concept of space and time, a certain use of actors. I also believe we're at a time in the development of creative work when a director's experience is going to be circular and interdisciplinary in the broadest sense. Take Luca Ronconi's case for example. He works in theater and television and, sooner or later, will make a film as well. I really think it's worthwhile to mix diverse experiences and that a film director should share what he knows with theater actors and teach them 'immediacy,' making a return to building a performance 'with their craft' rather than reverting to intellectually-contrived formulas.

1. Originally published in *Cinema 60*, 144 (March–April 1982). Next to Petri's text, the editor-in-chief Mino Argenteri added his own comment, to which Petri replied with the following article collected here, "Our Cinema Leaves the Left Indifferent."

And what about television?

Television is a medium that allows broadcasting an event live to millions of people. Unfortunately, that capability is only marginally employed, since many prefer to build an 'event' from the most routine and proven methods. Television shouldn't be an excuse to make pseudo-films, nor pseudo-comedies, nor pseudo-sport events. That's why I find theater more interesting than television. I even think that working in theater these days requires lots of ideas, many more than those expected of a film director.

Was your experience televising Sartre's Dirty Hands *also "pseudo"?*

Not at all. If you consider it closely, you will find that I didn't try to make pseudo-film or pseudo-theater but something truly and intrinsically televisual. To do that, I took screen size into account for every scene and worked intensely with opening shots and precision handling of the video camera. You asked me why I chose Miller. I chose the play because it's a contemporary work. I am not drawn to classics already incised in cultural history and the annals of the stage. *The American Clock* is a play we should have written in Italy, a work of great newsworthiness. Staging it was like making a film.

Let's turn to your own newsworthiness in film, and Todo Modo *in particular. At the film release, there was much controversy. You were accused of ridiculing the Christian Democratic government by portraying it as a self-devouring monster. After all these years and the wave of terrorism and the assassination of Aldo Moro, do you still find that portrayal valid?*

More than ever. I think the film resists a political stance as much as it does an aesthetic one. Of course, I am referring to a long period of time. We can all see today that Forlani appears more and more like Facta, the minister whose laziness cleared the way for Mussolini's rise to power. Let's hope that comparison doesn't end up having the same drastic consequences, but so far everything points to the worst. What's more, isn't it true that the Christian Democrats are self-destructive? Look at Andreotti, who is the party's most distinguished & intelligent figure, yet still someone you would be embarrassed to present to the public. Nonetheless, I'll say it again: he is the only Christian Democrat of international stature. I would also say that he is the only real challenger to the Left, precisely because of his lucid cynicism. We're living through a real tragedy for which *Todo Modo* was a precise metaphor. Before leaving the public hearing room of the parliamentary commission investigating Aldo Moro's death, Sereno Freato said: "Please note that we didn't kill Mino Pecorelli!" Don't you think that this way of "throwing their hands up" is even more absurd than my portrayal of the Christian Democrats? In short, the atmosphere they have created in the country is one of vendetta, so I still believe that *Todo Modo* was based on an accurate political model. Even in the D'Urso affair, if the country's leaders — Pertini aside — had shown a greater sense of State, the captive would have behaved differently toward his kidnappers.

Aren't you too pessimistic?

Too pessimistic? At a time when the commander of the Carabinieri has more political sense than the Prime Minister!

In the years immediately following the Second World War, things weren't easier than now, yet Italian film followed reality closely, it interpreted it, it unflinchingly took on the most troubling social problems. That's not the case today. You need only consider the rise of internal terrorism, and the scant attention Italian film has paid to it, to realize how much has changed.

There has undoubtedly been a decline in the political conscience of filmmakers, but there has also been a rise in the complexity of the political situation. In the postwar years, class struggle had clear connotations. Then came this very peculiar anthropological change that Pier Paolo Pasolini was the first to expose. The contradictions became greater and more complicated — everything became more difficult and less clear. Add to that the passing of several great filmmakers, such as De Sica, Visconti, and Pasolini himself, and the explosion of numerous "contradictions within the people." The directors who were most preoccupied with, and dedicated to, political film found themselves attacked more aggressively by the critics, censored by political parties, and generally regarded with suspicion, from organizations such as Lotta Continua to the conservative press. We continued to make films without anyone's help simply because we believed in them. There was no sense of internal adjustment on our part: we were attacked from all sides. There were filmmakers of my generation who, before the audience of Porretta Terme Film Festival in 1971, demanded to have the prints of *La classe operaia va in Paradiso* set on fire. Do you understand? They wanted to burn it! And you were there, so you might remember that no one came forward to call that man crazy. How can you lament the mediocre political sensibilities of contemporary Italian filmmakers when you never fought for, never defended, those who tried to keep talking about politics despite a thousand obstacles? If the Left blocks all forms of political inquiry and experimentation or better yet, if it is bothered by any independent voice within the worker's movement, how can you then bemoan the 'depoliticization' of filmmakers? I joined the youth movement of the Italian Communist Party at an early age, at 15 (in 1944). Two years later, I joined the party and I stayed until the events in Hungary. I left the Italian Communist Party in 1956 after founding a journal called *Città aperta*. I have maintained ties with the Italian Communist Party ever since, with issues of Marxism and Leninism, but I have always remained independent in my thinking and autonomous in my judgment and actions.

Did your stay in Genoa — home to Guido Rossa, the man who fought terrorism — provide any inspiration for your future work?

Several great Italian films were born on the wave of a great popular movement: the case of the Resistance and neorealism is one example. Similarly, a few of the political films that I and certain other directors shot between 1972 and 1974 came out of the great students' and workers' movements of that time. Then Italian society began to disintegrate and film, being a creative and communicative entity closely tied to social reality, suffered the consequences. Today, any rebuilding would require a pluralist effort rich in dialectical tension & hegemonic tendencies (an old communist vice) and show respect for different people and differing opinions. What is needed is a process of cultural and critical growth, a process that even the Italian Communist Party up until now hasn't sought with the required conviction. I want to share an anecdote I find meaningful: When I was Giuseppe De Santis' assistant, I went with him to visit Mario Alicata in Naples, where we met Giorgio Amendola. Amendola was already one of the most prestigious figures on the Italian political scene, and chided De Santis rather harshly, saying: "Why don't you make a lovely corsair film?" Poor Peppe didn't even have the heart to tell him that he couldn't make it because for three years he had tried unsuccessfully to put together a film about land occupation. If someone said the same thing to me today, I would reply: "I am not making it because you and I together haven't reached the point where directors can make films they care about rather than ones imposed on them by those pulling the economic and political strings." In short, I am not against 'social engagement' and political opinions, I am against censorship...

Concerning censorship, what do you think of the so-called 'young critic' who is prone to pay John Wayne the most swooning praise while tossing out anything that has the least whiff of an openly political work?

My generation really liked American cinema, but not those films where military propaganda takes priority. The John Wayne I liked, and still like, is the one you see in John Ford's films, not the gallant knight of the worst military aggressions. Also, as for militarism, it should be understood that for Ford, militarism was only a small component of a discourse that transcended it to arrive at an 'Americanism' that was one of the characteristics of the 'first generation' of American film. Even if today's nationalism is linked to that early moment — and these are but weak and circuitous links — Ford's Americanism is the mortar bonding together men of diverse cultural experiences and histories to serve a single goal.

And the inspiration from Genoa?

While working for a few months in Genoa, I had the chance, among other things, to consider a possible project on the drama of Guido Rossa. More accurately, the 'case' of Rossa & Berardi, two victims of opposite ways of conceiving the struggle and political militantness. Such an undertaking doesn't just spring from a director's head: it needs the approval and verification of the whole city and of the political and social forces at work there. It must confront the men and women who live there. If I were one of the promoters of this initiative, I would fight for it as a quest for the 'true facts' that lie behind these two tragedies, facts we only know today in incomplete and biased accounts gleaned from the press. The first objective, in my mind, would be to understand the chain of events so as to present them without prejudice, neither toward Rossa nor Bernardi.

§ 2.7
The Left Is Indifferent to Our Cinema[1]

There's always a little residual mistrust in the relationship between those who make films and those who must play the role of the conscience for the totality of cinema. Their rapport is indeed interdisciplinary, but as things have evolved bit by bit, it's also an inter-corporative relationship, and beyond its ideological, cultural, and political contents, there are also psychological and even physical dimensions.

I wonder to what degree this relationship explains one sentence of the 'footnote' that you graciously attached to my interview in the March-April issue of *Cinemasessanta* ("You Reproach Us, But You Have Never Defended Us"), an interview I gave to Umberto Rossi for a private Genovese network. Your sentence came in response to my statements concerning the film politics of the Italian Left. I quote: "However, it would bother us if Petri made allusion to certain assessments rendered by critics who weren't always favorable towards his films." Now, dear Argenteri, I hardly reach the paradox of Monsieur Teste ("*On ose me louer!*"),[2] but I never claimed cheap praise or stupid collusions by anyone for any reason, and you should know that.

So where does your notion come from? Perhaps, if I understand correctly, it is my "bellyaching" or "polemical" tone, as certain of my articles have been described. You see, I won't at all rule out that some searing whiplashes or other crippling pun-

1. Originally published in *Cinema 60*, 146 (July–August 1982). The article caused a series of reactions, published in the same journal in the following numbers, by Francesco Maselli, Sergio Frosali, Francesco Bolzoni, Ettore Scola, Giampiero Dell'Acqua, and Giuseppe De Santis.

2. "They dare to praise me!" The reference is to Paul Valéry's text *Monsieur Teste*.

ishments occasionally inflicted on me (whether with a frivolous smile, a knowing academicism, or the usual recklessness typical of critical terrorism) have left their marks. But I must ask: how could they not? It is also possible, however, that my "resentment" (admitting that it is resentment and not something more grievous and painful) is of a more complex and widespread origin. I urge you to take that into serious consideration. For example, I think that the indifference shown by the entire political, intellectual, and unionized Italian Left — faced with the cultural and human disintegration of our cinema as symptoms of a more general, & distinctly Italian, renunciation of self-respect — is hereafter part and parcel of our reality and, in itself, the essential condition. Second, I think that film criticism — with a few exceptions, including you — has contributed to that. It has apparently limited itself to going about its job while surrendering to the interchangeability of principles and transformism imposed by the mercantile needs of publishers, and in giving way to the allure of 'protagonism' that is so costly to filmmakers.

For my part, in the midst of this regression and hamstringing, I have tried to stick to etymology in considering the role of criticism. The critic develops a crisis in the work, in its language, in the history of works and language, to provoke a crisis of conscience in the reader/viewer as well as in the filmmaker. In order to avoid being an end in itself, however, shouldn't the critical process aim at what might be called an essential result, even given the prospects of so many other deeper crises, and thus even more essential? I say yes, I think it must. And I consider the critic's work sterile and un-creative if he lacks the drive to explore and live within the crisis of the work and of language, having already experienced the crises of his analytical tools, of his own criteria and of his own status. It seems clear to me that all the crises around these subjects start off separately but soon come together in the ongoing general and enduring crisis of culture and society. It is that crisis we mustn't forget if we are to get essential results for mankind out of our work as critics and creators.

It seems to me that only in this way can the etymology "crisis-criterion-criticism" be taken in its positive light rather than simply its negative and persecuting aspects. In the negative aspects of the critical process, we only come to destroy any possibility of the redemption of cinema.

We all agree that we've gone a long way down the path of destruction in Italy. Even so, among the few survivors we can see standing and solid amidst the ruins, is the material structure of criticism, which is both a corporation and a place of power. On the other hand, if it's true that criticism isn't essential to the material existence of cinema, it's equally true that criticism doesn't need films to survive — it can continue to exalt its purpose even in undertaking purely necroscopic work. And then there's always the emergency exit in the criticism of taste, that is hedonistic and an end in itself. Argenteri, you would say to me: don't filmmakers bear any responsibility? And I would respond that filmmakers, by their very name, are the most responsible for the destiny of film. Don't you see? The more difficult the situation and more sub-cultural the working conditions, the more filmmakers seemed hemmed-in by their own 'particulars,' that is, in their own affairs, in their own film, as though even a poetic, even a beautiful, even a very beautiful, film could make cinema. If you exclude the battles between the early 60s and the early 70s — a period immediately degenerated into violent political-corporative disputes — the rejection of film as a great collective and contextual experience returns to the tradition of Italian filmmakers. Out of that derives the eternal state of cultural poverty plaguing the vast majority of Italian filmmakers. Like athletes, they can only express their ideas in interviews — a fact already acutely analyzed for filmmakers and athletes alike in one of Musil's novels. In letting themselves be consumed as ritual objects typical of this society, nearly all Italian filmmakers have masked the intellectual and theoretical nature of their activity, especially from themselves. They've accepted a division of labor that creates innumerable differences and separations, among which the most important could be the separation of theory and practice. We all move about as if we are between the lines of some unseen organizational chart of a large, anonymous multinational society. Italian filmmakers as a social group feel right at home in this chart, especially the younger ones. The proof is that no one has worked systematically to improve working conditions outside the establishment. Their current silence, long and troubling, fits in with it all. Is it their latest and perhaps definitive act of acceptance of the great industrial and political strategies in the 'audio-visual' domain? Is it a conscious acceptance of their obsolescence? Or is it the mute and inconsolable expression of feeling inferior and impotent by those who see their lives menaced by forces clearly too big for them? Not a hint of resistance. Nothing but silence, frankly, which is so profound it smacks of guilt.

So my 'resentment,' if that's how you want to call it, is not about some fruitless collection of compliments. I can say that this is also about me, since I feel no less responsible than the others, and that's the truth. I feel, however, that I must at least take it up with those individuals and political forces that, in the past, have shown great interest in all of the problems facing film. In light of today's facts, the interest and solidarity of that time appear instrumental and propagandistic. That much is certain.

In parting, dear Argenteri, I would like to return to the interview that provoked this letter and correct at least two mistakes. Umberto Rossi has me saying I was the editor of *Città aperta*. That's not right. As everyone knows, Tommaso Chiaretti was the editor-in-chief. Rossi also wrote that Volontè "was inspired by the figure of the statesman from Bari," in other words by Aldo Moro, for his role in *Todo Modo*. No, Volontè was 'inspired' by my script and the character of M. included in the script, which I carefully prepared as an imitation of the behavior & political discourse of Moro. I know these minor corrections are also a part of the 'particulars,' but they need to be made.

3.
"NUOVA CUCINA"
(1980)

§ 3.1 Apocalypse Now [1]

Apocalypse Now begins where a lunch would end. In fact, the first scene of the film, which takes place during the Vietnam War, opens with an immense expanse of palm trees burning under a bombardment of napalm. Palm trees equal bananas. That is to say, if the palm trees are burning, *bananes flambées*, and therefore, a dessert that finishes lunch. *Dessert* literally means "to clear the table": "*desservir*" in French. After the *bananes flambées* everything is cleared away. And isn't every end of lunch a kind of little apocalypse?

This image is part of Willard's delirium. Willard is a young Marine captain who is an assassin for the American government. We see Willard in Saigon, closed up in a room in the grip of an alcoholic frenzy: a vaguely masturbatory scene. The young captain is punishing himself, wounding his hands with shards of glass and moving almost like a woman, in a naked semi-conscious state, in a kind of solitary orgy.

From the *flambées* bananas the camera slowly moves with a rhythm used for commercials showing a bottle of Martell cognac: the source of the only nutrition for Willard throughout the film. Cognac: another sign that lunch is over.

Instead the film begins. Willard is dragged and presented to the general. Finally he has a new mission. He must assassinate Kurtz, a high-ranking American officer who has imposed his personal power going beyond his status in some vague area between Cambodia and Vietnam. Kurtz orders and follows

1. Originally published in *Nuova Cucina* 5 (February–March 1980).

through on capital executions. He must in turn die so that his rebellion won't have any influence over the other officers.

To talk about Kurtz's assassination, the general invites Willard to lunch. A work breakfast, American-style. The menu is simple: roast beef, boiled shrimp, iced tea, Italian bread, and some indistinguishable vegetables. The film is vague on the vegetables. Olives are seen out of focus around the shrimp but they are olives as large as figs & maybe some pieces of pineapple. Coppola sacrifices gastronomic precision in favor of beauty and the marketing of the images. The general says that the shrimp are almost rotten, but he serves them all the same. Anyway, no one eats this lunch, not the general, not Willard, not the other officer present, not even a mysterious South Vietnamese woman who is the only character that occasionally timidly hints at cutting the beef. Maybe no one is eating because they are already consuming Kurtz?

Willard must return to the delta in a boat and meet Kurtz in his little fiefdom. The scene is substantially similar to that written by Joseph Conrad in *Heart of Darkness*, which apparently inspired Coppola.

The boat was outfitted with four sailors: two black and two white. First of all, Willard and his companions come upon a squadron of helicopters piloted by the air cavalry. The pilots specialize in destroying Viet Cong villages with napalm. The leader of the squadron is the always-spectacular actor, Robert Duvall. He dons a Stetson, goes surfing during the napalm bombardments, and at night barbecues mounds of steaks. But even in this Pantagruelesque barbecue scene, no one eats, not even the extras, who are usually famished. People just drink cans of beer of an illegible brand. The mystery of the brand of beer continues through the film because there are empty beer cans all over as mute testimony of a miserable alcohol diet.

Leaving Duvall behind, the boat reaches the delta in the most deliberate and inexplicable fasts. The sailors massacre Vietnamese women, smoke marijuana, drop LSD, drink beer: but that's it, no one eats. Not even Spam. So little by little, as they go deeper in the canals, their hysteria heightens, no doubt fueled by their disastrous diet.

The most touching gastronomical moment comes however after a Felliniesque interlude where strippers drop from the sky to excite the troops. One of the white sailors is named Chef because when he lived in his hometown, New Orleans, he studied to be a *saucier*. All of a sudden, Chef decides to make a pudding with mango sauce and goes ashore. Instead of mangoes, however, the ex-cook finds a tiger. The terror of this encounter unleashes a panic attack. In the midst of searing sobs and inhuman cries, the probably homosexual Chef (judging from the suspicious attention he gives to the younger black sailor) confesses his nostalgia for the Creole cooking of his native New Orleans and his horror of the boiled steaks of the Marine mess hall. The gastronomic wastefulness of the military has scarred him for life.

But this unhappy life will be brief. He will be the third out of the four sailors to die, decapitated by Kurtz's men. His head is dumped at Willard's feet like the pig heads in the food stores in Bologna during Christmas, but also like the mafia: a symbol of Coppola's Italian roots. Already in *The Godfather*, Coppola had a horse's head placed in one of his characters' beds. Out of the four sailors, only one young white man will be saved but buried in sand in a demented, Ophelia-like state.

In spite of all this, Willard reaches Kurtz's compound. He is revealed as the assassin and is immediately submitted to torture, which stops when Willard is offered a bowl of plain rice. Willard refuses, accustomed to his Martell diet.

Kurtz-Brando lives like a mystical body adored by great masses of indigenous extras. He dreams of an American military like that of the North Vietnamese soldiers driven by a moral imperative. The American soldiers who do not have this imperative are destined to lose. (Kurtz-Brando doesn't say that the North Vietnamese soldiers were forced to be heroic so that their nation could survive.)

At this point, the film once more picks up the theme of food. We are surprised to discover that Kurtz-Brando is the only character in his gastronomic (and otherwise) apocalypse who eats anything, albeit unwillingly. During a long scene where he tells Willard he wants to be killed by him, he lazily munches an unknown tropical fruit with a yellow skin, juicy like citrus if you notice the saliva that drips from the actor's lips.

Kurtz-Brando is made up to look like Lieutenant Kojak and seems even bigger than he was in *The Missouri Breaks* even though all he eats in the film is that little piece of fruit. Then the apocalypse doesn't really purify. Willard massacres Kurtz-Brando-Kojak in a dark-red apotheosis while Kurtz's followers sacrifice a cow at the foot of a temple. They cut up the cow with a butcher's expertise so that the carcass immediately has the look of a bloody beefsteak.

The films ends here with this intense image of a bleeding, yet still alive, steak. The biggest steak ever seen in film.

The steak becomes the symbol of the apocalypse. *Beef-Steak Now*. Oldenburg's steak, symbol of the American dream, of American protein-ism. A patriotic steak, which represents everything that went wrong during and after Vietnam in the waste, the massacre, the craziness, the food. Steak is also the symbol of death, of cannibalism, of the love of death. The many proteins to nourish a dream totally carbonized by napalm. A great collective dream that discovered the emptiness of human significance and instead became a nightmare. An enormous napalm barbecue for those who no longer want to believe in steak. The sad anorexia of exhausted cannibals.

§ 3.2
Ogro: Bread and Omelettes, Hammer & Sickle [1]

Ogro is the film reconstruction of the attack on Carrero Blanco and of the ideological-political debate that was carried on among all the attackers in all the proceedings before the attack. The terrorists were all ex-seminarians. The mystical aspect of their actions is well depicted in Pontecorvo's film. Even in the most insignificant of everyday gestures the terrorists of *Ogro* are chaste, lean, and monk-like. Naturally, also when dealing with food, they act like it is Lent. Every so often they assemble to eat together but it is assumed that they eat only food that is essential to living and sexually mortifying. Eating becomes a political rite: everyone is at the table ostensibly to eat, but the gathering is to discuss their political and militaristic reasons to stay together. The terrorists are from the Basque region but they work from Madrid. The film never reveals what is in their modest food bowls: is it Basque or Castilian food?

The Basque nationalists ate Basque or Spanish food? Was there any discussion among them about what to eat before or after the attack? Does a terrorist's food need be national-popular? There is only one person who courageously describes his food, the communist mason to whom the terrorists turn for certain of their excavations. The mason goes to work with a beautiful, large baguette of French bread filled with (if we are correct) an omelet. This loaf of bread and omelet is a symbol of the reasonableness and humanity of the character, and it also serves to demonstrate

1. Originally published in *Nuova Cucina.*

the indifference on the part of the mason towards the terrorists. He doesn't trust people like them. He says to himself: "I will give these crazy people a hand. But I will bring my own lunch." The loaf of bread is also a symbol of the internationality of the food of the proletariat. Bread and omelets, in all its variations: with onions, with zucchini, etc., it is the hammer and sickle of the proletariat gastronomy. The gastronomic class enemy pits as the symbol of his privilege caviar and blinis.

The head of the terrorists (political as well as gastronomic) is Volontè. The actor appears very fat considering what we see him eat in the film and considering all the ideological anguish that is tormenting him. A pudgy actor who doesn't enthusiastically throw himself at every edible thing means that he doesn't feel the part. Otherwise, he would have done something to lose weight.

And his weight clashes with the essential, sober, 'leanness' of the film: it is precisely because of his monasticism that we feel something for him. *Ogro* is very meticulous, but at the same time, in its own way, sweet, just like some simple Mediterranean flavors.

§ 3.3 Don Giovanni or Boiled Meat à la Dionysos [1]

Even from the very first images with which Losey begins the overture of *Don Giovanni*, it is easy to be transported to a rare state of mind, usually relegated to the sublime, and not just because over, inside, and around us we are enveloped by and surrounded by and penetrated by Mozart's music, or rather "Mozzart" as Da Ponte used to write either to be phonetically precise with a double "z" or just out of negligence.

We are confronted with the film. We are there, in a state of ecstasy, enraptured by the extraordinary technical magic that bursts from the screen: therefore, from the art that 'made' this film. An amazing magic that Losey wields in frame after frame under the most absurd technical conditions. The exceptional performance of the director and all who worked under him, especially at this time of complete artisanal barbarism in Italy, is a poetic fact of the highest caliber, for all that it implies: love for one's work, respect for the public, passion for culture, that is, humanity.

However, our spirit can also be touched by a certain discomfort that little by little could grow to be a punishment and a critical idea that we are facing an opera contaminated with some non-Mozartian anxiety. For example, from our specific point of view, we can immediately observe that the gastronomic *feeling* of the film, notwithstanding the recommendations of Da Ponte and "Mozzart," is pale, cold, and lacking in spirit. We are sad to say this, but it is true. Moving out from our tight visual angle, let's go to some more general observations.

1. Originally published in *Nuova Cucina* 6 (April 1980).

We can better explain by examining the visualization of the overture. Losey set his *Don Giovanni* on location in the Venetian lagoons and in their humid backcountry, drippy like some omelets, spectral like some blueberry puddings. A sky full of portent: an angry sea, swollen with poison. A lagoon boat transports to an isolated island some people in 17th-century costumes, all of them dressed in black or in white, the colors of death. The lagoon is a Lethe. Everything is already dead in the film, beginning at the overture. The boat docks. Among the ghosts, we recognize Don Giovanni and Donna Anna, who disembark and enter into a cavern of glassblowers. Here we see the first living thing in the film: the fire of the ovens, the presentiment of the infernal fire that will burn Don Giovanni alive. It will be this oven, turned into hell, which will swallow up Don Giovanni to burn him for his sins.

Mozart wove into the overture the musical elements that in the sixteenth scene of Act Two will announce the appearance of the Commendatore and will morbidly expand until Don Giovanni disappears into the fire. Losey thus needed to use images from the beginning that forewarned the spectator of the hellish destiny that awaited his protagonist. (Yes, but why that ghostly touristic wandering? Why those realistic glassblowers, a bit like Guttuso's painting,[2] and why that fire like a documentary on Murano glass? Why, then, this pain without irony?)

The idea that moved "Mozzart," aided by his librettist, is that of the would-be libertine, and then again, would-be only to a certain point. It is true that his music and his words bring to the listener the tragic sentiment of the character who is fighting against nature, against liberty, against instinct, but in the sweetly ironic way of a libertine rite that cannot be carried out. In fact, in the arc of the opera, Don Giovanni never 'gets the girl.'

This dualism in its entire poetic ramification is already present, note for note, in the overture of the opera, while in Losey's visualization only the tragedy is evidenced, in a style even apt for a funeral parlor. Someone is already dead: and this is a little random.

2. Renato Guttuso (1911–1987) was an Italian painter.

ELIO PETRI · "NUOVA CUCINA" (1957–1958)

Mind you, to film an overture was already gutsy: it is as if he filmed the *Jupiter Symphony* or *Sonata K. 367*.

Erotic Diet

However, gutsy or not, what is better than visualizing the overture playing on the libertine aspect of *Don Giovanni*? Why show a glassblower, a somber image far from Mozartian culture, instead of a hypothetic dinner of Don Giovanni's, in preparation for his raid on Donna Anna? 'Lust' is also 'gluttony.' What would a Venetian Don Giovanni do to prepare for his deeds? A light dinner but very attentive to the erogenous qualities of certain foods, of which, by the way, the Venetian kitchen is very proud? A dinner based on crabs or other lagoonal *coquillages*? A quick taste of swamp game? Light Friulian wines redolent of violets, raspberry, and almonds? Doesn't a dinner also have its tragic side?

Then Don Giovanni could move on with his body bewitched with love juices towards sex: the one and only goal of his existence; in this case, sex with Donna Anna.

But Losey needs the fire, the fire that presages the punishment. Yet fire was already there, ready — the fire of the Venetian cuisine. The fact is that Losey was thinking of a *realistic* fire that would immediately recall the inferno that would ultimately swallow up his protagonist. But hell is not realistic. It is a cultural idea that gets inserted into Don Giovanni's joyous existence. Unless in the glassblowing furnace Losey wanted to symbolize the future world of industry and technology, where our human instincts would be burned away; and, in the glassblowers, an obsequious proletariat. But wouldn't this be a too-convoluted interpretation for the limpid clarity of the Mozartian universe?

Da Ponte, who was a defrocked priest, describes 'his' hell like this: "Fire from different parts, earthquake, etc." And Molière in 1665, one-hundred twenty-two years previously: "*Le tonnerre tombe avec un grand bruit et de grands éclairs sur Don Juan; la terre s'ouvre et l'abime; il sort de grands feux de l'endroit où il est tombé.*" [3]

3. "Loud claps of thunder burst, and the lightning flashes vividly round Don Juan; the earth opens and swallows him; and big flames issue from the place where he went down." Molière, *The Plays of Molière in French, with an English Translation and Notes by A.R. Waller*, Volume IV (1664–1665) (Edinburgh: John Grant, 1907) 261.

Their hell is not realistic, just as the statue of the Commendatore is not realistic. They are both phantasmizations of the sexual & political *establishment*, of its punishment, and its manipulative power.

Don Giovanni Equals Dionysos

Why then did Losey need a realistic and not nonsensical hell, an earthquake measured by a Mercalli intensity scale and not with a child's fantasy? Did he want to 'really' punish Don Giovanni, and us too?

It can be said that the character of Mozart's Don Giovanni is *anti-Christian* and *Dionysian* in the Nietzschean sense, while Losey's is full of moral doubts, which makes him (with respect to Mozart's character) a Christian, a deviant, a pathological case study. In Mozart's opera, instead, it is the members of the *establishment* who obsessively reduce love to a sin of lust, deplorable victims of a sad sense of honor, enlivened by an insatiable desire for revenge. These deviate from a life lived for art, like the Nietzschean Dionysos and Mozart's Don Giovanni: they are the 'pathological cases.'

The Smell of a Woman

In Mozart-Da Ponte, Don Giovanni wants to live with all his senses: "Quiet! I think I smell a woman..." says this creature of Da Ponte (who incidentally already in 1792 wrote *Dithyramb of Scents*). Don Giovanni lives with all five senses ready for what Nietzsche called "life for life," of instinct, of sensuality, of love. He who doesn't love "the smell of a woman" and stops his sense of smell, vision, taste, touch, and hearing for fear of "beauty" & of "sensuality" will bring upon himself a world that in order to be moral is deadly, punishing, and anti-human.

'Lust' needs *all* the possible bodily 'sins.' In fact, Mozart's Don Giovanni moves about in a world where flavors, the fragrance of wines, and the wild sense of human odors have a great importance.

Instead, in the film, a glass of wine is had only after a good forty minutes have passed, during Zerlina and Masetto's wedding. We see an extra who hints at sipping wine without any Bacchic zeal, as if under the gaze of a Baptist preacher. In this scene, there are many baskets full of grapes & piles of apples, and no one avails themselves of these gifts from God. In fact, instead of eating them, the apples get thrown around. Incomprehensible, unless you return to Losey's American roots: either the idea of waste and abundance, or also, Puritan roughness.

After roughly sixty minutes, we see a toothless old lady in a basement who pulls up something from a pot of sauce, maybe a piece of cod. And what happened to the "chocolate," the "coffee," the "wines," and the "prosciutto" that Don Giovanni ordered Leporello to give to the guests? Notice that in this list there is nothing but 'superfluous' foods, therefore 'erotic.' Don Giovanni doesn't order roasts but "chocolate," that delicacy which was forbidden by the bishops in Spain because women loved it too much, so much that they brought it into church for vespers.

Losey sets Don Ottavio's aria *"Dalla sua pace la mia dipende"* outdoors in the fields. In the meadows, many peasants are lying down for their siestas like animals. But when did these peasants eat? And why not film their meal? Losey really censored, if not *castrated* food. Without a doubt, there is a greater meaning that permeates all his work.

The Magical Dinner with the Commendatore

And what about the dinner with the Commendatore? In Losey's film, Don Giovanni is seated by himself in front of an oddly set up table, and surrounded by his servants and their families (!). He stays by himself, crushed by his vices and by his fear of the dialogue he had with the Commendatore in the cemetery a little while previously. Elvira tries valiantly to redeem him. Don

Giovanni responds listlessly, anguished by the idea of sin and punishment: sickened by "Christianity."

Concentrating on the music and understanding the words, we realize that the feeling of the scene is completely the opposite. First, Don Giovanni eats like a horse. So much so that Leporello comments: "What a barbarous appetite! / What giant mouthfuls / I think I am going to faint."

And then Don Giovanni orders: "Plate!" and then: "Pour the wine." And after drinking exclaims: "Excellent Marzemino!" with the sharp ability to recognize this particular wine from the Trento area from the many other wines of the Veneto.

There is nothing penitential or pestilential in Mozart-Da Ponte's text. The music is serene and playful to the point of "your cook is so proficient / I would also like to try some," one of the lightest and sweetest airs of the whole opera.

Elvira arrives, darkly warning of redemption, and Don Giovanni greets her with gentility, ending with a most civil, "Let me eat / and if you like, eat with me" where, given their carnal relations, "eat" also stands for "making love."

Mozart's Don Giovanni, one step away from punishment, is still indulgent, serene, a *libertine*. Or rather: "free thinker," since before meaning 'licentious,' *libertine* meant "free thinker." Even after Elvira's invective: "Stay you barbarian / in your sickening stench / terrible example of iniquity," Mozart's hero answers in all innocence: "Long live women! / Long live good wine! / glorious support / of humanity," words that recall the wonderful part of the first act, where Don Giovanni sings a hymn to liberty that is marvelously represented by Losey, an old & courageous liberal.

Then the stone guest arrives and God saves us all. Here, Losey's Don Giovanni loses control just as do some fragile atheists in the face of death. The baritone Raimondi, excellent actor that he is, shows us all the nuances of his terror with his beatific face, devastated by expressions that go to the metaphysical.

ELIO PETRI · "NUOVA CUCINA" (1957–1958)

And yet, in the Mozartian text, Don Giovanni confronts the leader of the *establishment* up to the end. He says: "My heart is firmly in my chest / I have no fear, I will go," and he takes the luxury of insulting the great moralistic ghost, calling him "old fool." He has a slight moment of anguish when he takes his hand and doesn't hide his horror in seeing the flames. But these are perfectly understandable human emotions. Then he screams a simple "Ah!" and disappears.

You could say: "Well, the dinner with the Commendatore was written and invented by Mozart and Da Ponte, not Losey; so therefore, they wanted the punishment of Don Giovanni."

It is true, but we should not be so strict. Don Giovanni's end is in the myth: it is in Tirso de Molina, it is in Molière, it is in Goldoni, and all the other 17th-century versions, both Italian and not Italian. Even the Marxist Roger Vaillandin, in his *Monsieur Jean* (Gallimard, 1959) kills Don Giovanni under the Commendatore's portrait. The myth is the myth. It is culture. It comes from our mothers' milk. And the culture of Mozart and Da Ponte is already that which wants punishment for the erotic monster, degeneration of the procreative instinct and incorruptible enemy of the social order. However, the two artists 'recount' and sing the myth without any moralistic bent. Both of them, the divine prodigy and the little converted Jewish Casanova from Cèneda, did not participate in any execution. At most, with him they exhibit a childish horror faced with the idea of the flames. But that's enough. The rest of the opera bears witness.

Don Giovanni's music is always seductive; it is never sinister, guilty, or mournful. The only dramatic and macabre arias are sung by *establishment* characters: Elvira, Donna Anna, Don Ottavio, the Commendatore.

Even Zerlina is Don Giovanni's accomplice: "There you will give me your hand / there you will say yes," is a knowing accomplice, ready to stay with him to have fun even though she loves her intended. She is like Don Giovanni in a skirt: "I would be happy, that is true," sings Zerlina, "happy," if her senses were not entangled with thoughts of her wedding.

Don Giovanni is loved by women, as is Dionysos, who was considered the Jupiter of women. He is loved because he loves them. Doesn't he want to marry them all? Even Donna Anna must have felt something for him in the beginning, since her singing is so passionate, though disdainful. And doesn't the uber-religious Elvira say to Leporello when she mistakes him for Don Giovanni: "I am totally on fire for you?" and in that "totally" there is her whole body. Instead, Losey, when he tries to be a 'libertine,' only succeeds in putting on screen an Anglo-Saxon big girl, half-asleep, while Don Giovanni, dressed as always in black like a priest or a Fascist, sings his "Leave women alone? Crazy... you know that they are more necessary to me than the bread that I am eating." In the recitative, Don Giovanni leans on a girl's body as if it were the backrest of a bed. Losey's is a too-cold libertine, too sarcastic, taken from the *Playboy* calendar.

In the interest of the truth, it cannot even be said that Mozart's music is Dionysian if not in a few irrepressible, joyous, and fluent rivers of notes like Zerlina's aria: "Young girls who make love / seize the day," or in the successive aria of Don Giovanni's: "While there is wine / the head is warm." It is not totally Dionysian, but neither is it punitive. Mozart's philosophy is affectionate towards the innocence of this man persecuted by the *establishment*: it is a philosophy that melancholically considers the irreparable loss of the phallus, amputated by the Apollonian law of supreme order, of a form without imperfections.

Further, this nostalgic sensuousness in Mozart adds up to Losey's sentiment, which is openly desperate, full of mourning and full of negativity. What in Mozart is languorous and sweet poetic presentiment of death, in Losey's film is already a funereal rite, an *après coup*, it is hindsight, it is irrepressible. And in Losey there is also the mourning for the passing of Mozartian culture. This is the major contribution to a modern reading of the myth: Losey got to the heart of the matter, that of the paranoiac persecution of Don Giovanni. In the film, the plot is limpid and yet full of suspense. Paranoiac phantasms obsessively persecuting an anxious one. This is worthy of the best Hitchcock.

The technique itself chosen by Losey is marvelously obsessive. It is the technique of the 'long take' that collapses in one frame, in real time, from scene to scene, all the different actions of the characters, excluding the editing of short pieces, that is, the inlay work. A supremely ordered technique, almost neurotic, that requires a truly Apollonian formal discipline but that makes colder and ghostly the flow of the musical tempo, *which is never real*, the agitation of the characters, and the presence of the monumental and cadaverous location sets.

Is Losey's *Don Giovanni* too technical? We could say yes, while we doff our hat to the artist. And by 'technical' we mean here something inanimate and prejudiced, which makes everything work towards itself according to its needs. The respect for 17th-century iconography is rigorous: artists like Longhi, Guardi, and Canaletto would be proud. But we know how significant the rapport is between man & inanimate objects in the 17th-century painting: think of Chardin.

The bourgeois discovered in that painting the enchantment of objects: of a set table, of a piece of fresh bread like signs or traces of their cultural identity. The technique of the long take excludes the possibility to show this relationship because the camera must not stop on any detail no matter how significant. The long take is done for its own sake, for the movement of the camera that becomes romantic in and of itself and not only for the narrative of 'everything' that can be narrated. In this way, the kitchens in *Don Giovanni* are portrayed distractedly by Losey. Apples and pears drying by some decorator but without the idea of "those things" which was Visconti's taste: tactile, sensual, and gastric. So the table set for the Commendatore's dinner is botched: all of a sudden a roast arrives as if it were plucked from a delicatessen on Sixth Avenue. *Wolf's* let's say.

Boiled Meat à la Dionysos

On the other hand, a doubt comes to mind: what if Losey was right? What if Mozart's serenity is no longer possible for us? What if in our time of technique without philosophy it is no longer possible to enjoy Mozart's lightness without enduring impotent desperation? Maybe it is impossible for us to have anything but an Apollonian world, cold, rational, elegant, perfect, ascetic, forever detached from the goatish whiff of poor Dionysos (in his own way unfortunate: he was cut in seven pieces, by Juno's order, and all seven pieces were boiled. The idea of boiled meat, boiled meat *à la* Dionysos is not to be discarded). So: and if the sexual and political *establishment* has won? Eating and making love are acts that rob time from productivity. And Don Giovanni, whether diner or seducer, would never have been able to be a factory worker at Fiat. It would have been a union scandal. And so, instead of hell, a layoff.

ELIO PETRI · "NUOVA CUCINA" (1957–1958)

§ 3.4 Ex-hungry People Now satiated in Terrazza[1]

Hunger, like sexual desire, has always been depicted in only two ways: to elicit laughter or to elicit tears. However, apart from the social and populist leaning, everyone prefers to laugh about hunger and the hungry. Laughter dispels the condition, buries the symptom, and removes the problem. In a certain sense, laughter is the definition of an irresolvable knot. Don't we all like to laugh, albeit hysterically, at death? Bergson considers hunchbacks the funniest people. Now, what is a hungry person but a hunchback with his deformity in reverse? And the more insatiate and insatiable his hunger is, the more he will make us laugh or cry as a result of what Bergson called *répétition*.

Commedia all'italiana films have always played around with *répétition* dealing with hunger. Italian comedies at one time were replete with Totò, Aldo Fabrizi, Peppino De Filippo, Pietro De Vico, Nando Bruno, Giulio Calì, Luigi Pavese, Claudio Ermelli, Fanfulla, Erminio Macario, Alberto Sorrentino, Renato Rascel, Alberto Sordi, Nino Manfredi, and an infinite multitude of Neapolitan comics, all taken with their empty stomachs, with their internal 'hunchback.' In those times food was very important in our country because there wasn't any. Except for the well off, Italians didn't have much to eat. And among those who didn't have much to eat were the artists & intellectuals, just like the characters in the films. Writer Alberto Moravia said that for him,

1. Originally published in *Nuova Cucina* 7 (May 1980).

the most poignant memory of Fascism was the hunger of the intellectuals. And when he speaks about this hunger, he bursts into laughter.

'Eating,' along with 'family,' was the justification for every base act committed. Italians with guilty consciences still say: "I'm doing this so we can eat." Even the Caltagirone mafia clan would say that they did it to eat.

But during the second half of the 1960s, hunger seemed to disappear from our country.

It is true that also in Italy, and not only in India, every so often children and the elderly are found starved to death and being nibbled by mice, but it seems as though they lay there, dead, just to remind us of our difficult past.

If in Italy hunger isn't a collective problem anymore, we can no longer laugh or cry over the hungry. Instead of hunger, there seems to be a sentiment of satiety in people. But can you laugh or cry over satiety?

This seems to be the problem of Ettore Scola's film *La terrazza* (*The Terrace*, 1980), written by Age, Scarpelli, and the director. Really his earlier film *C'eravamo tanto amati* (*We All Loved Each Other So Much*, 1974) should have also been entitled "We Were So Hungry." Instead, *La terrazza* is nothing except "We Are So Full." We can clearly see that the comedies about hunger (if we can call them that) are dynamic, setting out to describe every single act that the Hungry Person contrives in order to fill his stomach; the comedies about satiety, conversely, are static, immobile, and serious. Hunger is a shortage that can be filled. Satiety is instead a state that can merely be contemplated. The Hungry Person runs after food. The Sated Person lets food run after him. In satiety there is less courting and seducing of food. The emptiness has been filled. Food is no longer outside; it is 'inside.' The internal hunchback has disappeared.

Let's say this: the primary problem of 'how' food is obtained becomes an ethical dilemma. Has the food been obtained honorably? The Sated Person would at first contemplate himself,

ELIO PETRI · "NUOVA CUCINA" (1957–1958)

his stomach, and the world with melancholic inquietude. His thoughts are post-prandial, a little sad, but also useless because at that point the deed is done. But in the next phase, if he is not an idiot or a prig, the Sated Person who has conquered his food problem, would be in a reflective state of mind and not in an active state of mind.

In Scola's film various Sated People do 'not' act: Marcello Mastroianni, Vittorio Gassman, Stefano Satta Flores, Jean-Louis Trintignant, Serge Reggiani, our Editor-In-Chief [Ugo Tognazzi], and their respective wives & lovers: Ombretta Colli, Stefania Sandrelli, Carla Gravina. For years they have all met at a friend's house to celebrate the rite of dinner on the terrace. When they first started the tradition many years ago, the dinner was an essential rite for them. They got together solely to eat together. In the succeeding years, each person resolved their lack of food problem. And so now yes, these Sated People eat together, but distractedly and not with Totò's great hunger. Their dinner is a simulacrum. They do it to see the decadence in each other, or to celebrate their successes, to solidify or reclaim alliances improperly named 'friendships,' and to combat their solitude so terrible among city dwellers. It is a Mass where the Enemy, that is to say who was not invited, is sacrificed. It is many things, but it is not a dinner.

What is left then in the dinner in *La terrazza* from the days when a dinner was a dinner? Surely the memory of hunger, which is transformed into nostalgia for hunger, understood as nostalgia for youth, since hunger is a particular aspect of that age.

The menu of the terrace dinner demonstrates what we are saying. How else, in fact, could we explain why the characters, all now in their 60s, find themselves around a table loaded with food? In the distribution of so many calories there is the desire to still 'grow' in spite of being already middle-aged. And there is also the ancient fear of not being able to satisfy oneself and one's guests. But Scola's menu is also rigorously neorealistic as it faithfully depicts the food that Roman women would offer at their house dinners at the time: mixed antipasto, *crudités*, salmon and onions, hot and/or cold *pasta fagioli*, *pasta al forno* and/or *alla matriciana* and/or *puttanesca* and/or *quattro formaggi*, roast lamb, pork loin, roast beef, salad and boiled vegetables and/or beans in tomato sauce, fruit, sweets, gelato, coffee, and liqueurs. A million calories, enough to support an entire nursery for a week.

All of these calories thoughtlessly engulfed, late at night, outside, with stomachs facing the westerly wind, can't help but cause serious nightmares, or insomnia, dyspepsia, and hypertension in people of a certain age like our Satiated crowd, as well as many other maladies that we will not mention because of our love for our Editor-In-Chief and the other Sated People.

For the neorealistic precision that Scola overlooked, it must be said that these dinners in Rome are usually ordered from places such as Ruschena or Vanni or Euclide, but the hosts love to pretend that they prepared the meals themselves. The basics of the meal: beans, pasta, lamb, more than showing their snobbism reveals their ill-concealed poor origin.

Once, all these things were desired, loved, and eventually possessed, tasted, devoured, and violated. And who had time to talk, then? But not now. The five Sated People in the film eat *distractedly*.

Why distractedly? It begins with the idea that nowadays our relationship with food, like our relationship with sex, is experienced with a sense of guilt for four reasons: a) because we fear that it might endanger our health; b) because we feel badly wasting time instead of doing something 'useful'; c) because we feel we don't deserve it; and d) because 'eating' is the first obvious cause of our daily struggle and sacrifice. All of these guilty feelings, it is understood, are included in the dark cycle of the Christian tradition that considers eating a sin of the throat; & this also influences lay eaters.

The distracting mechanism at work, just like a lapsus, is repression. Nobody pays attention while they are eating or rather to their guilty feelings about it. Eating becomes a lapsus. People are eating, but they would like to do 'something else.' Therefore people eat 'distractedly,' making conversation or even reading the newspaper.

This theme is relatively interesting but it is developed only in the episode containing Serge Reggiani. His character brings the lapsus to its extreme: he doesn't eat at all. He refuses to eat in order to punish himself. Reggiani is aware of the mediocrity of his life. And since he did what he did in order to 'eat,' he punishes himself through food, refusing it, as a symbol of his defeat and of his spiritual malaise. Reggiani's diet is thus: three olives and three lupines, also called in Roman '*fusaje.*' It is a very poetic diet because it recalls the lupine vendors the '*fusajari*' and in so doing, the places where he grew up: the cinemas in the suburbs, the little gardens, the little stores, the street, the piazza and the meeting places.

Reggiani's story is the most meaningful from a gastrological point of view and it is not by chance that it is the 'tightest,' the best told. The humor becomes cinematographic images and it is not 'told' through aphorisms or self-righteously like the other episodes, which are somewhat slow-paced. The other stories of the film are 'slow,' whether they are too long with respect to the core of what they are narrating or because the characters give the feeling that they are slow in keeping up with the times in which they live. And both they and the authors are not aware of this being *outdated*, and this is what stops them from being good narrative material, whether comic or dramatic. The five Sated People are simply 'latecomers' or never-arrivers, with apologies to our Editor-In-Chief, who is a genuine late-comer who doesn't rely on aphorisms or fake tears. Tognazzi's character is at least an avid eater and pleasure seeker. He pulls a slice of prosciutto out of the refrigerator and cuts it up with his fingers like the animal that he is, that is, a film producer. The others are intellectuals, parliament deputies, film students, and writers and they have to be true to their professions: they talk much and pretend not to eat much. They pontificate a lot but don't think a lot and don't reveal much of themselves or of their true 'selves.' However, if there is a positive spin on being 'satiated,' it is to have your mind cleared of the problem of hunger and, as a consequence, to be able to think about something other than your stomach.

But the characters in *La terrazza* are satiated in the dazzled way that is typical of prigs, and we won't really find out through them, since they are so disinclined to reflection and introspection, what happened in Italy and in their consciences during the years between the Great Hunger and the Nauseating Satiety, neither for laughing nor for crying. They express themselves through aphorisms and, as we know, aphorisms are neither sad nor funny. Aphorisms serve to cover the true internal dialogues. Especially the treacly aphorisms of the priggish are not funny, like the one murmured by Gassman: "We are tragic characters that cannot be played out in a comedy." Inside Gassman (who plays a communist deputy), we see neither tragedy nor comedy. A communist deputy these days is much more sarcastic, frustrated, melancholic, grotesque, cynical, romantic, and disingenuous than Gassman's senator, who instead recalls Paul Wegener's *Der Student von Prag* (*The Student from Prague*, 1935). And, as such, he doesn't make us laugh or cry.

In conclusion, Scola's film doesn't answer the question: can Satiety, like Hunger, make us laugh or cry? And it also doesn't answer the other questions that seem more important to the director and his collaborators. Perhaps a greater gastrological understanding could have helped. At this point it is clear: the absence of a real gastrological knowledge is a general lack among film people. It is just that Scola, Age, and Scarpelli voluntarily chose to make a film about a dinner, not on a conference at the Istituto Gramsci, with citations worthy of *nouveaux riches* of culture. And to really describe a dinner and all the social, political, and even ontological implications, one must focus on the dinner itself, as we see in the masterpiece of this kind of genre: *Dinner at Eight* (1933) and *La Grande Bouffe* (*The Big Feast*, 1973).

Permit me a last observation. Our Editor-In-Chief's character is the stupidest and most vulgar character in the film. When will we understand what a most sensitive and refined soul is that of the Editor-In-Chief and how he scrutinizes us all from above, including Scola, Age, and Scarpelli?

§ 3.5
La città delle donne (City of Women)[1]

In our notebook we read the following notes: "*La città delle donne* starts at 4:25 pm. Right away, before the protagonist, Marcello Snaporaz, starts to dream: a sad little bottle of mineral water on the little table in a train compartment (without a brand on it; apparently no one paid for product placement), *no one drinks it*. 4:50 pm: a waiter arrives at the feminist conference at the Hotel Miramare with a tray on which there are three brioches, some cappuccinos, two beer bottles (also without a brand). We don't know, and won't know, who ordered this stuff (Marcello-Snaporaz takes the tray around the hotel to justify his presence among the feminists. 5:25 pm: the extraordinary and monstrous fireman of the Miramare Hotel offers to accompany Marcello-Snaporaz to the nearest station by motor scooter. Instead she takes him to a greenhouse where we see a stuffed cat and a live chicken. She offers him an egg but then right after she goes for him and offers him to suck her right breast; Marcello-Snaporaz refuses and only touches it with his index finger. The *egg-breast* association is that both are to be sucked, but *nobody sucks anything*. 5:35 pm: tough feminists drinking Coca-Cola in a car, chewing bubble-gum, all drugged up; one has a stomach ache and is complaining painfully, but *it is not indigestion*. 5:45 pm: the appearance of the first whisky, a drink that will return at regular intervals, sipped *indifferently* by Mrs. Snaporaz. In the

1. Originally published in *Nuova Cucina* 8 (June 1980). The director of *La città delle donne* (1980) is Federico Fellini.

shrine to the ten thousand lovers of Sante Katzone, there is one photograph of a woman with a biscuit in her mouth (fellatio?). 6:10 pm: appearance of *champagne* in the little fest for the Sante Katzone's ten-thousandth intercourse: *no one drinks it*. Quasi-contemporary appearance of a giant 5-layer cake with ten thousand candles: *no one eats it*. 6:20 pm: still during the little Katzone party, extreme long shot of two women among the crowd of guests, *out of focus*, visible only by a gastronomic eye; two anonymous extras lapping gelato (fellatio?); the Katzone banquet is based on Roman cuisine: mixed fried food, phallus-shaped sautéed rice cones (Katzone's furniture is also phallus-shaped, except for a labyrinthine tropical plant that recalls a vulva); many erotic fruits, pineapples, and bananas: *that no one eats*. 6:30 pm: three apples and three onions appear but only to be used in an exorcism that induces Snaporaz to sleep and rids him of bad spirits: naturally, *no one eats them*. There are two shots of the kitchen: the first in an *anti-maschilista* sketch in which an actress throws a steaming plate of spaghetti at her husband, a mime who looks like Frankenstein's monster; this monster *doesn't eat the spaghetti*; he prefers anal sex; the second kitchen scene takes place in the hallway of the feminist tribunal but *no one is cooking anything*. 7:00 pm: in the train compartment, Snaporaz wakes up, reappearance of the water bottle, *intact*. 7:05 pm: *La città delle donne* ends."

After I read these notes, I wondered if the deliberate not-eating of the characters of *La città delle donne* reveals our greatest film auteur to have a cold, sinister, food idiosyncrasy, a worrisome peculiarity about food, not even explainable by the historic binge fest that is *Satyricon*.

But this would be the quickest and also the dumbest way to examine the film, which is much more complicated than extreme gastronomes and radical feminists realize or can admit. As always, the problem is to focus on what one sees and not have preconceived ideas.

ELIO PETRI · "NUOVA CUCINA" (1957–1958)

"Silent Concert" à la John Cage'

As we know, food is often in Fellini films. It is there, present, described if not with care, at least with respect. But no one eats it. Food is mute in the shot but visible as if to call attention to the fact that it is not eaten. Food in the film performs a kind of 'silent concert' *à la* John Cage. Its mute yet insulting presence as food that is not properly used, that is, 'eaten,' has the potential 'disorientation' of those details that when you are dreaming, clue you in that you are dreaming. As we all know, when we dream, reality is rendered quite normally but with strange elements, and only one is really needed to undermine the credibility of all the rest. Dreams have been creatively imitated by the Surrealists during this century, whether in painting, in film, and in literature, taking in (if you can say that) an idea that is part of art and clearly emerged previously in the consciousness of dark and gothic Romanticism. To stay within the field of cinema, this method is clearly used in the lunch depicted by the master of surrealistic *dépaysement*, Luis Buñuel, in Le charme discret de la bourgeoisie (*The Discreet Charm of the Bourgeoisie*, 1972). The participants of that lunch are blithely sitting at the table while eating, but they are sitting on toilets instead of chairs. This change of functionality of two tools of normal daily life renders the scene paradoxical, just as oneiric elements do. Ironically, this tells us: watch out, you who are eating, you are practically sitting on toilets since that is the endpoint of your mouthfuls. Above all, however, it underlines how the different gestures and postures of eating and defecating, in humans, are absurdly equal & become interchangeable. Just as in a dream, the chairs turned into toilets are the 'disorienting' element of the scene.

Food has the same function in La città delle donne: it is there, but not eaten for the simple reason that the film, though it is surrealistic only on the surface, is the rigorous reconstruction of a dream: Mastroianni-Snaporaz's dream. And food constitutes its symbolic 'disorienting' element. It seems to indicate that Fellini's film is not a surrealist nor 'gothic' one, notwithstanding its dreamlike bent, because it clearly distinguishes wakefulness from sleep and does not promote a mythic representation of life as a dream, nor does it contain a premonitory reading of visionary elements. What kind of dream is Snaporaz'? Let's see.

La città delle donne is the masculine version of *Alice in Wonderland*, that is: "Alicus in the Land of the Vagina" (after all, didn't Alicus help the Dioscuri to find Helen, who had been kidnapped by Theseus?). During a train ride, Snaporaz, a masculine Alice verging on 60 years old, while entering an old unused tunnel (Alice's rabbit hole?) begins to dream about his trip in a female wonderland.

You Never Eat in Dreams

We should observe right away that in general *we never eat in our dreams*. Food, which comes to us while we sleep through our awareness when we are awake, is filtered, manipulated, changed, and mystified by the sexual components of the dream, which appropriate it until they become one with it. No one eats in dreams because in that mysterious place called the "unconscious" (and it is time to change this name), food and sex belong to the same sphere of desire. The 'egg' and the maternal breast and the breast of one's lover are the same thing to suck, to nourish oneself, to bodily and affectionately feed oneself. In the first days of life, food, love, well-being, pleasure — or the converse, if there is no breast or if it is 'bad' or 'anxious' — all get mixed up.

Fellini doesn't only prohibit his characters from eating, but also from flirting. He also curtails their sexuality. There is food, but nobody eats it. There are men and women, and they don't make love. The only food 'eaten' in the film (and it is a simulacrum of food) is the gelato that the two girls are licking, out of focus and in an extreme long shot. And even the licking of the gelato cone (simulacrum of sex) recalls the breast and wellbeing, at this point quite far away, out of focus, and in the extreme long shot of the past. The only sexual act depicted by Fellini is the one mimed by two feminist actresses in the kitchen to deride the down-home lasciviousness of men. The kiss by the mysterious female traveler in the train, the only sexual element in the film, is given greedily, as if to an ice cream, and the kisser will evade Snaporaz for the entire dream. Snaporaz is therefore an anxious dreamer who is missing the 'breast,' the source of food and love and security. (The etymology of the word "Roma" in antiquity was thought to be either "strength" — *forza* in Italian — or "breast" — *poppa* in Italian).

A Romance Spectacular

To further understand the 'non-eating' in Fellini, we should speak about the formal aspects of Snaporaz's dream. In our opinion, Snaporaz-Alice's dream is narrated in the form of musical theater. The narrative rhythm of the film resembling a series of *entr'actes*, the kitschy visual elements, the alternating pieces of dance and narrative sketches, are all there to prove that. Even Luis Bakalov's *romance* music tells us continuously and with humor that we are in a musical. Snaporaz is dreaming a *romance* show in every sense: whether in the sense of 'sentimental telling,' or of 'idyll' or 'musical romance.' Snaporaz dreams this way because the men of his generation — born between the 1920s and 1930s — were strongly influenced by the sexual & sentimental culture of American musical theater that for us Italians operates on the sexual archetypes of the Catholic and Petrarchan cultures.

The archetypal male in this culture is Fred Astaire, and Snaporaz identifies with him. Fred Astaire is the only wonderful male that has the privilege to dance and to flirt with the thirty-six or seventy-two or one hundred forty-four Ziegfeld girls.[2]

Ziegfeld was the almighty God who gave to Astaire (who was romantic, sweet, whimsical, an incredible dreamer and dancer-lover, but still a child like Alice) the most beautiful women that could be imagined: beautiful, maternal, at once housewives,

2. Ziegfeld Girls were the chorus girls from Florenz Ziegfeld's theatrical spectaculars known as the Ziegfeld Follies (1907–1931), which were based on the Folies Bergère of Paris.

virgins, saints, and whores. (In our society, love & sex, and also family, are lived in a form of *romance*, of perennial musical, of eternal sentimental fashion show.)[3]

Alice in the 'World of Fred Astaire'

So it could also be said that Snaporaz is Alice in the world of Fred Astaire. And if we think about it, in American musicals, which are also dreamlike spectacles, food is generally prohibited. Fred Astaire and Ginger Rogers don't eat; nor do the thirty-six or seventy-two or one hundred forty-four girls of the god-almighty Ziegfeld. These marvelous creatures can be presented, as if in a dream or in a surrealistic painting, dressed like edible things: carrots, peas, etc., but *they never eat*. They are the food to be eaten, like the little soubrettes dreamed up by Snaporaz with butts like cream and meringue.

Even in the musical that is the form of Snaporaz's dream, nothing is eaten, just as in dreams, because the desire for nutrition is mixed up and sublimated into the desire for romance. But what causes Snaporaz-Alice-Astaire to dream such an unquiet, exhausting, and unappetizing dream, even sexually speaking?

Snaporaz, or rather the 'typical' petit bourgeois born between 1920 and 1930, gets to his sixties and feels the end of his life approaching. He constantly asks himself in the film: "But where is the station?" meaning 'station' as 'death.' He asks more with impatience than fear, as if the trip that started in that 'rabbit hole' abandoned gallery was boring him. Around Snaporaz the world is crumbling: moral values, aesthetics, religion, politics, a huge downfall. Snaporaz can take anything except the tainting of his myth of Ziegfeld just as he is reaching the 'station.' He can't accept the idea that the numerous Ziegfeld girls can change into creatures of 'progress,' which is both mythic and fleeting. This really frightens him because the real center of his egocentric youth, and this really is not a contradiction, has always been the woman, the *woman-romance*: he staged the musical of his life for her.

3. Florenz Ziegfeld, Jr. (1867–1932), popularly known as "Flo" Ziegfeld, was an American Broadway impresario.

At the time of his dream, Snaporaz's concept of *romance* has been torn to pieces by feminist radicals. They deride and profane it with their vulgar protest-imitation of masculinity (the costumes and behavior of the 'feminists' and 'rowdies' in the film are the freest and most rigorous documentation of the current feminist vulgarity; they are matched only by the horrid behavior and costume of Katzone).

Snaporaz-Alice-Astaire is therefore squeezed between the opposite extremisms of the fanatic and castrating feminists and the fascistic masculinity of Katzone, which is dominated by the idea of sexual performance as *record*, or a workaholic's goal where the erotic is raised to the equal of a productive exercise ("Dux" is written on the street that leads to Katzone's villa).

Snaporaz's Narcissism

To his chagrin Snaporaz is neither an activist nor a Katzone: he doesn't yearn for power. The type of petit bourgeois that could identify with Snaporaz has dismissed from his childhood the purely petit bourgeois tendency to radical and messianic 'purity' (along the lines of Mussolini-Curcio-Negri), to preserve the desire of seduction and fairy tale, the talent for game and myth. In fact, tyranny finds complicity in the Snaporaz of the petit bourgeoisie only thanks to an unclear and mythic identification or relying on his undefended erotic *trance* state: on his unbounded narcissism and on his puerility. 'Sexually' or 'sentimentally,' in fact, Snaporaz is still lost in his dream of an ideal woman, which took root in him as a child. The ultimate marvel that *La città delle donne* presents to him is really 'his' woman, but degraded by the feminists to the role of a doll. According to Snaporaz's canon of archetypes, this doll has breasts like a woman of Attalus, she is wearing a white wedding dress, she has the glamorous face of Virginia Mayo, and around her head is a halo, just like his childhood Madonna, because, don't forget, Snaporaz also believed in the Madonna-mother.[4] Snaporaz's Ideal Woman, in

4. Virginia Mayo (1920–2005) was an American film actress.

other words, is a horrendous caricature of the Petrarchan ideal; she represents its unveiling into a 'thing.' It is the fruit of feminist realism, cruel as well as inescapable. However, Snaporaz wants to live in peace with his doll, at least until he reaches the 'station.' The fact is that his ideal appears like a prize in an amusement park once and for all and establishes Snaporaz as a child.

"Where is the station?" There it is, up there in the sky. The voyage continues in a blimp and the Ideal Doll becomes the balloon. Snaporaz climbs up to the boat. The Ideal Doll and the boat, along with Snaporaz, ascend into a dark, mournful, and murky sky: the sky of death. The boat *is* Snaporaz's existence and it hangs there in that image, even though it is a caricature, always unreachable. Snaporaz and his feminine archetype go up, up, up in the sky to the end. Like vultures, the feminist guerrillas attack the blimp, but Snaporaz's voyage to nothing continues.

The Station, Death, the Woman

As in all decadent and crepuscular myths, in *La città delle donne* Death and Woman are identified with each other. Aren't the orgasmic moans of the ten-thousand lovers in the "columbarium of love" built by Katzone also moans of agony, in a true requiem conceptualized by Fellini as the *forte* of his musical?

During his dream, Snaporaz realizes that he will die without ever reaching his Ideal Woman. His sixty years don't matter: he, like Alice, is still a child and yet he must die without reaching 'his' woman. It is clear that Snaporaz never really made love to her and never fully fed on her except in his fantasies. And this is the sweet neurosis of his life, his particular kind of chastity. The sweetness of his life, the lullaby of his narcissism, is all in his infantile running after an unachievable archetype that is so deeply rooted inside him that it makes his life 'bi-sex.' Snaporaz never really made love: more than impotent or anorexic, he will die a virgin. And in his dream, food, like his Ideal Woman, stays intact, unconsumed, uneaten, & intangible. It is there to adorn Katzone's table like one of those happy banquets that follow a burial.

In essence, *La città delle donne* represents the detailed inventory of the imagination of an Italian man born between 1920 & 1930, of the archetypes that shaped him, of his sexual toys, of his puerility, and of his sexual-political terrors. Snaporaz is situated in a poetic museum of cultural horrors. And here is also the political aspect of the film: it is a spontaneous confession, bordering on grotesque self-criticism, on the part of a great male child-Alice of the Italian 1900s. And if Fellini is self-critical, his self-criticism belongs to the genre that Sartre considered the only one possible: the one that is not imposed by someone else's power and intolerance.

To want to pass Fellini as the Joseph De Maistre of our cinema is the fanatic demand of people who no longer have eyes to see and ears to understand.[5] But we know that fanatics are deaf and blind. Conversely, and luckily for us, besides a fresh new viewpoint, Fellini also has stunning ears. Just think of the dialogue of this film, which is also an inventory, in the form of a nursery rhyme, of all the decipherable and indecipherable kitsch that is constantly spoken in this Wonderland that is Italy.

As a critical question, however, it would be important to remind Fellini of Pascal's saying, cited from Joseph De Maistre himself: "When you write a book, what is revealed at the end is what must be placed in the beginning." We don't know for sure if Fellini in making this film had in mind a similar principle. If, in other words, his film at times suffers also visually from an uncertain layout; if what the director discovered "at the end" was 'situated' by him at the beginning; and if that uncertainty doesn't end up 'disorienting' without reason. Maybe not to have an intention was Fellini's intention. But even the oneiric is, in its way, intentional. And it is our fear that the lack of intention can culminate in an excessive lightness of thinking, barely concealed behind an excessive & glamorous richness of imagination.

5. Joseph-Marie, Comte de Maistre (1753–1821) was a French-speaking Savoyard philosopher, writer, lawyer, and diplomat.

§ 3.6
Kramer vs. Kramer[1]

We are not ashamed to say that while watching a film or reading a book we are still moved to tears. I use "we" because of the constraint of a century-long journalistic tradition, to use "we" instead of "I." In that "we" the whole editorial board of a newspaper is represented, from the editor-in-chief to the copyeditor and the typesetter. And this bold ellipsis also includes the reader's opinion, the only one that, in fact, should be understood as 'in progress.' Obviously that "we" is purely hypocritical. And not only because it seems a snobbish *pluralis majestatis* that tends to bully the reader, but also because in newspapers, as anywhere else, opinions have always been different (thank God), and today more than ever. For example, we don't know if our editor-in-chief, Ugo Tognazzi, cried like we did while watching *Kramer vs. Kramer* (1979). Who knows? He is an unpredictable man, our editor-in-chief, and he could have cried like a baby, but also sneered like a loyal follower of the pirate Lafitte.[2] In this sense, however, it is necessary to clear one possible misunderstanding. The pirate Lafitte could have easily been 'sentimental' and could have easily been moved to tears, as the rare documents on piracy attest and as the wonderful 1930s Hollywood films about pirates confirm. A 'sentimental' person is not necessarily a 'good' soul, in the sense that even the sarcastic Brecht gives to the word. A sentimental person is simply someone who cries easily. He cultivates feelings inside, and little by

1. Originally published in *Nuova Cucina* 9 (July 1980).

2. Jean Lafitte (c.1776–c.1823) was a French pirate and privateer in the Gulf of Mexico in the early 19th century.

little he forgets what caused those feelings, their roots. In this way, he can be moved to tears while watching a fictional scene in a film, and yet he is indifferent in front of a real event that is very similar to the film scene. A sentimental person usually cries by imitation, after seeing other people cry. More specifically, he cries to 'identify,' that is to say, in a given situation-simulacrum he finds a reason to picture himself in it. Memories are also a good reason to cry sweetly, bitterly, and even happily. In sum, a sentimental person cries over himself, because of the residual layers of 'good feelings' that were injected in him as a child, or even before he was born, and that 'life' quickly proved to be unrealistic. He cries because he is still a child: misunderstood, repressed, abandoned, betrayed, and slightly paranoid. He can also cry because he feels 'bad,' a bad child who is unable to have real feelings while he should have been 'so good.' He is a bit hysterical. In a way, a sentimental person is like those fools who believe they are Napoleon: he 'believes' that he is good. For example, a sentimental member of the Red Brigades can easily tear up while watching a film about the killing on Via Fani,[3] maybe thinking of the policemen who were killed, but also remembering his own emotions during the killing. Or an executioner can be moved to tears while reminiscing about one of his difficult executions. A sentimental person, while reading *Les Misérables*, could identify with Jean Valjean and cry like a baby, but then kick a real escaped prisoner, or little orphans, or beggars, or other outcasts, and support the death penalty. In other words: it is easy to cry over the life of fictional characters because it doesn't cost us anything. On the contrary, it saves us the trouble of being moved by 'real' life. What is really difficult for many of us is to put ourselves in the shoes of someone who has a difficult life, and help him, and in so doing have a real relationship with others and with life itself.

So, is the person who cries at *Kramer vs. Kramer* a 'bad' person? This is up to only the person himself, if he or she can unravel the thick and inscrutable thread of good and bad with which we are woven. We just want to point out that tears burst out of

3. Via Fani is where the kidnapping of Aldo Moro took place in 1978. During the attack of the Red Brigades on Moro's escort, several policemen were killed.

ELIO PETRI · "NUOVA CUCINA" (1957–1958)

our eyes for many reasons, among which there is also goodness. Another one is naïveté.

For example, we cried during *Kramer vs. Kramer*, but for gastronomical reasons. In Benton's film, in fact, the importance of food in the life of a nuclear American family is described with rare attention: we could say that food is the link that ties all the little weepings to the general cry over the dissolution of the Kramer family. The drama of Ted, Johanna, and Billy Kramer is indeed a gastronomical one, which at the end reaches a true catharsis and is built around a French toast that becomes the symbol of familial unity. The culinary adventure of the male Kramer begins with Johanna's retirement from her roles as wife and mother. Up to this point, Johanna had diligently carried out her role as the manager of her small nuclear family: she was a cook, a waitress, a servant, an ironing lady, a wardrobe lady, a nurse, and a doctor. As she writes in a letter to her son Billy, she leaves in order to "find something interesting in life." She departs one evening, suddenly, while Billy is asleep, leaving her husband incredulous and appalled.

When the next morning Billy can't find his mother, he starts to cry. To reassure him, it is enough that Ted prepares him the same French toast that his mother used to always give him for breakfast. The French toast here represents the snobbish attitude of the American middle class, always looking for exotic flavors due to the lack of truly unified national cuisine. But more importantly, the toast indicates that the continuity of affections is rooted in food, which for a child becomes the symbol of his parents' love, or lack thereof. In our civilization, at least up until this moment, it is surely the mother who dispenses the food, that is to say the reassurance and the wellbeing, the certainty of life and pleasure. As much as a father tries, what can he give a child to suck?

Predictably Ted, faced with the problem of the French toast requested by Billy, immediately makes a mess. He gets measurements and cooking time wrong, and he almost sets the house on fire. If our editor-in-chief had been Billy's father, then the child's life would have been very different. First of all, two or three other mothers would have appeared. But Hoffman is no Tognazzi. Things get worse. From the toast on, Ted experiences a series of culinary Waterloos. Billy misses Johanna, who could cook and thus could give him warmth, and he can't stand Ted, who presents him with strange and unpredictable food; he doesn't know how to love him yet.

On top of that, Ted accepts the challenge posed by his runaway wife and engages in complicated recipes such as a *steak aux oignons*, which Billy decidedly refuses, preferring some chocolate ice cream. Father and son dine on squalid tables that recall the cafeteria of RAI TV studios. The dishes look and taste like in-flight meals on airlines such as Pan Am or Alitalia: the wet and greenish color of peas, and the brownish yellow of the side carrots paint an unforgettably sad stain on the screen.

We counted in total: three breakfasts with cold milk and bread substitutes, such as flakes; and three breakfasts between lunches and dinners in the film. These rituals are sad, without Johanna, and completely Oedipal since Johanna was a mother for Ted, too. Father and son are like two sad Oedipus orphans who lost Jocasta. Despite a curious dialogue on soda and graffiti in which Hoffman, to interest his son, talks about the soft drinks he used to drink as a child, the atmosphere of the interaction between him and Billy is quite squalid. We wonder: would this atmosphere have been 'warmer' if Johanna had stayed? Isn't sad repetition the only possible atmosphere of a nuclear family lunch? The family lunch 'theater,' reduced to just a very few regular characters in its modern version, is a bare chamber theater, in which tensions are represented without any possible mediation, filter, or distraction. What would have been different if Johanna hadn't left? Ted and Billy would have probably eaten better, and Ted would have talked obsessively about his work with his wife, a thing that he luckily spares his child. Is that all? Perhaps yes.

Besides, Ted is very appreciated at work. He is a creative director at a New York ad agency. But little by little, as his relationship with Billy becomes more 'maternal' and 'professional,' with the constant sacrifice of his time, grocery shopping, frenetic rushes to pick up Billy at the end of school, and monotonous work in the kitchen, his ambitious drive and energy at work diminishes.

It is at this point that Benton portrays the social significance of the American lunch and keenly introduces the theme of the work lunch, a very common ritual in America, & now also in Italy.

One day, Ted's boss invited him to lunch. It looks like a regular work lunch. Finally some good food, prepared by a professional cook. At the end of the meal, Hoffman has a righteous post-coital expression of a person who just ate a good plate of pasta. All of a sudden, his boss tells him: "I'm letting you go." Which means: "I am firing you." The boss is a good 'democratic' and 'down-to-earth' kind of guy, who invites his employees to lunch. He has only one pet peeve: he can't stand when the productivity of his employees is impacted by personal problems. In this case, he first warns them, then he fires them, but during a lavish lunch. *He invites to lunch the person to whom he wants to deny money for food.* It's one of the most sado-democratic ways to fire a poor man. At least in Italy we don't invite to lunch those who will be fired. Here we send a letter and that's it, without mixing the aesthetics of interpersonal relationships, conviviality, with business. And that also saves the money for the bill.

After this incredibly cruel lunch, which for Ted is filled with bitterness, for a long time there are no more moments in the film that are dedicated to food. The legal part of the film begins: Johanna is back in New York and wants full custody of Billy. She is more positive about her role as a mother, now that she has found a job that she likes. But Ted also likes his role as father-mother, although he is going through a professional crisis. And he, too, wants full custody of Billy. No more same-sex meals in the film, but a harsh trial, during which, in a sort of cannibal banquet, father and mother try to devour each other in order to have Billy back (probably to devour him, too). Here, there is much to cry over. Johanna cries, and even Ted tears up. You can just imagine my tears.

Johanna wins the trial; Billy is 'hers.' One morning, Ted and Billy are at home waiting for Johanna to pick up the child. Here we come to the cathartic moment of the film. What does Ted do while waiting? He prepares Johanna's specialty, the French toast, with a great chef's *brio à la* Tognazzi. Now he is both father and mother, so Billy helps him, with a sort of male complicity: he dips the bread slices in egg and passes them to Ted, who cooks them. Food becomes the purifying and cathartic element of the now solid relationship between father and son. The two could now live well, even without Johanna. But the law is against the father and it rewards the mother's betrayal. Billy cries. Ted cries. We cry. Johanna arrives and while everyone in the movie theater is sobbing, she cries, telling Ted that she can't take Billy away from him. The movie ends like that, with a hurricane of tears that sweeps us all off our feet.

Once we regain control of our lachrymal glands, we can now reason. It is true: Benton made a very interesting analytic use of food, revealing its symbolic affective content. But he used it mostly in an emotive way, to have the spectator deeply touched over the destiny of the two males abandoned and betrayed by the woman. The director completely identified with the teary character of Ted (or Billy?). Every time we see Ted and Billy eating alone and sad, we are led by the director to feel, along with them, betrayed by Johanna. "Our mother," "our wife" shouldn't have pushed us to this point. If it doesn't reveal an intellectual failure of Benton, this use of food is at least very manipulative. We wonder: why force the audience to cry only over Ted's culinary sufferance, without ever hinting, in a honest and efficient way, at the long eight years that Johanna spent in the kitchen before her fatal decision? Benton doesn't even attempt to tackle the complex issue of the immobility or interchangeability of family (but also genetic, social, historical) roles, not even for humor. Is the mother's role purely biological? Women have milk in their

ELIO PETRI · "NUOVA CUCINA" (1957–1958)

breast, that is true, but for this reason are they destined to spend their whole life in the kitchen? How much and which part of the female role does not derive from economic history? Has the young and 'abandoned' Benton ever wondered what would happen to our economy if all the mothers did what Johanna did? Besides the strict view of the kitchen as 'sacrifice,' — and not instead as a playful possibility — Benton is a careless traditionalist on everything else as well. He doesn't even touch, with suspicious prudishness given the topic, upon the sexual aspect of the Kramer's crisis. What kind of husband and lover can a fanatically productive and ambitious man like Ted be, completely self-absorbed? Further, Johanna's competitiveness with Ted can't be explained with the usual penis envy, or as the manifestation of her unreasonable narcissism. This film's take on this aspect, while it serves the patriarchal and moralistic view of Benton well, does not bring to light the real motives that are at the basis of many family breakups and that are destroying the institution of marriage, at least the kind that is lived as a company in which the woman occupies the lower echelons. Let's be honest: at least Johanna's escape forced Ted to become the father he had never been.

In conclusion, we must add that while watching Johanna and Ted's behavior on screen, for example their stubborn way of fighting over the 'male-doll' Billy ("He's mine," "No, he's mine"), we see them as children in need of French toast, or a doll, to shield themselves from their insecurity. The puerility of the parents is perhaps the hidden theme of the film, but Benton did not develop it. His film would have been less dramatic, and it wouldn't have won its four Academy Awards, nor had the great success that it enjoyed. And we wouldn't have cried.

Recipe for French toast: beat the eggs, whites included, one egg per person; mix them with milk; dip bread slices in the mixture; cook the bread in butter, in a pan. About cooking times, we should ask Tognazzi. And we should also ask him if he cried while watching *Kramer vs. Kramer*. If he did, we should tell him to be ashamed: he is a ninny like me.

IMAGES

Nello Poletti (Marcello Mastroianni) and Adalgisa De Matteis (Micheline Presle) in a scene from *L'assassino* (1961)

Nello (Marcello Mastroianni) and Adalgisa (Micheline Presle) in a scene from *L'assassino* (1961)

Cesare Conversi (Salvo Randone) and Graziella (Angela Minervini) in a scene from *I giorni contati* (1962)

Elio Petri and Cesare (Salvo Randone) on the set of *I giorni contati* (1962)

Elio Petri and Antonio Mombelli (Alberto Sordi) on the set of *Il maestro di Vigevano* (1963)

Elio Petri, Marcello Poletti (Marcello Mastroianni), Olga (Elsa Martinelli), and Caroline Meredith (Ursula Andress) on the set of *La decima vittima* (1965)

Elio Petri and Caroline (Ursula Andress) on the set of *La decima vittima* (1965)

Elio Petri and Caroline (Ursula Andress) on the set of *La decima vittima* (1965)

Prof. Paolo Laurana (Gian Maria Volontè) and the Priest of Sant' Amo (Mario Scaccia) in a scene from *A ciascuno il suo* (1967)

Prof. Laurana (Gian Maria Volontè) and Luisa Roscio (Irene Papas) in a scene from *A ciascuno il suo* (1967)

Flavia (Vanessa Redgrave) and Elio Petri on the set of *Un tranquillo posto di campagna* (1969)

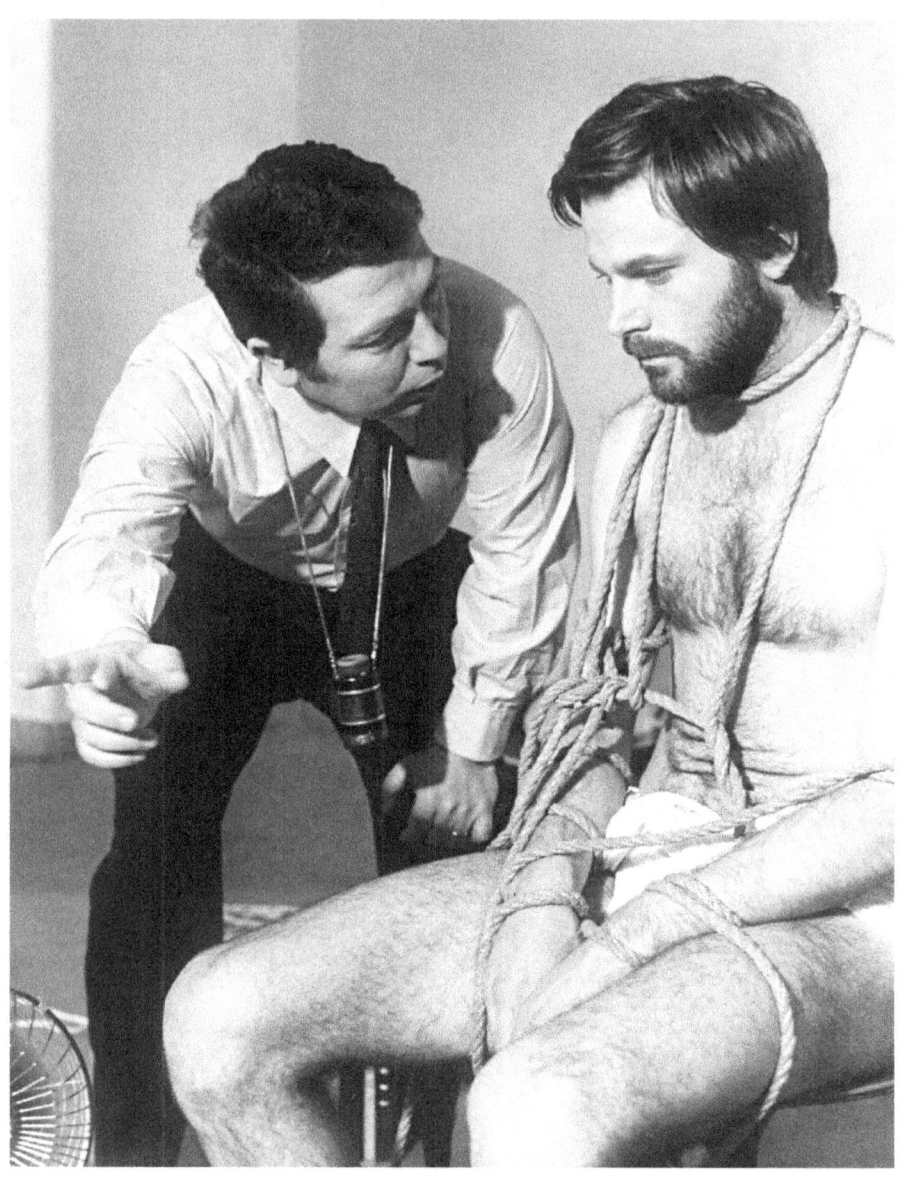

Elio Petri and Leonardo Ferri (Franco Nero) during the shooting of *Un tranquillo posto di campagna* (1969)

The Chief (Gian Maria Volontè) on the set of *Indagine su un cittadino al di sopra di ogni sospetto* (1970)

Augusta Terzi (Florinda Bolkan) and The Chief (Gian Maria Volontè) in a scene from *Indagine su un cittadino al di sopra di ogni sospetto* (1970)

Elio Petri during the shooting of *Indagine su un cittadino al di sopra di ogni sospetto* (1970) in Rome

The Chief (Gian Maria Volontè) and Elio Petri on the set of *Indagine su un cittadino al di sopra di ogni sospetto* (1970)

Lidia (Mariangela Melato) and Lulù Massa (Gian Maria Volonté) in a scene from *La classe operaia va in paradiso* (1971)

Albertone (Mario Scaccia) in a scene from *La proprietà non è più un furto* (1973)

The Butcher (Ugo Tognazzi) in a scene from *La proprietà non è più un furto* (1973)

Total (Flavio Bucci) in *La proprietà non è più un furto* (1973)

M. (Gian Maria Volontè) on the set of *Todo modo* (1976)

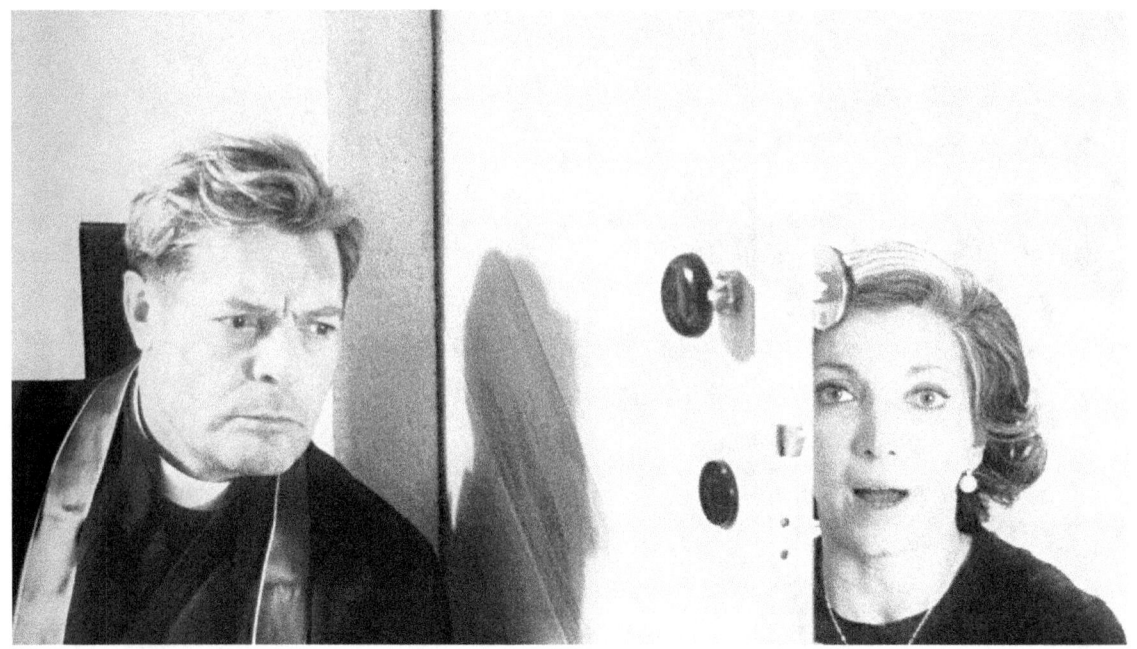

Father Gaetano (Marcello Mastroianni) and Giacinta (Mariangela Melato) in a scene from *Todo modo* (1976)

Father Gaetano (Marcello Mastroianni) leading the group of politicians gathered at the Zafer Hotel in a spiritual exercise (*Todo modo*, 1976)

Fedora (Angela Molina) and the Man (Giancarlo Giannini) in a scene from *Buone notizie* (1978)

Elio Petri with part of the cast on the set of *Buone Notizie* (1978)

Elio Petri on the set of *La classe operaia va in paradiso* (1971)

Composer Ennio Morricone

Set Designer Dante Ferretti

Screenwriter Ugo Pirro

4.
COMMENTS ON HIS OWN FILMS
(1976–1979)

§ 4.1 Short Tracts on *A Ciascuno il suo* & *Todo Modo* [1]

1. *Dostoyevsky & Sciascia: Why?*

A director's head works in an eccentric way, or mine certainly does. Facts that would be incomprehensible in an intellectual's head can happen in there. It is only from the distorted perspective of a filmmaker like me that one can talk of the kinship between Dostoyevsky and Sciascia, or at least between some of their novels. I admit that the two writers appear to be scandalously different. As much as the materials of the first are eruptive and verbally liberating, those of the second seem frugal, prudish, even lazy — as if they were permeated by an attitude of strict skepticism. It is true that Dostoyevsky's self-declared and sarcastic, even fantastic anti-Illuminism is apparently, from a semantic point of view, the polar opposite of Sciascia's subtle and piercing "Voltaireanism." However, regardless of literary taste, to a filmmaker's mind the two writers share some things that make them translatable into the director's own language. I will list them here. First, there is the passion for a mysterious plot that develops around what seems to be a great mystery but is not, for example, a plot that symbolizes the relationship between the individual and the social dimension, as if this relationship were based on a criminal basis known but forgotten by everybody. Second, there is a use of dialogue that reveals the common tendency to 'theatricality,' and thus, a vision of society as 'theater' or spectacle. Third, there is contemporaneity, or the impossibility of escaping from their contemporaries

1. *A ciascuno il suo* refers to the novel by Leonardo Sciascia and the eponymous film by Elio Petri. In the U.S. market, the titles of each work have been translated differently. Sciascia's novel was translated with the title *To Each His Own*, whereas Petri's film was first translated as *We Still Kill the Old Way*, then changed into *To Each His Own*. Currently, a U.S. version of the DVD is not available.

and themselves, a desire to stay rooted in existential time and attached to personal responsibility. Finally, there is the irony, or the manifestation of an aesthetic discomfort, of an ethical and political uneasiness that makes both writers 'others' in their own literary societies.

Through a certain cinematic lens, these things form the basis for a film; they would have made both Dostoyevsky and Sciascia highly transposable into film. This kind of filmmaking does not renounce the *intention*, contrary to Adorno's statement about cinema: "True intentions would be possible only through the renunciation of intention."[2]

Now, choosing Sciascia as the source of my film already implies that I am imposing an agenda on myself. And that I intend to impose my agenda on others, too.

2. *A Ciascuno il Suo: Sciascia's Sensuality*

Sciascia is a prude. That is true. But he is also sensual. Or better still, his sensuality consists of his prudishness, which is a stylistic one, a verbal one, but it is also a form of reticence about things and about the 'words' used for the senses. This sensuality, to me, seemed to constitute the *volonté de jouissance* of *A ciascuno il suo*. It is in this novel that Sciascia reveals all of his seduction.

In *A ciascuno il suo*, all reality's mystery is centered on a woman, specifically on her body and her clothing. The male protagonist, Professor Laurana, cannot unravel this mystery because he is unable to understand the language of reality through her and his own sexuality. Sciascia casts a light on the woman that creates a big, thick, black shadow all around her that is as sensual as mourning and that covers everything else.

The woman, Luisa, appears in very few places in the book. The first time is when Laurana visits her, right after her husband Roscio has been killed. Luisa says of herself: "And that is how it will always be. [...] Always dressed in black, always..." She is a widow, but she is always dressed in black because she is both object and

2. "Wahre Intentionen wären möglich erst beim Verzicht auf die Intention." Theodor W. Adorno, *Minima Moralia: Reflexionen aus dem beschädigten Leben* (Neuauflage: Suhrkamp, 2003) 142. Theodor W. Adorno, *Minima Moralia: Reflections from Damaged Life*, tr. E. F.N. Jephcott (London: Verso, 1974) 142. [TN]

victim of a sexual, death-driven desire. Her little daughter says that she is "prettier" when she wears black. And Laurana thinks: "The child's right."[3]

The second time that Laurana goes to Luisa's house is to look through the archive for a political dossier that the dead Roscio wanted to send to Rome in order to denounce the illegal activities of an unknown notary in town. "The Signora had lent her hand to the search; she was squatting before the bottom drawer of the desk, framed in the square formed by the play of light and shadow, nakedly female, her face mysteriously concealed beneath the dark mass of her hair. Laurana's thoughts dissolved in the black sun of desire."[4]

There is a third encounter between the two characters: it is very brief, on November 1, at the cemetery. Luisa says of herself that she is "living, yes, but how unhappily, accursedly alive" (the sensuality of the cult of the dead in front of "unhappily alive" & "alive"); "she sighed and brushed away invisible tears" and, while greeting him, "it seemed to Laurana that when Signora Luisa shook his hand, she held it for one meaningful moment and that there was a gleam of imploring understanding in her eyes." During her frequent kneeling in front of her husband's tomb, the woman "allowed a glimpse of the abundant, languid nudity of a Delacroix odalisque, and as the Signora got up she had necessarily exposed a further whiteness of thigh above her tightly drawn stockings." And that movement, "Laurana noted, was attentively awaited and spied upon by a group of young bloods nearby." "'What a people,' he thought, but his contempt was shot through with jealousy. [...] Laurana did not stop to think that he, too, had voraciously caught the white gleam of flesh between black and black, and that he had noticed that group of young hoodlums for the simple reason that he was of the same breed."[5] (There is a "gleam" of understanding in the gaze, like the "gleam" of her flesh against the black of her clothing).

Then, on a bus directed to the "county seat," the fourth encounter: "She was sitting up front, her black-stockinged legs in

3. Leonardo Sciascia, *To Each His Own*, tr. by Adrienne Foulke (Manchester, UK: Carcanet Press Ltd., 1989). In Italian: *A ciascuno il suo* (Turin: Giulio Einaudi, 1966) 51.

4. Ibid., 72.

5. Ibid., 111–113.

line with the open door" (the sensuality of "black-stockinged" and of "open door"). During the trip, she talks so stupidly that "Laurana actually felt as if his ears were stopped." But "the more closely, the more pitilessly he observed her to detect some mortal flaw, to uncover some perversity, the abundant grace of her body, [...] her heavy hair, her perfume that barely concealed the acrid scent of bed and of sleep, aroused in him a painful, a physically painful desire." And "Laurana recognized in his turmoil the impediments of a long-ago indoctrination into sin — the *turn of the screw*, in a word — and of terror about sexual things that he had never shaken off; indeed, the more actively his mind was engaged, the more fiercely they assailed him."[6]

The sum of these four apparently fortuitous meetings would be an appointment that Laurana and Luisa set up in order to together find a way to inculpate Rosello, her cousin, his confidante, and finally the one who ordered Roscio's murder. But Luisa will not go to the meeting place, the Romeris Cafè in the county seat, and instead the professor will be kidnapped, killed, and buried "under a heavy pile of lime, in an abandoned sulphur mine halfway, as the crow flies, between his home town and the county seat."[7] (In that "heavy pile of lime" the "dark mass" of sex seems to be burned to ashes and reconciled).

The four brief encounters and the last appointment (missed the way a sexual act can be missed), like so many *turns of the screw*, will cause Laurana's death. Instead of a sexual encounter, death.

Laurana is sexually impotent: thus, he is also politically impotent. He discovers that in his hometown a political murder has been disguised as a crime of passion even though later in the story, its political motivation is overshadowed by one of passion. The murder seems to have developed with the complicity of the Church. The professor communicates his findings to a notary associated with the Christian Democratic Party in town, who is the nephew of the town's priest.[8] He is the killer, but Laurana does not know this. When he starts to suspect something, he

6. Ibid., 118–120.

7. Ibid., 138.

8. The Christian Democratic Party was an Italian political party founded in 1943. It was a Christian centrist organization comprising both right-wing and left-wing factions that dominated Italian politics for almost 50 years from 1944 until its demise in 1994.

seeks support in Luisa, the killer's lover and accomplice, even just for the pleasure of touching her, of feeling the "blood that grew hot as he sat beside her." Luisa was "evil [that] had become incarnated, had been obscurely, splendidly transformed into sex."[9] This "obscurely" is a long shadow on the whole of reality, not only on sex. Reality, filtered through the impenetrable shadow of that "dark mass" made up of the Church and of sex, is unintelligible.

I made the film because *A ciascuno il suo* is the sensual and ironic portrait of a humanistic and sexually impotent intellectual. For me, the political aspect of the book consisted essentially in this mingling of sex with the whole of reality. That the book on first reading was also a strong civil and political denunciation was true and important, but secondary for me. The Church is the instigator of the murders. In the shadow of the Church, politics and murder go hand in hand and the killer remains unpunished. But, most of all, it is in the extremely long and sensual shadow of the Church that Laurana received his "long-ago indoctrination into sin," which is his political and sexual impotence.

In the film, I tried to be as clear as possible, notwithstanding Adorno's other statement: "The clear formulation, even though esoteric, leads to consumption," and I changed the structure of the novel considerably, but always trying to retain Sciascia's sensuality in the images.

3. *Todo Modo: Une Comptabilitè Obsessionelle*

Nine years later, politicians, financiers, industrialists, notaries (among them, perhaps, also the unpunished killer from *A ciascuno il suo*) will gather at Zafer apparently to undergo the Spiritual Exercises,[10] but really so as to continue to weave together their illegal activities and their power plays. They are forced by Father Gaetano, the priest who runs the hotel, to recite the rosary together:

> "their voices, although lifted in the Our Father, the Hail Mary, the Gloria, sounded a tiny note of terror and hysteria. The voice of

9. Ibid., 119.

10. St. Ignatius de Loyola's spiritual exercises are religious praxes that consist of structured ways of praying, meditating, and breathing, in order to repent and purify the believer's soul. They were a widespread praxis among members of the Christian Democratic Party in the years prior to the shooting of *Todo Modo*.

Father Gaetano, which alternated with theirs, was distant & cold; uttered by that voice, expressions like [...] 'ancient serpent,' 'sword that will pierce the soul,' were infused with an entirely physical import — they were no longer metaphors, but actualities that were becoming, that already were, real, there on the frontiers of the world, the frontiers of Hell [...] and at that moment [...] in all their abject mystifications and grotesqueries [there was] some genuine feeling — genuine fear, genuine distress — as they moved back and forth in the dark, reciting prayers, in what truly equaled a spiritual exercise. It was almost as if they were, and felt themselves to be, despairing in the turmoil of a hellish pit, on the point of metamorphosis. Dante's inferno of the thieves came readily to mind."[11]

This extremely theatrical scene appeared to me, the first time I read *Todo Modo*, as an appalling, even pitiful metaphor of Christian Democratic power exerted by its politicians, who were like prisoners inside a dark and obsessive labyrinth.

From the perspective of Ignazio's "little theater," I have thought a lot about what Barthes (Loyola) wrote: "Obsessional neurosis has been defined (Lacan) as a 'defensive decomposition comparable in its principles to that illustrative of the *redan* or the obstacle.' This is precisely the structure of the *Exercises*. [...] The obsessional character of the *Exercises* blazes forth in the accounting passion transmitted to the *exercitant* [...]. The accountancy is obsessional not only because it is infinite, but above all because it engenders its own errors: being a matter of accounting for his sins [...] the fact of accounting for them in a faulty way will in turn become an error that must be added on to the original list; this list is thus made infinite, the redeeming accounting of errors calling up *per contra* the very errors of the account."[12]

The ways that power has been administered by the Christian Democrats in Italy over the past thirty years exactly resembles the process described by Barthes, but in an even more 'sinful' sense. The Christian Democrats in power do count their mistakes and crimes, but only to hide them: and the fact that they hide them

11. *One Way or Another*, tr. by Adrienne Foulke (New York: Harper and Row, 1977). In Italian: *Todo modo* (Turin: Giulio Einaudi Editore, 1974) 41–42.

12. Roland Barthes, *Sade, Fourier, Loyola*, tr. by Richard Miller (New York: Farrar, Straus and Giroux, 1976). In French: *Sade, Fourier, Loyola* (Paris: Éditions du Seuil, 1971) 69.

becomes "in its turn, a sin that will add to the original list," and so on into infinity, obsessively, unless there is a *redde rationem*.[13]

Ignazio's "little theater" is sadistic in that "the master is he who speaks, who disposes of the entirety of language; the object is he who is silent, who remains separate, by a mutilation more absolute than any erotic torture, from any access to discourse" (Barthes, *Sade* I).[14] Also, it is sadistic in its capricious repetition, in its rituality, in its *concevoir l'inconcevable*:[15] which is to say, to conceive the exercises as the place of high tension coming closer to God through the word, while leaving to the patient-sinner only the material *mise-en-scène* of hell. In fact, from the very moment that the patient-sinner enters Ignazio's theater, which is built like stairs that seem to climb upwards, but really lead downwards, he is lost, because his guilt is — in the perversity of Ignazio's spirit — irredeemable.

This sulfurous and sarcastic idea was the *brio* of Sciascia's book. But I believe that I forced the writer's hand and built *Todo Modo* exactly as if it were a spiritual exercise, even in the police investigation assimilated into the exercises! I follow, as much as possible, Ignazio's cadence. And I admit that I forced Sciascia's hand again in making the film more explicit than his book, through my personalization of the denunciation.

In the book, there is the story of a courtship between a priest and a lay artist who arrives in Zafer because his car breaks down. The two characters look for each other, study each other, they discuss, but in the end, they court one another. There is, in this courtship, something obliquely sensual, like in every collusion, even the intellectual ones. The lay artist is a *repressed* believer, the priest is a *repressed* atheist, and every aspect of their personalities, in the couple that is created, can again be broken down and give birth to more 'doubles': the *repressed* mystic again reflects a *repressed* atheist, and so on.

The story of this complicity was interesting and meaningful, even though it became an obstacle to my goal, which was essentially political. I wanted to make a film against the party that

13. Latin in the original. "Final reckoning."

14. Barthes, ibid., 31.

15. French in the original. "To conceive the inconceivable."

governed Italy for thirty years and shipwrecked the country, politically and culturally. Another collusion firmly established itself over the past thirty years between the Church and the Christian Democratic Party: I wanted my film to talk about this, through the metaphor offered by Sciascia-Loyola.

I decided, perhaps cruelly, to eliminate the character of the lay artist and to substitute it with a Christian Democratic politician, who at the same time was the most recognizable and the most emblematic of all the living ones. In this way, a new guide-character was created, "M.," in which the personality and the demeanor of Aldo Moro are reflected. For many years Moro carried his power like a cross on his shoulders, and the torment of this sort of exhausting spiritual exercise was clear in his emaciated face, in his somewhat lost behavior, in the bitter grimace of his mouth, in his sickly gaze. He took onto himself the impossible endeavor of mediating between the utopian and the wheeler-dealer souls of his party, between his party and the leftist parties, between the poor and the rich, between the exploited and the exploiters, and as the cross of mediation weighed on him more and more, it looked as if it could crush him at any given moment.

Moro too, like Loyola and Sade, conceived of the unconceivable: a change that did not change anything, a movement that could develop into immobility, a whole that seemed empty, a Left that would go Right, a Right that would go Left, but always complicit with the worst part of his party. In the meantime, the cultural and social fabric of the country, in this metaphysical tension, was falling apart, rotting, and dying, and is still dying.

From such a perspective of death, I imagined that M. had a veritable vocation for martyrdom and it seemed to me that, among the murders that occur throughout the spiritual exercises, the final and most significant one had to be his own murder, even insinuating that he, himself, was the instigator. (The Christian Democrats in *Todo Modo* were like Luke's pigs in Dostoyevsky's *The Demons*, and like these same 'demons' seem to be irresistibly drawn to slaughter. Are they right-wing demons?)

I forced Sciascia's hand also in the tone of the film, which became that of a grotesque black farce, and by doing so it seemed to me not only to follow Sciascia's indication — "in all their abject mystifications and grotesqueries" — but also to evoke the climate of the blackest of farce that one could, and still can, breathe in Italy. I am not sure if I succeeded in my intention to be clear. Perhaps this time I proved correct Adorno's statement: "the formulation [is] unclear & unprofessional according to its immanent criteria."

However, Sciascia, in the midst of the controversy that the film caused upon its release — during the electoral campaign — defended the film *Todo Modo* against all its critics, who were a majority worthy of the "Historic Compromise."[16] He recalled Pasolini's wish to put the Christian Democrats on trial for political misconduct. This came through about Sciascia despite all my manipulations and the distortions of his text & its "sensuality."

For this, I must still thank him, and most of all thank him for his lesson on style.

---

16. The term "Historic Compromise" (*"compromesso storico"*) refers to the accommodation between the Italian Christian Democratic Party and the Italian Communist Party in the 1970s, after the latter embraced Eurocommunism under Enrico Berlinguer. The 1978 assassination of Christian Democratic Party leader Aldo Moro put an end to it.

§ 4.2
Todo Modo

Interview with Jean A. Gili [1]

Todo Modo (1976) is based on the eponymous novel by Leonardo Sciascia. How did you approach the original text? How did you adapt the novel into a screenplay?

From my perspective, the only viable approach to the text was a political one. Sciascia's book could have lent itself to other interpretations, that's for sure, but when I decided to adapt it into a screenplay, I had only one goal in mind: that is, to damage the Christian Democratic Party (DC), even with the most prejudiced perspective. That was at the end of 1974. Since then many things have happened in Italy, among which two elections that have acquired an apocalyptic tone thanks to priests and Americans. There have been bloodbaths, tragi-comic scandals, hundreds of bombings; the economic crisis has reached perhaps irreversible levels, and all is wrapped in the fetid cloud surrounding the rotting body of the State institutions. Today, I would do my film against the DC again, since I am now more than ever convinced that its leaders are responsible for the present degradation of Italy's social and political life. In the past thirty years, they have ensured the continuity of the Fascist state, the restoration of the worst capitalistic models, and the return of political methods based on a pre-fascist and cronyist parasitism and on corruption. In the Americanization of this country, a process irrationally imposed from above, the Christian Democrats threw the country into a cultural misery that is the main cause of cultural desperation, cultural idiocy, and cultural impotence. They are shielded by the parasitic elements in every social class, which are most responsible for the cultural shipwreck of the 1960s and represent

1. This interview was originally published in French in Jean A. Gili, *Le cinéma italien* (Paris: U.G.E., 1978).

the sick part of this country. Given this situation, not only would I approach *Todo Modo* in the same way, but I regret having at times given in to that 'measure' or 'good taste' that seems to have become the distinctive stylistic feature of the present political-cultural wretchedness. I regret not having been more partial and not having shown more openly and without qualms my disgust, which is the common disgust of all Italians. I believe we must defend the right of every Italian of my generation to be partial and disgusted once he has reached, after thirty years, the conclusion that through the DC our worst national characteristics, such as slyness, opportunism, and conformism, have returned. It is a right we have earned in many years of opposition, though often weak and ineffective, to the DC's deathly course of action. Those who were young when Fascism fell, who witnessed the betrayal of the simple and human hopes for a better society on the part of the bourgeoisie and its representative Party (in this sense, the DC is the direct heir of Fascism), and who grew up amidst the increasing smell of corruption of the capitalistic human and social tissue, have the right to be partial and disgusted. But all of us share the right of feeling nauseated and revolted by the certainty that what is done is done, that the values that made autonomous the culture of the Italian proletarian classes are now gone forever. At the moment, the petty bourgeois ideology has won through corporatism.

Why did you feel the need to give your political characters a more direct link to Italian reality? In particular, I mean the relation between actor Gian Maria Volontè and politician Aldo Moro. Further, do you think that a non-Italian viewer, who won't be able to pick up on this link, will watch the film with the same interest? Don't you think that the nature of the relationship of film to viewer will change'?

In order for my political attack to be comprehensible, all the references had to be clear and unequivocal. In Sciascia's book, the dramatic mystery is played on a dualism between a lay artist (a painter) and a priest who is half-saint, half-devil. Together, they sing the praises of humanistic culture and weep over the end of a civilization. The painter is a repressed mystic, the priest is a repressed layman, and every part of their personality can be divided in an ulterior double: the repressed mystic produces another repressed layman, and so on, in a never-ending reproduction (like the optical illusions of the mirrors in a shop). The two characters court one another; in fact, we can say that the book is the story of their courtship. In a way, they are accomplices. Both consider themselves above the group of Christian Democrats that is gathered in the Zafer Hotel to practice spiritual exercises. In reality, they consider themselves above everyone and everything, in the name of culture, and in this they are twins. In my opinion, the 'lay' intellectual has the same responsibilities as the 'mystic' intellectual. But I needed to express another dualism that I observed with my own eyes, and that is much more dangerous for Italian society, between the Church and the State. We can say that a Christian Democrat is a repressed priest, and that a priest is a repressed Christian Democrat. They live in an embrace that looks more and more like a *rictus*, like a psychophysical imperfection, like a 'Siamese-ism,' and they are tied to the same destiny. The priest is forced to justify any immoral action of his partner to contain the more and more severe usury of the ecclesial institution. The politician must support and be part of every abuse of power and clerical interference in order to obtain the priest's complicity. This relationship is created in a situation of ambiguity, suspicion, diffidence, & contempt, which are natural human feelings in our society, but they are ten times stronger due to the sense of necessity that forces them to collaborate. This dualism, to me, was more interesting than the one in the book. And in order to make it clearer, I not only substituted the character of the painter with a Christian Democrat, but I made sure that he was also recognizable. Then I turned the priest into an American-style businessman, at least in his behavior. In the film, the layman ends up being more religious than the priest, who, instead, acts in the rushed and violent way that is typical of businessmen (there is also a hint of a courtship, but only on the part of M., who appears to be attracted by the priest's virility; M. uses confession almost as an excuse for carnality). After all, the thirty-year old iconography of the Christian Democrat leaders — which by now resembles that of the *Commedia dell'arte* — inevitably recalls grotesque and slimy characters, oily church mice with a feminine strut and with difficult, incomprehensible speech. They are *clercs manqués*, just like the Nazis were *artistes manqués*. They also recall priests in their certainty of having been invested with a mission. Among all Christian Democrats, the one who appeared to me the most emblematic and the most dangerous was Aldo Moro. Moro has been the protagonist of the Leftist-Centrist experience. He succeeded in taking on the Socialists in the political coalitions of the 1970s, when the great crisis of that developmental model, which is now at its zenith, was already in place. Skillfully, he made them co-responsible for all the mistakes that the Christian Democrats have made in the previous fifteen years. He is now trying the same thing with the Communists. He is mellifluous. He is madly ambitious, but he forces himself into a façade of exacerbated modesty. He utilizes the language of an 'educated' man, behind which he hides his lack of vision, which he tries to mask as 'progressive.' But from the analysis of his political action, one can guess a political thought that fully corresponds to the Pauline rule: "Everyone should remain in the situation in which he was when he was called."[2] He acts so that nothing will change while trying to convince everybody of a constant change. As a consequence, the social tissue of the country is getting weaker, older; it is coming apart & dying. He embodies a comic version of the *Leopard*, since he even convinces himself of his innovative abilities, like a good reactionary. His attempt to mask stasis as movement is taking its toll on him. In fact, he even appears to be sexually ambiguous. He is lifeless, rarefied, diaphanous, absent, and immersed in sublime conflicts. In reality he is the most coherent interpreter of the petty inter-

2. See 1 Corinthians VII:20.

ests of the Italian petit bourgeoisie, especially from the South, which is tied to its privileges while disguising its lowly intentions with the highest goals, almost inspired by God. In sum, Moro is a man who is at the same time on the Right and on the Left, which puts him in a sort of void, a truly emblematic position for a leader of the DC. This void also corresponds to that 'indifference' that St. Ignatius requests from a man of faith. We can say that the only thing that does not leave Moro 'indifferent' is his Party's interest. However, we can also say, in Moro's 'defense,' that his psychological characteristics are those of many small Italian bourgeois from the so-called 'liberal' professions: deviousness, duplicity, and laziness, rooted in and clinging to their privileges. He is just like his electors & his Party's friends. In the film, M., the character played by Volontè, shows all of these characteristics but he expresses them most strongly in his actions. The film is the story of a deathly dualism, of an impossible return to faith on the part of a power group that even sports religious symbols as their political banner; it is the story of a series of spiritual exercises that is destined to turn into a slaughter, because the negative forces, the dark ghosts emanating from the participants, must necessarily come down on themselves.

In the book, the murders are not explained. The same happens in the film. Do you want to present it as a form of self-destruction? By choosing the driver as an executioner, it may look like an execution. What is the meaning of the film ending, for you?

How do I see the ending of my film? First of all, it is the logical conclusion of the spiritual exercises, that is to say, of an ascetic *happening* in which the subject is methodically thrown back to the hell of the Catholic 'self,' of a truly particular psycho-drama in which the 'patient' always has the role of the sinner predestined by St. Ignatius' perverted spirit, which is to be crushed under his guilt complex. The exercises are the attempt, also perverted, to experiment from inside the neurosis of one's own body, of the division of one's soul, and of God's silence. The set is fixed, the roles are fixed, and the rhythm is fixed, and yet within these predetermined parameters there is the chance of an open-ended conclusion. Will our sinner be able to come out of the tunnel alive? I don't think so. The metaphor of the spiritual exercises is valid only if it ends with the irreparable loss of the patient-sinner, since this is the hidden and neurotic goal of St. Ignatius (and Father Gaetano). We can say that the political test that the current DC has been conducting in the last few years seems, just like a spiritual exercise, doomed to its own condemnation and extinction. Roland Barthes says about St. Ignatius' exercises: "The obsessional character of the *Exercises* blazes forth in the accounting passion transmitted to the *exercitant* [...]. The accountancy is obsessional not only because it is infinite, but above all because it engenders its own errors: being a matter of accounting for his sins [...], the fact of accounting for them in a faulty way will in turn become an error that must be added on to the original list; this list is thus made infinite, the redeeming accounting of errors calling up per contra the very errors of the account."[3] The way the Christian Democrats exercise power in Italy resembles exactly the process described by Barthes, but upside-down. To clarify: the Christian Democrats govern and count the mistakes and the crimes they are often responsible for, but only to hide them and by hiding them, they become "à son tour une faute qui devra s'ajouter à la liste originelle," and so on until the *redde rationem*. The exercise of power has become, for Christian Democrats, a sort of perennial feeling of being accused, as if they had to make up for the 'sin' of having usurped power. Under this aspect, to keep repeating their mistakes, as the Christian Democrats are doing, equals a suicide. The final sequence of the film can thus be interpreted as a suicide, but only in this sense. From the point of view of immediate political satire, which is my favorite interpretation, the film resonates with the absurd atmosphere in which the Christian Democrats, and the secret services of the whole world, have kept Italy for the past ten years. It is the atmosphere

3. Roland Barthes, *Sade, Fourier, Loyola*, tr. by Richard Miller (Berkeley & Los Angeles: University of California Press, 1976).

of a bad *Guignol* in which anything and its opposite can happen, as long as people are pushed to vote for the agents of order. For the last ten years, elections in Italy have occurred amidst murderous bomb explosions, like the religious celebrations in Naples that become spiritual only with firecrackers. Kidnappings and killings follow one another like in the screenplay of a bad noir series.

Keeping with the idea of the 'black' farce that I wanted to make, I shot the film with the idea that the man behind all the murders was M. himself, who eventually, as an admission of impotence, would order his own execution. But at the same time, regardless of whatever objective perspective I adopted, the ending of the film always becomes a *redde rationem*. Whether the protagonists eliminated one another, or M. ordered theirs and his execution, or someone else from his Party from Rome decided to destroy them for an inexplicable scheme, or the CIA decided to kill all of them due to their proved incompetence, or the massacre was caused by a social uprising, or God (at this point allied with Communist party?) decided to get rid of his corrupted sons, in all of these cases the massacre takes on the objective value of a punishment, of a *redde rationem*. In other words, the ending of *Todo Modo* metaphorically represents a Christian Democrat's nightmare, which is to say, a dream for the rest of us.

You show that power took these men and led them to corruption. The problem is: is power corrupting in general, or is it this specific kind of power that generates corruption?

In some ways this question is not exactly about the film, which is metaphorically concerned with a specific and identifiable situation. However, I can quickly explain why I don't agree with the tendency of some 'radical' intellectuals to consider 'power' as a sort of devil's spawn. Power is determined historically, and it belongs to those who own the means of production. The giant ensemble of the institutions and the instruments of exploitation and coercion that compose the defense and offense apparatuses of the dominant class constitutes 'power,' which is the 'power' of capital. In our historical period 'power' is always discriminating: it is built on the exclusion from any of its parts those who are excluded from the means of production. Power in a society divided into social classes is necessarily corrupting because it is the reflection of a concept of a social life that entails a divided, separated humanity in which the relations of production are based on exploiting the other. In this kind of society, the individual follows a utilitarian way of living aimed at obtaining his own wellbeing at any cost: and if that happens at someone else's expense, so be it. In this way, he is exposed to the loss of the possibility of his own total conscience of the world and he is destined to corrupt his own humanity. Therefore, in my opinion, power that is based on exploitation is corrupting, and an individual who accepts his own alienation is corruptible. But we do know, even in this historical period, societies that apparently are not divided into social classes. They have displayed, and still display, irrational and shameful tendencies to an authoritarian degeneration, which is the typical form of corruption of the forms of power they expressed. These societies are still anthropologically rooted in the present historical cycle and negatively reflect the structures of the society divided in social classes, of which they are direct filiations: they constitute their 'double' I could say. In every place of these societies, the human and social relations are still based on the division of labor, on hierarchy, on the separation between 'city' and 'country,' on selection, and on the bourgeois notion of *productivity* and *normality*. The means of production are now in the hands of the State, but it is an arrogant minority that decides about their use. The individual is 'manufactured' according to vertical structures based on the old taboos: sexual repression and guilt. These societies are unfair despite the apparent disappearance of social classes. This is because bourgeois 'rationality' survives in them through the division of labor that, if it doesn't create true conditions for the 'private' withdrawal of the surplus value, surely favors the persistence of inequality, which is one of the main causes of social malaise and of corruption. The kind of subordination that the old and the new forms of power require from the individual, or 'subject,' is based still on a pyramidal structure with the image of God at the top: "Everyone shall obey the authorities because there is no power that does not derive from God" (Romans XIII:1–2).[4] I would rather say that there is no power that does not derive from the rapport of production, and this is what needs to be radically changed if we really want to change power. The foundations of the rapport of production are laid outside and inside the individual in a continuous exchange between this 'outside' in the objective reality, in factories, schools, & centers of power, and this 'inside' in the complex cultural structure that defines us. To consider power in general as a source of irresistible corruption is, then, like rejecting reality as a whole, a sort of infantile autism. But it is also an idea that can hide a total and passive self-abandon to the power of 'power.' To moralistically reject power is the blindest obedience to 'institutional authorities,' and is a way to ensure the protection of 'god' (or the 'rapport of production'), since the rejection implies the end of every conflict, while every change generates harsh conflicts. This rejection defines one's position before power, and of the reality that is expressed within it, only as impotence. On the contrary, power must be *seized*, outside and inside, against exclusion, division, corruption, and illness. And it must be seized again every time it's necessary since its particularity is that it goes back to excluding, dividing, corrupting, and generating malaise. It must be seized again and again, day after day, in any way, 'inside' and 'outside,' with patience.

4. The exact passage: "Let every soul be subject unto the higher powers. For there is no power but of God: the powers that be are ordained of God." King James Version. [TN]

Father Gaetano is a very ambiguous character. He introduces himself as an evil priest, but at the same time he states that the Church is made great by evil priests. The Church itself becomes a power structure. Do you agree with this analysis?

Father Gaetano is particularly ambiguous because among the 'ambiguous' characters that characterize the late-capitalist, or pre-socialist, period, that of a priest of 'power' is the most ambiguous of all. He has chosen false conscience as the only way to live, more than anyone else, more than intellectuals and politicians, and he is fully aware of that. We could say that his awareness of his own falsity is at such a high level that it resembles a state of folly. He is with the poor and the rich, but he really is with the rich. He is with the weak and the strong, but he really is with the strong. He is in the past, present, and future, but he really is with the past. He is with power and against power, but he really is with power. He is ascetic and against sin, but in his voluntary sexual marginalization is his sin. He is outside the world, but in it. He is broken, as incomprehensible as a schizophrenic, just like one of the representatives of secular power to whom he is tied. Father Gaetano's real 'power' is in his knowledge that everything has already died, including God. And it is this knowledge that he tries to impart to M., who is stuck at a less refined stage of conscience. M. is simply an authoritative personality; Father Gaetano is authority itself. Father Gaetano's function is to remind the secular power that without his protection, without the Church's protection, the political and social efficacy of the Christian Democratic Party would be irreparably compromised. The priest must gain back the authority it has lost. In order to escape man's law, which is threatening him due to his illegal affairs, he must fully re-acquire his role as a judge. (This becomes another source of ambiguity: he is simultaneously the accused and the judge). A priest can decide to be with Paul: "Servants, obey your masters with devotion and fear as if they were God himself, and not men,"[4] or with James: "And now to you, rich ones! Cry and

4. See Ephesians 6:5–8 (KJV): "Servants, be obedient to them that are your masters according to the flesh, with fear and trembling, in singleness of your heart, as unto Christ; Not with eyeservice, as menpleasers; but as the servants of Christ, doing the will of God from the heart; with good will doing service, as to the Lord, and not to men: Knowing that whatsoever good thing any man doeth, the same shall he receive of the Lord, whether he be bond or free." [TN]

wail over the salary you took away from the workers who harvested your fields!"[6] Father Gaetano this time decides to make it clear that the Church could, if it wanted, be against the rich: however, he will suggest to M. that he accepts without hypocrisy or false shame his mandate as the defendant of the exploiting classes, because in this theme lies their common salvation. The priest uses the guilt complex of M. and of the others as his own self-defense. (In this sense, the film is also the story of a confession that is both uninterrupted and continuously interrupted by the free absolution among accomplices). In order to survive, the priest and the Church need corruption and the collaboration of the secular power. Sin & death are the Church's two instruments of negativity, which priests manipulate to preserve all those social structures — negative, inhuman — that guarantee man's immutability.

Todo Modo carries along a discourse on schizophrenia that is analyzed from a political point of view. This problem of schizophrenia is tied to that of power and of the relationship between practice & theory.

In this case, in order to have a clear picture of the problem, I believe it is necessary to ask ourselves about the social and psychological meaning of the choice to become a priest or a leader of a political party such as the DC. Among the possibilities that the division of labor offers to the petit bourgeoisie in this period, those who decide to become priests are also consciously choosing to become 'representatives' of God. Those who choose to become politicians are also deciding to become representatives of the representatives of God. A young man who makes one of these choices is full of pride and conformism. Both professions are among those with the least amount of risk from a social point of view. One just needs to simply learn the technique of preservation and deferment. One sides with 'god,' and, as it is known, with 'god' one finds safety, & privilege; there are believers who are 'beloved,' but also those who are 'unworthy,' and that com-

---

6. See James 5:1-6 (KJV): "Go to now, ye rich men, weep and howl for your miseries that shall come upon you. Your riches are corrupted, and your garments are motheaten. Your gold and silver is cankered; and the rust of them shall be a witness against you, and shall eat your flesh as it were fire. Ye have heaped treasure together for the last days. Behold, the hire of the labourers who have reaped down your fields, which is of you kept back by fraud, crieth: and the cries of them which have reaped are entered into the ears of the Lord of sabaoth. Ye have lived in pleasure on the earth, and been wanton; ye have nourished your hearts, as in a day of slaughter. Ye have condemned and killed the just; and he doth not resist you." [TN]

poses a divided humanity. For their whole life, they will have to tortuously sublimate petty bourgeois ambitions with power, charisma, with false words and mannerist behavior. They will spend their time, more than others, looking differently from what they are, and professing coherence between theory and practice, which they will have fruitlessly followed. Such men are destined to have a hallucinated view of their work, and thus of their power, which they will see as a 'mission,' and to an alienated form of existence, cut off from any link with nature and other people's real necessities. The division of labor requires them to be broken, schizoid, and as incomprehensible as schizophrenics. But much more dangerous.

Why did you find it necessary to preserve the grotesque-comic style of your previous films when dealing with a topic of direct political intervention?

People are accustomed to looking without 'seeing' the facts of daily life and specifically those pertaining to politics. The latter are part of a routine managed by an elite that has its own incomprehensible code, a way to face problems that is completely removed from everyone's life. In other words, people have the tired look of those who have seen too much. In a political film, blatancy must be challenged, in the sense that showing the *obvious* is less *obvious* than what it appears, but it must be done without sublimating the topic. The obvious must be made less banal. It is dense with a meaning that must be returned to the analysis conducted by the eye. As Brecht says: "The realist constantly confronts ideals with reality and constantly rectifies its images… it does not limit itself to represent reality, but it makes it prevail over idealization." So, in order to highlight the monstrous element of a political fact buried in obviousness, a corrective operation — a rectification — which will exaggerate the representation, is necessary. The 'rectification' of the comic and dramatic elements that coexist in a fact, especially a political fact, leads directly to a grotesque exaggeration. This has always been, with different degrees of artistic and critical conscience, the way of popular theater, which has always employed all the comic and dramatic elements that *obviousness* would make available to achieve a greater 'effect,' a further meaning. Now, in the representation of the Christian Democratic *milieu* there was no other choice: Christian Democrats are already grotesque without a 'rectification.' The rectification was used to diminish the effects instead of magnifying them: and that was a mistake.

§ 4.3
Todo Modo

Interview with Simon Mizrahi[1]

The problem is that not even the Italian spectator easily understands the grotesque aspect of some characters. But I believe the discourse should be broadened. I believe that all men of power are ridiculous because there is a strong and comical discrepancy between their arrogant attitude and the extreme fragility of their human destiny. In this sense, both the enlightened attitude of a nation's president — of whatever nationality and political faith — and the slightly mad arrogance of postal employees, office bosses, and city policemen, are laughable. Whoever believes to be in a position of superiority, to have a 'mission' to fulfill, makes me crack up laughing. Now, since everyone more or less, even simple family 'fathers,' believe that they are playing a 'directorial,' 'formative' role, we have a double phenomenon in the current Western way of life (including also the so-called Socialist countries): on one side, everyone tends to haughtiness, to pomposity, to self-importance, & to affirm their role as irreplaceable; on the other side, as a consequence, these same people cannot look at the comedic side of others' situations, since they should first laugh at themselves, at their own pomposity and folly. I believe that this problem is generally widespread and not only specific to Italians. I don't think that John Ford is any less ridiculous than Sergio Leone, or that Giscard's pipe is funny enough to make the French laugh. We should get used to laughing more about the men who hold power, but only to laugh at ourselves.

[1]. This interview was previously unpublished: a few excerpts from it could be found in the press kit handed out at the release of *Todo Modo* in France. The list of questions has been lost.

Once we have established that people are not used to 'seeing' the comedic side of their 'representatives' — who are also 'representative' of the average comedy, it is also true that in Italy people cannot 'see' because their eyes are tired from having seen too much. The exhaustion is caused by *routine*, and vice versa. There is also the weariness of *déjà-vu* (and *déjà-vécu*) that comes from the great daily pressure of the mass media, a pressure that trivializes our entire existence, both public and private, if there even is a difference. The purpose of a political film is to contribute to de-trivializing both the way to see and what there is to see. The blatancy that surrounds our daily life must be challenged, since it is a mask for the tragic and comic aspects of life. This coating is rich with meanings that must be made apparent again to the retina of the eye and of the intelligence. Brecht says: "the realist compares ideals with everyday reality and he continually adjusts his images of reality."[2] This adjustment — or correction, or expansion — of the dramatic and comic elements of reality brings us directly to the grotesque, which is the style of *Todo Modo*. Besides, this has always been, with differing degrees of critical and artistic conscience, the way of popular theater, which has never rejected the mix of the comic and dramatic that surrounds us, nor its *adjustment* in order to reach an ulterior effect, or a deeper meaning. Now, in Italian political reality the comic elements are more apparent, and that is what differentiates it from the French. Compared to Chirac's martial attitude, Moro might seem more comical, but we should look beyond what is merely apparent. Surely a court of political characters (the whole ensemble of the leaders of the Christian Democratic Party) that moves as if in a church, slightly leaning forward with a hunchback, with a feminine strut and speaking in a polished, almost religious way, is definitely comical. The typical Christian Democrat of the last thirty years — by now worthy of the *Commedia dell'arte* — recalls more Molière's *Tartuffe* than Shakespeare's *Coriolanus*. That is not my fault, but my responsibility is to have dared, together with the actors of the film, to study thousands of pieces of foot-

2. Petri may have this passage in mind: "The critical element in realism must not be suppressed. It is decisive. Even if it were possible, mere reflection of reality would not serve our ends. Reality must be criticized by giving it shape, it must be criticized realistically. For the dialectician the decisive element is the critical factor, herein lies the tendency." (GBA 22.I:136) Bertolt Brecht, *Werke: Große kommentierte Berliner und Frankfurther Ausgabe*, ed. Werner Hecht et al., 30 vols. (Frankfurt am Main: Suhrkamp, 1988–2000). [TN]

age that showed the behavior of Christian Democrat leaders, and to have studied them in the behavioral context of the whole Italian petite bourgeoisie. But even the dramatic elements, in light of the particular Italian economy that lacks so many resources and of the recent political history, are livelier in Italy than in other countries marked by advanced capitalism. I believe that these dramatic elements, based on a great irresponsibility of the government's politicians and economists, are absolutely present in my film. *Todo Modo* is a mix of tragedy and comedy, just like the events from which it is inspired.

I chose Sciascia's novel because the typical condition of our current Catholic ruling class is narrated in the form of a metaphor. What is Sciascia's book? It is the story of a series of spiritual exercises for the highest Christian Democrat leaders that is destined to transform itself into a slaughter, since the negative forces, the dark ghosts that come from its participants, will come down on them. It is, as we will see, an exemplary story: it is what is happening now, as it was perceived by a writer who knows all the subtleties — and the historical and cultural references — of Italy's political life.[3] We can say that the political test that the current DC has been conducting in the last few years seems, just like a spiritual exercise, doomed to its own condemnation and extinction. Roland Barthes says about St. Ignatius' exercises: "The obsessional character of the *Exercises* blazes forth in the accounting passion transmitted to the *exercitant* [...]. The accountancy is obsessional not only because it is infinite, but above all because it engenders its own errors: being a matter of accounting for his sins [...], the fact of accounting for them in a faulty way will in turn become an error that must be added on to the original list; this list is thus made infinite, the redeeming accounting of errors calling up per contra the very errors of the account."[4] The way the Christian Democrats exercise power in Italy resembles exactly the process described by Barthes, but upside-down. To clarify: the Christian Democrats govern &

3. From this point forward, although a significant part of this particular answer repeats comments made in the previous interview, we chose to leave the repetition since removing it would distort the coherence of the answer. [TN]

4. Roland Barthes, *Sade, Fourier, Loyola*, tr. by Richard Miller (Berkeley & Los Angeles: University of California Press, 1976). Petri quotes from the original French edition.

count the mistakes and the crimes they are often responsible for, but only to hide them and by hiding them, they become "à son tour une faute qui devra s'ajouter à la liste originelle," & so on until the *redde rationem*. The exercise of power has become, for Christian Democrats, a sort of perennial feeling of being accused, as if they had to make up for the 'sin' of having usurped power. It is to better express this mechanism, which is common in Western culture, so I had to tamper with Sciascia's novel and use only the idea of the exercises as slaughter, and of the priest as both the judge and the accused. In order to enter more directly into the matter, I had to more directly rely on reality. Instead of the dualism on which the book was based (between a priest and a lay artist), I directly chose the dualism of a priest-Christian Democratic leader, a double figure on which all of Italy's political life of the last thirty years has been based. I also structured the whole plot according to St. Ignatius' Exercises: that is to say, I divided the film into the days and the meditations predetermined by St. Ignatius, and to each of the meditations corresponds a specific, and even ideological, role of the narration.

I will report here two comments that Sciascia made after seeing the film in Palermo, in a very simple theater: he was accompanied by a journalist sent to Sicily specifically to find out his opinion about the film adaptation of *Todo Modo*. The first comment was: "The film [...] acquires an exceptional power. It is traversed by a metaphysical fury, so that the proletarian executioner becomes a sort of exterminating angel, and vice versa. [...] *Todo Modo* is a Pasolinian film, in the sense that Petri did today what Pasolini wanted to, but couldn't do: put the Christian Democratic ruling class on trial. A trial that becomes an execution." And here is the second comment: "Yesterday I saw a picture of Moro in a newspaper getting ready for a television political program with greasepaint and face powder, and I immediately thought of Elio Petri's film *Todo Modo* and of Gian Maria Volontè. In the film, he interprets with extraordinary imitative virtuosity the character of "M.," which all the viewers unanimously identify with Moro in his physical appearance and in the way he talks and moves. And I thought that in that film a paradox was at work, a reversal of things and time, an overturning of reality: as if it weren't Volontè who put makeup on his face to look like Moro and imitate him in his speech and gestures, but rather it was Moro who tried to look like Volontè in the film and who, looking just like the honorable M., prepared to enter the political slaughter that Petri's film, with inverted symbolism, foreshadows and anticipates for the Christian Democratic Party." I have only cited these two comments because they both reflect in the film, both for the reference to Pasolini and for the duality Moro-M., a Pirandellian style.

All the rational and traditional doubts that might arise while watching *Todo Modo* should have no answer, since I believe that the Italian political life of the past ten years is full of unsolvable mysteries. Besides, the film aims to raise a series of questions and to leave them unanswered and to create another parallelism with Italian reality: is it important to know whether M. was kidnapped by the CIA, or by the Italian SID,[5] or by French or German intelligence? Is it crucial to know whether the *chauffeur* was the only assassin, or if he had accomplices, and whether Father Gaetano knew the truth? Is it essential to know what evidence senator Voltrano gave to M. and the content of his letter? I don't think so. The explanation to all these grotesque problems, which are so similar to those we see in our daily political life, can be anything, and it doesn't really matter. Are the Red Brigades the violent outcome of a metaphysical extremism, or rather a product of the CIA, or of another secret service? Who could ever answer to this crazy question? Was Feltrinelli killed by the SID, or by the Red Brigades as a product of the CIA, or other secret services? Who killed the judges in Palermo, in Genoa, in Rome? Was it an extreme rightwing movement that wants to keep the country on the verge of a civil war, or rather

5. The "Servizio Informazioni Difesa" (SID) was the intelligence agency of Italy from 1966 to 1977. In 1977, after the former chief of the SID was arrested for "conspiring against the State," the SID was replaced by a civilian institution, SISDE, and a military one, SISMI.

an extreme leftwing movement that is exploited by the Right for the same purpose? Who killed Calabresi? Like in the film, before trying to answer these questions we need to realize that they are absurd, that the problems they pose are preposterous and they hide other political and economic realities. The questions are lunatic, just like the reality that produces them, which is based on division and sickness. Keeping with the idea of the 'black' farce that I wanted to make, I wanted to find rational-literary comfort in the idea that the man behind all the murders would eventually, as an admission of impotence, order his own execution. But the narration acquired an objective value, which gave the whole mechanism a sense of *redde rationem*. Whether the protagonists eliminated one another, or M. ordered theirs and his execution, or someone else from his party, from Rome, decided to destroy them for an inexplicable scheme, or the CIA decided to kill them all due to their proved incompetence, or the massacre was caused by a social uprising, or God (at this point allied with Communist Party?) decided to get rid of his corrupted sons, in all of these cases the massacre takes on the objective value of an exemplary and well-deserved punishment. In other words, *Todo Modo* represents, metaphorically, a Christian Democrat's nightmare, and as such it is irrational, mysterious, and unavoidable.

The sexual behavior of M., who is a typical representative of our culture, is based on an extreme need for orality. His *vaniloquence* is oral, as is his dependence on Giacinta's breast, which is also the symbol of the mother. Further, M.'s attachment to the (mother) Church is once again a dependence on the maternal breast. Because of all of these symptoms, M.'s sexuality is stuck in a specific pre-genital period. Such fixation causes a latent homosexuality in this character, which remains unexpressed and keeps the character suspended in a perennial indecision, a game of continuous disguises that, in the specific field of politics, become tactics, ambiguity, and political polyvalence. His latency forces him to a more general apathy; even his goals are latent, and he cannot be either a revolutionary or the progressive man he aims to be. Like many of his contemporaries, M. acts so that nothing changes, because if anything really changed, he would be forced to make a sexual choice and dissolve his latency. He is, however, compelled to show the desire, or the will, for change. This neurosis, which is common in our culture, has been studied in an essay that Sigmund Freud wrote in collaboration with Ambassador William C. Bullitt on Woodrow Wilson (*Woodrow Wilson: A Psychological Study*, 1967). In the book, the authors demonstrate the folly of a quintessential product of Christian culture, his identification with the figure of Christ as a neurotic sublimation of his latent homosexuality. This material on Wilson is, quite alarmingly, very relevant today and can be useful to understand the attitude of politicians belonging to our culture, of any nationality, even not coming from a Christian background. It also helps to understand the more general notion of power as sublimation, a problem that affects all levels of society and all professions. In fact, M. is not only a politician; he is also the representative of a certain Italian male culture (only Italian?) from which women are excluded. Giacinta is by M.'s side only to offer him support through her body. He sucks from her the nourishment from which he draws his balance. She must give him the certainty of his quasi-divine uniqueness. All of M.'s business is among men; even religious matters are exclusive to the male gender. Who commands over the sexuality of men and women, who are clearly separated, is the priest, who sets the boundaries of a double morality and experiences in himself the separation of sexes, in a sort of bisexuality that is not only biological, but also cultural and social. He experiences all the sins, male and female, through his religious role, and he must endure them in his own flesh. All these characters therefore suffer from an ill sexuality, which is repressed for religious reasons and which pushes them to ambiguous and insincere behavior that is based on fake ideologies, on the systematic use of lies, on the exploiting of a guilt complex to achieve power, & on a split between what they really are and what they would like to be. Their psychological condition is similar to ours, with the difference that they inhabit places of power where decisions are made.

[The end of the answer is missing.]

§ 4.4
Le Mani Sporche

The Plot of the Three Episodes[1]

I.

We are at the end of the Second World War in Illyria, an imaginary country in Central Europe that is at war against the USSR & allied with Nazi Germany. German troops have invaded Illyria as the war is heading towards defeat. Olga Lorame, a leader of the clandestine Proletarian Party, is listening to the Soviet radio, which invites Illyrian soldiers to surrender. Enter Hugo Barine, a youth of twenty-three years who has just gotten out of prison. He was incarcerated for two years for the murder of Hoederer, the leader of the Proletarian Party. Hugo was also part of the Proletarian Party, & the reason for his crime seems to be jealousy. Hugo looks bitter, as if he experienced a great disappointment; he accuses Olga and the party of trying to poison him during his imprisonment. Olga rejects the accusation. But that same evening, two members of the Proletarian Party come to kill Hugo. The woman tries to stop the assassination and asks to speak with Louis, an important communist leader. Hugo's execution, the reason for which is still unclear, is postponed until midnight. It is for Olga to decide whether or not the young man can be part of the party again. The woman interrogates Hugo about Hoederer's death, and she appears anxious to confirm that it was a crime of passion. Instead, the young man is uncertain about the real motive behind his actions. To clarify his mind, he tells the whole story.

1. This document was written for the Press Office of RAI in Rome, in August-September 1978. The text is not signed, but it is attributable to Elio Petri.

Two years prior, Hugo was a Party journalist. At that time, Olga and Louis were part of the dogmatic section of the party, which was openly hostile to the changes proposed by Hoederer. In fact, in order to take the party into the government, Hoederer was ready to compromise with the historical enemies of the proletarian workers: the bourgeois and the ruling class. In order to prevent this change, Louis and Olga deemed Hoederer's death necessary. They designated Hugo the assassin, since he was a young man from the high bourgeoisie.

Hugo thus moves to a country house where Hoederer is hiding from the police and becomes his secretary. Jessica, his very young wife, accompanies him. The relationship between husband and wife is like a continuous comedy in which they pretend to be different from what they are in order to hide their desperation and disaffection. Jessica is also very curious about Hoederer, whom she feels attracted to before even meeting him.

Two of Hoederer's bodyguards come to search Hugo's room and he tries to stop them: he is afraid that they might find the gun he hides in his luggage. Hoederer reminds all three men of the revolutionary discipline: class differences and different ways of being communist should be set aside before the party's interest. In the luggage, Hoederer finds only some funny pictures of Hugo's childhood. His suspicions seem to vanish. But when the politician leaves, Hugo restates his intention to kill him. Does Jessica believe him or not? Will she instead think that even the murder is a chance for a new game?

2.

Ten days later Hoederer is still alive. Why didn't Hugo complete his mission? Is his victim's charming personality the reason for his uncertainty? Jessica is more and more attracted to Hoederer, who instead accepts her presence with the diffidence that is typical of an old-fashioned man; he considers her a danger to his own equilibrium.

Hoederer, perhaps to set a trap or just in need of a friend, opens up to Hugo. Is Hoederer doubtful about the political course of action to take? Knowing that some people in the party want him dead, he feels rushed to achieve a political compromise. It seems like he's inviting Hugo to move quickly. Then comes a crucial day for Hoederer. He is going to make his historical enemies meet: Karsky, the head of the Pentagon, and Prince Paul, the son of the ruler, that is to say, the representatives of the bourgeoisie and of the ruling class. The moment to fulfill his mission has come for Hugo too: he can kill Hoederer precisely when he is about to complete his "political betrayal."

Karsky tries everything to sabotage the meeting. Many years of class rivalry and hatred cannot be easily overcome. Yet, he must eventually give in to the alliance between Hoederer and Prince Paul. Hoederer's line proves to be successful. The meeting, however, is interrupted because a bomb is detonated against a wall nearby. Would Hugo have fired his gun if someone else hadn't thrown a bomb and destroyed Hoederer's studio? Even Hugo will never know, as his actions were carried out while drunk. Out of his mind, Hugo vents his rage by screaming against the attackers and declares his philosophy of death, which now dominates him.

At night, Olga slips into Hugo's room while he sleeps. She was the one who set off the bomb since she was certain that the young man had betrayed the trust of his comrades. Olga and Jessica had never met before, and Jessica doesn't hold back her sarcasm towards the other woman, whom she considers her rival. When Hugo wakes up, Olga tells him that their comrades consider him a traitor and that, if he doesn't want to be killed, he must kill Hoederer. Hugo is forced to reaffirm his intention to kill Hoederer. He will decide the following day.

3.

For the first time, Hugo asks for Jessica's help. The young woman expresses her discomfort. She replies that for nineteen years she has been living in the world of men without permission to touch what was on display. It is then too much, she continues, to expect that all of a sudden, she understands and agrees. Instead,

Hugo reproaches Jessica for never loving him, for never being his woman, for denying him even the pleasure of the senses. Suddenly Hoederer arrives. Jessica, who found a new stimulus with Hoederer, wants to save him, so she starts an ideological confrontation between the two men, hoping to convince Hugo of the righteousness of Hoederer's ideas. Accused of being a traitor to socialism, Hoederer patiently explains the reasons for his realistic line of thought. "We have to acknowledge," says Hoederer, "that we are a minority and that a proletarian revolution would be wiped out by a counterrevolution." He wants to pursue socialist ideas, that is for sure, but not through a bloodbath. Neither would the arrival of the Soviet Red Army solve the problem. Socialism cannot be built on foreign bayonets, even belonging to another socialist army, but rather on a daily political struggle that will expose one by one all the contradictions of their class enemies. Hugo passionately defends his ideas and states that the party will be corrupted soon. His words have an effect on Hoederer. Perhaps they make him nostalgic for Hugo's youth and his passionate way of being a Communist. But it is just for a moment. Hoederer reiterates his positions and accuses Hugo of loving his principles more than he loves people. Instead, Hoederer loves humans with all their flaws. He is used to being nauseated, while Hugo is pure, but his purity resembles death. Instead of dreaming a proletarian revolution, Hugo dreams of blowing up the world. Hugo is an intellectual, and intellectuals are never true revolutionaries.

The meeting doesn't go like Jessica had hoped. When Hoederer leaves, Hugo reaffirms his intention to kill him. The next day, Jessica sneaks out to go see Hoederer. The old man is brusque and unfriendly, but the woman confronts him with the intent of saving both him and Hugo. Jessica also reveals her feelings and the danger she is facing. Hoederer decides to confront Hugo and give him the chance, if he is able, to shoot him. Hugo's arrival interrupts the meeting. The two men are now alone and Hugo is very nervous: he must prove, as his last chance, his ability to carry out the gesture that Louis, Olga, & other comrades expect of him.

Hoederer plays with him, he encourages and also opposes Hugo, and he shows courage & real faith in his ideas. He voluntarily turns his back to Hugo, waiting and hoping with well-hidden fear that the last meeting will make the young man desist from his murderous intent. Hugo, gun in his hand, realizes that he can no longer kill the old man since he cannot kill what he represents, also for himself. Hoederer has won, and Hugo breaks down and seeks comfort in him like in a father. But the situation soon takes a turn for the worst. When Hugo comes back to the studio, he finds Jessica in Hoederer's hands. Perhaps seduced by Jessica's amorous advances, or simply in need, after such tension, of a moment of tenderness, Hoederer is found in what appears to be an ordinary betrayal.

What pushed Hugo to shoot? Jealousy, or the disappointment toward the man who had won his heart with his moral solidity? What made him reacquire his determination as an assassin? If he weren't assigned that mission, in the same situation, would he have killed? It is Hoederer himself who defines Hugo's gesture a "crime of passion," with his last breath. As a politician, he fears that what he has prepared and not yet concluded might die with him; in this way, he also saves Hugo.

Back in the room with Olga, in the present of the narration, Hugo's long talk is over. Though there are ambiguous elements, the woman sees a possibility to save Hugo and rehabilitate him for the party, the proletarian political cause, &, perhaps, herself. But the illusion is short-lived. Hugo cannot agree to renounce his identity and disappear anonymously in the ranks of the party, thus confirming the hypothesis of a crime of passion and agreeing that Louis' political ideas have become the official party's course of action after Hoederer's death.

Hugo takes a decision that pushes him, as Hoederer has predicted, toward death. Perhaps to find his purity again. He runs out of the house and toward the assassins sent by the party, who are waiting with their weapons in hand. "Not salvageable!" he yells. Then gun shots are heard off screen.

§ 4.5
Le Mani Sporche

Short Notes, Preliminary Observations

1. *Before Going to Bed*

Should we challenge television's total power to substitute for all that exists? Before television there was football, newspapers, movies, classical theater, variety theater, games, salons, boxing, track & field, country fairs, patron saint's festivals, parliament, literature, and concerts. Now television has superseded all that preceded it as a pastime until-something-happens, or until it is bedtime, or until it is time to die. It has not yet substituted for bodily functions or other functions with a metaphysical cast such as the daily mass. But often, when metaphysical functions border on the theatrical, such as the papal mass in St. Peter's Cathedral at Christmas, television captures us with an intense and blind confidence in the religious validity of the broadcast images. Let's look for a moment at the example of the mass. Someone believes in God and goes to mass. To celebrate the mass, there is a well-defined space: the church. The church can be a temple designed by Borromini, or a hut in the heart of the jungle. And the faithful agree that this Baroque temple, or this hut, is the house of God. All the rites that bring men closer to God are celebrated in this house and for Catholics, the mass is the foundation of these rites. Whoever chooses to attend mass goes because it is there in their past that they were led to experience Christ's sacrifice. Thus their behavior, in theory, and often in practice, is that of deep immersion in the transcendence and meditation of life's religious values.

The fact of physically being in the church, mentally and bodily, is the essential condition for the mass to be effective for the believer. Of course, mass doesn't require our presence to take place. It can be celebrated in an empty church without changing its religious value, since what takes place in the ritual is perfect in and of itself. But a believer knows that the validity of mass requires his physical presence if he is to truly prove his faith. He who isn't there hasn't *seen* the mass, since mass is only visible to those who are physically there. Like the world, which is visible and livable only by the living. The world, like mass, would continue to exist even without witnesses. To witness its existence one must come to the world, just as the believer must go to mass to experience for himself Christ's sacrifice. So then, what religious value can Christmas mass have for someone who watches it on television filmed by cameras, even when celebrated by the pope? He is not in attendance at Saint Peter's, thus the mass has no meaning for him. It will mean something to the *cameramen*, but not to the viewer at home. For him, this mass will have an ornamental value. Instead, via the television, there is the figment of what the mass could have been if he, instead of being in the midst of eating nougat and dried figs, had gone out into the cold, all the way to St. Peter's Square, slipped into the crowd and reached the church where, despite the pompous grandiloquence of ceremony and the distracting clusters of lights that surround the cathedral to enable the television taping, there would be an actual mass with the actual celebrant, the true blood of Christ, the true house of God, and the actual physical presence of other believers. He could have melded his desire for purity and the absolute passion there with them and among them. Does the television viewer experience a love for mass, or for television? Is it a love of the house of God, or of his own house? Is it a love of the collective values emanating from the house of God, or a love of his own private space? This discourse, with a few small, commonsensical changes, could be extended to football, literature, the salon, games, parliament, & all the rest.

ELIO PETRI · COMMENTS ON HIS OWN FILMS (1976–1979)

2. Mass and Football

Those who go to mass go to find or retrieve this wellspring of emotion (even physically) that distills and flows from every detail of the ritual and from the place where it occurs: from the candlelight, from the worn marble floor, from the presence of others, from the actions of the priest who is at once public and private, from the scents, from the hue of the darkness, from the extraordinary height of the ceiling, from the stillness. All these, and many more details, which each person perceives according to his point of view, achieve a level which isn't just transcendence. It is the experience of life, childhood, the memories of those who came before us, the brevity and vanity of life, our own existential anguish, our own imperfection. Those who go to mass go because they love all these things and because there is an 'affective conscience' from this wellspring of emotion which accumulates during the mass. They go to mass to try to experience and retrieve these emotions of infinity, to live and relive, and live again this sacrifice to the rhythm of the changes these sensations take with the passing of time, which is a metaphor for the life and death of Christ, but also for their own life and death. Even the unpleasant ideas that might come of this rite, the sense of the futility and absurdity of being *here*, the sight of negative details like the distraction of certain churchgoers, or a particularly ugly Mannerist painting, or the awkward presence of the beadle who circles around without any regard to the orderliness of those present, or a child's laugh rising through mass as though at the fairground. All these are part of the metaphor of the mass and need to be experienced to be fully understood. Those who go to a football match go because they love to walk to the stadium with their friends, the waiting in the stands, the pre-game discussions, and the rain if it rains; and the sun if it's sunny; and the smell of the freshly-cut grass, and just the fact of being there, one among many, and the shouts, and the sweat, the smell of sweat, and the partisan posturing (theirs and the others), and the being there with the twenty players, and the unexpected chances and the lucky moments that follow, and suffering through unexpected mishaps and then, finally, they love the end. All of the sensations and impressions that then become ideas, make up a football game, much like the mass, a metaphor for life, of the 'result.' A metaphor that, interrupted at this point which we all anticipate with impatience, becomes a metaphor for the end, that is, for death. Without all that, what would a football game be? Only a very banal way to kill time. Those who sit in front of the television to look at, and not to 'see,' the mass or the football game, have a practical reason since they have time to kill to rob the 'experience' of those present at mass or at a game. This kind of viewer, as one of the two poles of the event, embodies all negative connotations: laziness, irresponsibility, and the unconscious desire to denigrate the event. He faces none of the risks that go along with attending these events, with actually being there. Above all, the risk of not being able to do anything other than what they're doing. Those who go to a game or to mass know that during the ritual period of time required for the completion of these two events, they can do nothing but be present at the game or at mass. If the game doesn't interest them, or if they can't concentrate on the mass, they might wish to be elsewhere; they might blame themselves for not anticipating that eventuality. But regret and blame are some of the risks the spectator must accept so the event can be as animated and authentic as possible. They themselves are part of the event. The event must become the only one possible out of all those that could happen, and thus the metaphor is complete. This is the life we are given to live, and it is the only one, unique and irreplaceable. Instead, the television viewer can jump from event to event. He can stop an event and turn it into another one. Mass can, *ipso facto*, turn into a commercial for absorbent towels or candy. Football and Beethoven can cancel each other out until the end of the broadcasts. The only possible metaphor in this case is that of the vague anxiety of the *tedium vitæ*, of the disaffection of things and their value as metaphor. The end of television programming each night leaves an emptiness much more serious and agonizing than an empty stadium after the football game. This emptiness is general and ill-defined; it is the emptiness a child feels when his toy breaks, an emptiness that darkens the whole night ahead and the day that preceded it. It is an emptiness that cannot be filled. The metaphor of this emptiness seems to be the sum of many parts, but it is only a summary. It doesn't describe individually all the metaphors experienced by those at the game, or the mass, or the concert, but blends and nullifies them all. *Tedium vitæ*, the satiety after the meal, one's vague sexual thoughts, the sense of inutility, the indetermination of one's own physical and spiritual availability. All these merge into a confused mixture that should be cleared soon to ease sleep.

3. Televisual Reality

Therefore, those who watch a game or mass on television don't really like games or mass. They like the generic emptiness, laziness, fatigue, their own home, and the time that passes in bits of one program and another, and not the solidarity of the ninety minutes of a game or the thirty minutes of a mass that become a thousand, ten thousand, and a million in the imagination and the unity and the amplitude of the metaphor. Such a person likes neither mass nor the match but the image transmitted by the television set. He likes television for its immense (although mistaken) possibility of space. He loves the TV set more than television itself, as an instrument of knowledge. In the technological amazement of playing with this magical object, he loses his critical and self-critical capacity. Everything is great. He prefers to 'look at' rather than 'see' what others have seen for him. He likes to stay home in his sanctuary where he feels the safest, and in this way avoids all contact with outside reality. In actuality, he decides to ignore it. In so doing, his house mutates (often to the rhythm of rapid and irrational successions) into a religious sanctuary of football fever, or a theater or a salon or newsroom or parliament. That is, into something it is not and cannot be; into nothing. As a result, the home loses its sense of being a private place that the television viewer hoped to conserve by spending the evening 'within its walls.' This aspect of the television-home relationship might be social, though only in a morbid way, when the viewer has never experienced in person the particular metaphors that derive from going to church, or the theater, or the stadium, or the cinema. But if he were a moviegoer, theatergoer, stadium-goer, or concert-lover, then the diminution of his social aspirations is clear. His social stagnation is such that it takes on its own metaphoric value when compared to the social stagnation of a society as a whole. Simply put, this seems clear if you allow yourself passionate reflection, imbued with a passion for everything (since everything matters) and, to begin with, a passion for the welfare of the 'TV viewer,' a reflection that thereby wouldn't want to minimize, banalize, fragment, or justify everything with desperate rationalism and bureaucracy. (After all, who is more desperate and blindly rationalistic than a bureaucrat?)

4. A Few "Whys"

A pressing question: after such a preamble, why make television-theater and not theater-theater? Why produce *Le mani sporche* for the so-called small screen and not for the real stage? The responses to these questions, which while deserving an explanation also bear the mistake of a moralism — inevitable in this moment of moral fluidity — and will be vastly diverse. In giving the answers, the actors and directors — those who in the case of *Le mani sporche* go from the exterior to the 'interior' of the television as an institution — would provide multiple examples of a no less inevitable 'bad faith' precisely in Sartre's sense, when he wrote: "One can stumble into bad faith in trying to be sincere."[1] Thus, attempting to respond may be a stupid, and certainly hopeless, undertaking. To be comprehensive would require first answering questions like: "Why be an actor? Why be a director?

---

1. "Thus the essential structure of sincerity does not differ from that of bad faith since the sincere man constitutes himself as what he is *in order not to be it*. This explains the truth recognized by all that one can fall into bad faith through being sincere. As Valéry pointed out, this is the case with Stendhal. Total, constant sincerity as a constant effort to adhere to oneself is by nature a constant effort to dissociate oneself from oneself. A person frees himself from himself by the very act by which he makes himself an object for himself. To draw up a perpetual inventory of what one is means constantly to redeny oneself and to take refuge in a sphere where one is no longer anything but a pure, free regard. The goal of bad faith, as we said, is to put oneself out of reach; it is an escape." Jean-Paul Sartre, *Being and Nothingness*, tr. by Hazel E. Barnes (New York: Washington Square Press, 1992) 109–110. This, and all of the following notes in this section, are those of the translators.

What's the point of being either today, giving the general social and cultural crisis? Why do it when everything is disintegrating and collapsing around us, when cinema is no longer cinema, and theater no longer theater, and nothing is anything specific anymore? Why be an actor or director in light of the crisis of the marketplace?" The questions can run on and on. Everyone could give their answers: from above, from below, and above all, from their age. Kids do things because they are confronted with them. In youth, you are searching for your identity, doing one thing and then another. When you are older, you do things even though you have already learned that you often do things alone, that searching for yourself is a false goal, that you do things in order to stave off death. You do them to make money. You do things to gain or defend your popularity. You do things to stand out from your contemporaries. You do, you do, you do just to be. Because you must in order to be. You do. Kids do things because they don't know how to do anything yet. Adults do things because they don't know what else to do. The kids have to prove themselves to themselves, to others as if to say: "I am in the world." The older people do things to prove they still can, as if to say: "I am still here." They do things for social promotion. To defend their place in the world. They do things because it is 'nice' to talk about themselves to others. We are actors and directors because it is 'nice' work compared to all the crap work that there is in the world. And exactly in all the degradation in the world of values, social issues, institutions, represented within us and outside, our 'game' is a source of life & liberty. A game, but a passionate game. A knowing game. Sartre: "The game is a kind of marking out and investigation. The child plays with his body in order to explore it, to take inventory of it; the waiter in the café plays with his condition in order to *realize it*."[2] This is exactly our scenario. And it is the case also of the young man in Le mani sporche, Hugo Barine. You could play with the TV set and with Le mani sporche the way Barine plays with politics. It is enough to know this. Television exists. It provides work, therefore a passionate 'game.'

2. Ibid., 102.

§ 4.5 · SHORT NOTES, PRELIMINARY OBSERVATIONS

Why not do television? You can't escape from its all-encompassing power, from its amazing capacity to condition and manipulate. It's true. It is useless to think that we can by ourselves and only one time turn it around. The system won't change. The work will be hard, hours long, the budget low, the threat of the institution looming. And afterwards? The broadcast will quickly pass in a single 'flash' of an evening, of course, given a context that is totally controlled by others. And through the television in the house-church, house-theater, house-cinema where the spectators, more or less undressed and satisfied or nervous and tired, waiting for it to be bedtime, would have the chance (either by happenstance or by choice) to come upon *Le mani sporche* probably for the first time. This would be the first time many would have heard of Sartre, would have seen a 'difficult' piece of theater and would have the choice at that moment to do something else to fill their evening. To deny this situation, to not make *Le mani sporche*, or rather to not 'dirty' our hands in a work that is not film since we don't have to make a film, not a theater piece since it is not in a theater, not television because it is not specifically made for television, it would be only an 'apparency' for the audience that wants something from us. The majority would probably want a soap opera? On the contrary, I think that this 'situation' would be accepted just as it is and always as a 'game.' But every game has its rules.

5. *Theater and the World*

The rules of our game, with *Le mani sporche*, are simple: to prevent the television viewer from considering *Le mani sporche* as 'true' in the televisual sense, in the TV series sense, 'true' in the sense of 'realistic,' of "that's exactly how things happen," of "you think you were there," of "it was just like that," in the sense of 'literalness,' which is precisely that of television production. Sartre wrote this play along the strict lines of nineteenth-century French dramaturgy without reserve, or as he would say, in completely bad faith. There are many *coups-de-théâtre*, situations are taken to the limits of the most pure artifice, personal conflicts are built around appearances — although these aren't verifiable — of this 'real-real' we all 'pretend' to know. The 'real-real' apparencies do not interest Sartre. They are sheer pretexts to the creation of his myths. Sartre aims to show his own self-doubling in Hugo-Hoederer, in pure-impure, in subjective-objective, in metaphysician-realist, in true-false, in playful-serious; and he does it with extreme 'theatrical' lucidity, in employing the theater as the best means of representing the falsity of his — and our — state of secession. He wrote every word of the play 'inside' and 'outside' the characters and situations, so that the spectator has the same possibility of entering or exiting 'reality' as it is proposed by the play, to evaluate, judge, 'live' the hopeless fiction of this reality; continually recalling that it all takes place in a theater, in revealing the doubt that *everything* is but theater, fiction, comedy, that *everything* is 'false': that life itself is false. The theater becomes the world. Theater & world — two entities dedicated to staging fictions. And yet one must pretend that life is important well before coming to the theater to search for significance. You have to pretend to not know about death. One must pretend that everything that happens is 'real.' You must pretend to take on these borrowed ideas like costumes in front of others who themselves must pretend, so as to guarantee the continuity of life and the denial of death. You must act like nature and society are the same thing, as if an executive order was the same as a clap of thunder, as if unemployment was the same as a flood, as if war was the same as an earthquake, as if socialism was the calm after the storm.

6. *The Free Mortal*

In the theater and in the world, we pretend to live to avoid dying. Sartre said: "We ought rather to compare ourselves to a man condemned to death who is bravely preparing himself for the ultimate penalty, who is doing everything possible to make a good showing on the scaffold, and who meanwhile is carried off by a flu epidemic."[3] "But the unique quality of death is the fact that it can always before the end surprise those who wait for it at such and such a date."[4] Wouldn't this "scaffolding" stand in for the "stage"? And this desire to "look good" be a role "well played"? "Thus death is not *my* possibility of no longer realizing a presence in the world but rather *an always possible nihilation of my possibles which is outside my possibilities.*"[5] "Thus it is necessary to consider our life as being made up not only of waitings but of waitings which themselves wait for waitings. There we have the structure of selfness: to be oneself is to come to oneself."[6] "If this is the case, we can no longer even say that death confers a meaning on life from the outside; a meaning can come only from subjectivity. Since death does not appear on the foundation of our freedom, it can only *remove all meaning from life*. If I am a waiting for waitings for waiting and if suddenly the object of my final waiting and the one who awaits it are suppressed, the waiting takes on retrospectively the character of *absurdity*."[7] "My project toward a particular death is comprehensible [...] but not the project toward my death as the undetermined possibility of no longer realizing a presence in the world, for this project would be the destruction of all projects. Thus death can not be my peculiar possibility; it can not even be one of my possibilities."[8] "It [death] does not penetrate me. The freedom which is *my freedom* remains total and infinite. Death is not an obstacle to my projects; it is only a destiny of these projects elsewhere. And this is not because death does not limit my freedom but because freedom never encounters this limit. I am not 'free to die,' but I am a free mortal. Since death escapes my projects because it is unrealizable, I myself escape death in my very project. [...] Therefore we can neither think of death nor wait for it nor arm ourselves against it; but also our projects as projects are independent of death—"[9] I am not condemned to die. "I am condemned to be free." I would say that some of these quotations could be said by Hugo, the rest by Hoederer during the performance.

3. Ibid., 683.

4. Ibid., 686.

5. Ibid., 687.

6. Ibid., 688.

7. Ibid., Part Four, Section II, "Freedom and Facticity: The Situation."

8. Ibid.

9. Ibid.

ELIO PETRI · COMMENTS ON HIS OWN FILMS (1976–1979)

7. *Hugo has no Project*

At the start, Hugo waits for the Hugo who "must come." His own project is still inconclusive & vague, despite the apparent 'purity' of his ideas, since he still hasn't decided that death is foreign to human projects. In the play, he tells us his purity resembles death. It isn't a project; it's a state, like death is for the dead. Hugo can't keep to himself his sense of unreality toward his presence in the world, and thus brings it up constantly because he still has not experienced death as outside his possibilities. To put it bluntly, Hugo is suicidal. He says he wants to die. He says that we are true only when we are dead and six feet under. In the end, he dies willingly and by choice. His project remains in limbo. Only death is true; the rest, the modifying of reality — thus the project — cannot be true: in its shadow, it seems absurd. Even Hoederer's death isn't part of his project. To cause a death or to die is the same thing: you are always alone. (Killing is to be killed). Sartre is *against* suicide, since he is *for* a project. "Suicide can not be considered as an end of life for which I should be the unique foundation. Since it is an act of my life, indeed, it itself requires a meaning which only the future can give to it; but as it is the last act of my life, it is denied this future. Thus it remains totally undetermined. [...] Will the outcome not show me that other solutions were possible? But since these solutions can be only my own projects, they can appear only if I live. Suicide is an absurdity which causes my life to be submerged in the absurd."[10] The only way to give significance to his own life is to have a project. If this project is confused with death, if death becomes the project, if to cause or experience death becomes the goal, then life is absurd. For that reason, Hugo feels all the absurdity of his life as well as the absurdity of Hoederer's death. And Hugo is without a project. And it is for this reason that he isn't even capable of understanding whether he killed out of jealousy or to eliminate an "enemy of the people." He is not "salvageable" because he belongs to death: that is what he cries out at the end.

10. Ibid.

8. *Hoederer and the Idea of Death*

Hoederer has *his* project. He experienced death as apart from his project, as foreign to social reality. "He attributes reality more to the world than to himself," as Sartre said about those who live in "the spirit of seriousness."[11] Hoederer is a revolutionary who wants to change the world, to eliminate class, to create a socialist society. All means are valid, even political assassination. But the idea of death inherent to political assassination is not the goal of his project — since it would turn it into the absurd — but only a means. (It seems to me one can dispute that; whether death, in intervening as a means in the struggle to realize a project doesn't automatically become a goal — as I believe — and whether such a discourse is only between the lines in *Le mani sporche* or, instead, is front and center.) Hoederer is this project. He hurries to accomplish a tactical advance of this project, since he feels his own death could slow down its realization: project and death come together but are never confused in his conscience. If, for him, death were mixed with his project, it would become absurd. For Hoederer, this is impossible. Death is not part of the reality of the world. The world isn't absurd, it *is*. It *is* unjust, it *is* imperfect, it *must* be changed. The world is, was, will be. It was and is unjust, and it will be better. Hoederer *is* entirely of such hope (hope will not die with Hoederer — hope is socialism). Reality, hope, party, socialism are beyond his own death. Hoederer is sheltered from the absurdity of his own death and simultaneously shields his project from death. For Hugo, death is his project. For Hoederer, he himself is his project. Hoederer is an instrument of socialism, of a collective project. His death, along the path of socialism, will be a mere accident. The party, socialism, the world become the same thing. And as the world remains indifferent to our death and continues to turn, it will be the same for the party and for socialism. No 'doubling' then, for Hoederer. He can't tolerate any hallucinations. Everything for him is true and real. It's for that reason that everything he

---

11. Cf. these two relevant passages on the spirit of seriousness: "The spirit of seriousness has two characteristics: it considers values as transcendent givens independent of human subjectivity, and it transfers the quality of 'desirable' from the ontological structure of things to their simple material constitution." "Many men, in fact, know that the goal of their pursuit is being; and to the extent that they possess this knowledge, they refrain from appropriating things for their own sake and try to realize the symbolic appropriation of their being-in-itself. But to the extent that this attempt still shares in the spirit of seriousness and that these men can still believe that their mission of effecting the existence of the in-itself-for-itself is written in things, they are condemned to despair; for they discover at the same time that all human activities are equivalent (for they all tend to sacrifice man in order that the self-cause may arise) and that all are on principle doomed to failure." Ibid., Conclusion II, "Ethical Implications."

'touches' or 'says' is *true*, is *right*, in the eyes and ears of Hugo and Jessica. That this characteristic of Hoederer is unambiguous is yet to be shown. There are traces of Hugo in him, of the youth he also was, of the 'purity' & the idea of death that he then had. Hugo asks him: "Are you afraid?" "Of what?" Hoederer responds. "Of death," says Hugo. Hoederer replies: "No, but I'm in a hurry" (which can also be understood as "I'm impatient.") "I'm always in a hurry. Before I didn't mind waiting. Now, I no longer can." This "being in a hurry" does not refer to the arrival of the two plenipotentiaries, but to death. Hoederer is in a hurry, as is Hugo; for Hoederer too, despite his project, hurries to compare himself with Baudelaire's *Le Vieux Capitaine*.[12] At this point in the play, he is in no hurry to meet the two men "before" the party comes to kill him. He makes it known to the regent's son and to Karsky in the next scene. He only says he is in "a hurry to die" since that directly answers Hugo's question: "Are you afraid of dying?" He hasn't in the least pushed death away. And we have the lingering doubt that Hoederer harbors traces of suicidal tendencies. He turns his back on Hugo, knowing Hugo is armed. In the conventional type of dramaturgy chosen by Sartre, such a move signifies: "You're not capable of killing me, Hugo." But Hoederer also wants to tell himself, "if he kills you, so much the better, your haste will be satisfied." Is there an explanation for the presumed suicidal thoughts of Hoederer? I think so. Indeed, he has the doubt that his political leanings aren't right, that the project of socialism would be better off not uniting with the opponents of communism. He says to Hugo, "We are never completely sure that we're right. Are you sure you're right?" And Hugo says yes. And Hoederer tells him that he has doubts of being wrong precisely at the moment that he dares Hugo to fire, as if to say, "if you want to shoot, understand that you may be right and I wrong; I could be an impediment to socialism." But in reality, Hugo, too, has this doubt of being wrong. Hugo and Hoederer resemble each other in their bad faith. However, a person must "act," even in bad faith.

12. Petri is referring to the concluding section of the poem "Le Voyage" from Baudelaire's *Les Fleurs du Mal*: "O Mort, vieux capitaine, il est temps! levons l'ancre! / Ce pays nous ennuie, ô Mort! Appareillons! / Si le ciel et la mer sont noirs comme de l'encre, / Nos c'urs que tu connais sont remplis de rayons! / Verse-nous ton poison pour qu'il nous réconforte! / Nous voulons, tant ce feu nous brûle le cervau, / Plonger au fond gouffre, Enfer ou Ciel, qu'importe? / Au fond de l'Inconnu pour trouver du *nouveau*!"

9. Sartre's Revolutionary

It is interesting to note that Hugo and Hoederer, despite certain ambiguities in their depictions, respond to the idea Sartre had developed of dogmatic materialism (Garaudy 1956, PCF 1946)[13] and of the 'true' revolutionary. Hugo represents dogmatic materialism while Hoederer is the true revolutionary. One is converted to materialism, Sartre writes, "as one is given to religious life. I would be tempted to say," he continues, "to define materialism as the subjectivity of those who are ashamed of their own subjectivity... [The Stalinist] believes in Marx, Lenin and Stalin; he accepts the principle of authority and, lastly, he retains the blind, calm faith that materialism is a certainty."[14] With this faith, Sartre writes, "[the young] are hounded even in their thoughts, which are poisoned at the roots, being condemned either to serve a philosophy they detest or, for reasons of discipline, adopt a doctrine in which they cannot believe. They have lost their carefree attitude proper to their age without acquiring the certainty of maturity. They are no longer footloose and yet they cannot commit themselves. They remain at the gates of communism without daring to enter or leave."[15] That is Hugo. The revolutionary, on the other hand, according to Sartre, has a *particular* repugnance for the idealistic tendency aimed at representing "changes in the world as governed by ideas, or better, as changes in ideas. Death, unemployment, poverty, hunger and strike-suppression are not ideas. They are everyday realities that are experienced with abhorrence.[16] [...] The revolutionary, crushed beneath reality, refuses to let it be conjured away. He knows the revolution will not be a mere consumption of ideas, but that it will cost blood, sweat, and human lives. It is his business to know that things are solid and can, at times, pose insuperable obstacles, that the best-conceived project encounters resistances that sometimes make it fail. He knows that action is not a happy combination of ideas, but a whole man's effort against the stubborn impenetrability of the universe. He knows that, when the meanings of things have

---

13. Petri is citing Roger Garaudy, et al., *Mésaventures de l'anti-marxisme* (Paris: Editions Sociales, 1956). PCF is the Parti Communiste Francais. For an examination of Sartre's relation to the PCF in English, see "Political Theory and Practice," Nik Farrell Fox, *The New Sartre* (London & New York: Continuum, 2003) 113–148, & 157–159.

14. Jean-Paul Sartre, *The Aftermath of War (Situations III)*, tr. by Chris Turner (Oxford & New York: Seagull Books, 2008) 185.

15. Ibid., 149-150.

16. Ibid., 233.

been deciphered, there remains an unassimilable residue — the otherness, irrationality, and opaqueness of the real — and that it is this residue that eventually stifles and crushes."[17] [...] In a word, the revolutionary's realism requires the existence both of the world and of subjectivity. More than this, it requires such a correlation between the two that one cannot conceive a subjectivity apart from the world or a world that would not be illuminated by the effort of a subjectivity."[18] Only human subjectivity reveals the adversity of the real, in and through the project that one hopes to realize by projecting one's self into the future. "[It] is by projecting themselves forward, by committing themselves to undertakings, that revolutionaries transcend the present. And since they are human beings acting like human beings, we must attribute to *all human activity* this ability to 'rise above.'[19] [...] But if he does, indeed, plan to 'change the world,' as Marx expressly states, that means he is originally a being for whom the world exists in its totality; this is something a lump of phosphorous or lead will never be, being merely a *part* of the world, played upon by forces to which it uncomprehendingly submits. This is because he transcends the world in the direction of a future state from which he can contemplate it, for it is by changing the world that we are able to know it."[20] And that's what Hoederer wants to be.

10. *A Family Group*

That's why Hugo loves Hoederer. (*Le mani sporche* is also a family drama, in which Hoederer is the father, Olga is the mother, Jessica and Hugo are the children, the party is God — while in Sartre's project it is man who becomes God, God who sees and decides all, even deciding to treat us like objects. Hugo wants to be like Hoederer, like the 'father': a way of 'having' him, possessing him in order to reject him. In his ambivalence, he loves him and hates him. Their relationship is also sexual. Possess or be possessed by Hoederer? And Olga? She protects him like a

17. Ibid., 234.

18. Ibid., 236–237.

19. Ibid., 243–244.

20. Ibid., 245.

mother, she gives him money, she opens her bedroom to him, she christens him Raskolnikov, she gives him advice regarding his 'uncle' Louis. Even Jessica — who everyone or everything wants to 'have' — immediately sees Hoederer as a 'real' person whose lips can't lie — with 'real' sexuality. And who, if not a father, can be so 'real'? The father is the first 'real' person to appear to us, even on the sexual level. And she wants to 'have' him for herself, to steal him from Hugo, like she wants to steal Hugo from Olga. When Jessica says: "He's my little brother," she means: "with him I play games, with you, I want to make love. Like a father, you *must* teach me about everything, even my body, even my sexuality."

11. *Purity, Obscenity, Games*

Hugo sees in Hoederer one of his possible projects actualized. Hoederer is the Hugo that Hugo wants to become. Hoederer is Hugo's ideal, what Hugo is not. But the fact that Hoederer already exists as the finished, tangible, and real model is a source of hatred for Hugo, since he, in his youth & purity, likes Hoederer and does not want to lose him. He does not want to become someone that precise. In getting rid of Hoederer, he uses death to get rid of his possible project. Death, however, cannot harm Hoederer's project, which is socialism. Hoederer chose to remove death from his project, although not completely achieving his goal. Projected into the future of socialism, it is as though Hoederer never died. Hugo's purity has the opacity and inflexibility of raw, inert materials; he loses all transparency of purity from the moment he hides behind an indecisive subjectivity, unable to make choices, the tension toward oblivion and death, the sense of the vanity of everything, and thus the unconscious desire to be projected, the desire that socialism doesn't exist, there is no future, that it all dies with him. "A bomb and the world disappears, and I with it." That's his favorite 'non' project. This is *his* purity. A purity tinged with the impurity of the lack of conscience & knowledge, and the rejection of reality. The obscenity of Hoederer, on the other hand, is so transparent that it is pure. It hides nothing, and in becoming one with the project, with the 'purity' of the project, it itself becomes purity. It is an impurity that, ridding itself of the idea of death and decomposition, becomes purity. It is Hugo who has the dirty hands of desiring death and oblivion. Hoederer has the clean hands of the 'true' revolutionary. Can we say that this is Sartre's game? I think so, since the artifice of setting, the theatrical touches, the situations that 'ring' false — in sum the 'ingredients' employed by Sartre to write this play — are as a whole symptomatic of the 'game,' up until the last situation, that is, the last reply. A passionate game ("Every human existence is a passion," says Sartre),[21] but still a game.

12. *Play & Seriousness*

Jessica and Hugo play. In writing *Le mani sporche*, Sartre has something in common with them. Hoederer, Olga, Louis, do "not" want to play. They are "serious." They are full of the "spirit of seriousness," which is opposed to playful activity. "Revolutionaries are serious." "The serious attitude involves starting from the world & attributing more reality to the world than to oneself…" (Revolutionaries "come to know themselves first in terms of the world which oppresses them, and they wish to change this world. In this one respect they are in agreement with their adversaries, the possessors, who also come to know themselves and appreciate themselves in terms of their position in the world. Thus all serious thought is thickened by the world; it coagulates; it is a dismissal of human reality in favor of the world." "It is obvious that the serious man at bottom is hiding from himself the consciousness of his freedom; he is in *bad faith* and his bad faith aims at presenting himself to his own eyes as a consequence; everything is a consequence for him, and there is never any beginning. That is why he is so concerned with the consequences of his acts. Marx proposed the original dogma of the serious

21. The exact quote: "We will consider then that all human existence is a passion, the famous *self-interest* being only one way freely chosen among others to realize this passion." Sartre, ibid. 1992, 796.

when he asserted the priority of the object over subject. Man is serious when he takes himself for an object."[22] Hoederer, Olga, Louis, they all take themselves for objects, for instruments, for people given a mission by history, or by God. On the other hand, "Play [...] releases subjectivity. What is play indeed if not an activity of which man is the first origin, for which man himself sets the rules, and which has no consequences except according to the rules posited? As soon as a man apprehends himself as free and wishes to use his freedom, a freedom, by the way, which could just as well be his anguish, then his activity is play. The first principle of play is man himself; through it he escapes his natural nature [God]; he himself sets the value and rules for his acts and consents to play only according to the rules which he himself has established and defined. As a result, there is in a sense 'little reality' in the world. [...The] function of the act is to make manifest and to present to *itself* the absolute freedom which is the very being of the person."[23] Jessica, Hugo, & Sartre "play" in the sense that they do not renounce their own freedom, they assert it minute upon minute, and neither do they renounce the possibility of a "game" inherent to the spirit of seriousness. All three are theatrical. Sartre writes for the theater. Hugo and Jessica make 'theater' of their very lives and they 'also' use it to express their tendency toward seriousness. These two young people play to such an extent that they continually have to point out 'when' they are being serious, as though it's a rule of their game. For them, seriousness is a game. They are always using the words "game," "role playing," "fiction," "comedy," "theater," to continually remind themselves & the audience that they're in the middle of playing, even when it doesn't 'seem' like it. But who is playing if not Sartre, who is the man incarnate who created them and speaks through them. Who, if not him, made the rules for this game we are playing with *Le mani sporche*: with him and his characters, and we the actors, the director, and above all the viewers?

22. Ibid., 580.

23. Ibid., 581.

13. Seriousness & Bad Faith

In various ways, Sartre comes out against "the spirit of seriousness," above all by showing his serious characters to be of "bad faith." Hoederer, Olga, Louis, all have bad faith throughout. (Hoederer has bad faith because, as previously mentioned, he leaves himself, as an opening to freedom, the "freedom to die." In some ways, his haste to die runs contrary to his "project." He plays with Hugo when he dares Hugo to kill him, he plays with Jessica when he gives into the temptation to help her achieve her sexual freedom.) (Olga plays with feelings in separating the party from love, she plays with the love and desire she shows for Hugo. The problem for her can be reduced entirely to a fiction in which Hugo 'pretends' not to be Raskolnikov and 'pretends' not to have killed Hoederer. She hides from the party and from herself the sexual origins of her desire to save Hugo). (Louis pretends to hate Hugo's anarchic intellectual side, while he hates his rivalry with Hugo, too ashamed to admit it, over the love of Olga). (These are the three characters of bad faith.) (Slick and George seem to be the only two free from bad faith. They are workers who want to change the world. They don't have any bad faith but they try to play 'bodyguards,' which is not their profession. At least they give the impression of being serious without seeming to be & without wanting to be.) But Sartre declares himself more explicitly against "the spirit of seriousness" to the point of affirming that "the main consequence" of his theories "must be to make us repudiate the *spirit of seriousness*."[24] "Many men," Sartre writes, "know that the goal of their pursuit is being…"[25] This knowledge leads them to attempt to establish projects. But within the limits that their attempt "still shares the spirit of seriousness and that these men can still believe that their mission […] is written in things, they are condemned to despair; for they discover at the same time that all human activities are equivalent […] and that all are on principle doomed to failure. Thus it amounts to the same thing whether one gets drunk alone or is a leader of nations.

24. Ibid., 626.

25. Ibid., 627.

§ 4.5 · SHORT NOTES, PRELIMINARY OBSERVATIONS

If one of these activities takes precedence over the other, this will not be because of its real goal but because of the degree of consciousness which it possesses of its ideal goal [...]." [26] "I never encounter anything except my own responsibility. That is why I cannot ask, '*Why* was I born?' or curse the day of my birth or declare that I did not ask to be born [...]. I encounter only myself and my projects [...]. I am condemned to be wholly responsible for myself. [...]. It is precisely thus that the for-itself apprehends itself in anguish: that is, as a being which is [...] compelled to decide the meaning of being — within it and everywhere outside of it. The one who realizes in anguish his condition as being thrown into a responsibility [...] has no longer either remorse or regret or excuse; he is no longer anything but a freedom which perfectly reveals itself and whose being resides in this very revelation." [27] "To be free means to be continually in the instance of freedom." Playing, freedom, responsibility, choice: they all run against 'the spirit of seriousness.' To be serious is to accept that life has value in itself. Freedom and playing require spending every moment of existence searching for the reasons to live.

14. *Triply Theatrical*

The two characters who carry the "play" on their shoulders, Jessica & Hugo, are also part of Sartre's "game." And they do it according to the rules established by others, refusing their roles to invest themselves in the different roles that they immediately reject. Jessica and Hugo thus make the play, with *their* play, doubly theatrical, since, as it happens, they never stop reminding the audience that they are performing a *play within the play*. But *Le mani sporche* has an additional theatrical direction, since this produces the state of *bad faith* in which Sartre puts all his characters. "In bad faith there is no cynical lie nor knowing preparation for deceitful concepts. But the first act of bad faith is to flee what it can not flee, to flee what it is. [...] If bad faith is possible,

26. Ibid.

27. Ibid., 556.

it is because it is an immediate, permanent threat to every project of the human being; it is because consciousness conceals in its being a permanent risk of bad faith."[28] The fact that the characters are placed in an infinite perspective of acts of bad faith makes the theatricality of *Le mani sporche* indescribable, since nothing is sincere in itself. From Sartre's lines, everyone plays someone whom they are not, even Sartre himself in his desire to exchange the cloak of philosophy for that of politics. And every act of bad faith is reflected in a parallel act of bad faith, even if of a different category. Bad faith in love is reflected in bad faith in politics, bad faith at the root of the party is reflected in bad faith directed toward the outside and vice versa, to the point that the play itself is a play of bad faith in which nothing is sure and nothing is true, except for the objects: Hoederer's coffeepot, the pistol, Jessica's clothes strewn all over the place, Hugo's typewriter, the photographs in Olga's room. A play in which all the characters never stop asking one another to trust and pretending to do the same, while they refuse it within the conscience of their own bad faith and that of others. So no real confidences can come out of it, not even for themselves. Their confidences kill. If nothing is sincere, if nothing is true, if no one is in 'good faith,' if everyone is in a play, that means that existence itself, lived this way, is not authentic. So in the theater, an infinite perspective of theater is reflected. Inside the theatrical construct, you are in a *whole castle of artifice*.

15. 'Our Game'

In this sense then, *Le mani sporche* cannot be 'true' unless it is as theatrical as possible. In this sense, the play cannot be presented 'to the letter.' It mustn't seem realistic. It mustn't be televisual. We find ourselves once again before this box endowed with a screen on which pass images programmed and broadcast from far off, and which is called a television set. In front of it, once again there is a man in slippers called a TV viewer. Everything

28. Ibid., 70.

that emanates from the TV set has an air of reality. The viewer's consciousness of the performance is based in large part on realism or literalness. Television 'says' it, so it must be true. The viewer didn't want to or couldn't go to the theater. Perhaps he reached the despairing conclusion "that all human activities are equal," that to read a book, go to the theater, make love, get drunk, are all the same, so he might as well accept the substitute of television that at least lets him stay in his cocoon. Our 'game' consists of breaking this illusion for him. We need to take him back to the theater, restore *Le mani sporche* to him for what it is: theater within theater, theater in the world. We need to constantly remind him that our game is the 'play' of theater, that theater and television are two different forms of 'play,' that everything presented to him as televised reality is a fiction. We need to constantly remind him that the essence of *Le mani sporche* is a triple theatricality: to not do so would be a betrayal of Sartre, of *Le mani sporche* and its philosophical content, as well as of the meaning of our 'game.' Everything: the set, the comportment of the actors, the lights, the camera positions, all must converge to bring the viewer to the theater. He should never have the idea that we are preparing him for a "good night's sleep" after viewing. He should see through Hugo's anguished eyes. All should seem simultaneously 'true' and 'false' as it does to Hugo. The wallpaper of the stage backdrop should seem more true than his wallpaper at home, but each door should open onto oblivion, and everything to him should seem *too* true to be true. That one day on this planet, sealed in a villa that could be in Hungary but *seems* to be a French villa, there would be men 'dreaming' to kill, to kill themselves, and their project would be socialism, that is, a society of free and equal beings, and that death, too, both theirs and that of others, would be one of the means of achieving their project. And all that in arguing, reasoning, 'talking' amongst themselves and in living, should seem to the viewer, as it seems to Hugo, to be 'true' and absurd: to be theater. The setting for our game must be beyond the small screen, outside the house where the TV set acts like Hugo's eyes. It must remain theater. The theater is the world and the history of the world.

Who should be at the theater this evening besides our sole, isolated interlocutor in slippers? Who can keep him company besides the characters in *Le mani sporche*?

16. *Stalin Among Us*

The beginning. The theater vestibule. In the background, the curtain is still down. We hear the audience's chatter. A man enters view with his back to us. He wears a threadbare overcoat and black hat. He carries a valise. He advances slowly, his back still to us, through the crowd. He stops at the edge of the stage. The house lights go down. The single beam of a spotlight lights the man's head. The curtain rises. The set is hidden behind a painted backdrop of an enlarged painting by Magritte: a suburban home with a single lighted window and a lamp. A clear sky stretches overhead. Now the young man turns to face us. He has a very young face, with razor stubble, feverish eyes and a sardonic smile. The man approaches the stage, the spotlight still trained on him. Slowly, we turn away from him to discover the theater's royal box and the solitary figure sitting in it. It's an old man with a large moustache. He wears a white military parade jacket, a medal and gold epaulettes: he resembles Stalin. The public takes notice of the young man with the valise in the theater. They watch the young man. The spectators are all young like him, but with long hair and beards and dressed like young militant leftists. The young man with the valise, dressed like a bourgeois out of the 1930s, is now on stage. He looks up at the royal box. Following his glance, we see the mustached man in parade uniform. His resemblance to Stalin seems more striking. Is he Stalin's ghost? Actually, he's an actor dressed as Stalin to remind us not only what he looked like, but of Stalin's presence among us. The young man climbs the stairs to the proscenium. He stops pensively in front of the Magritte backdrop, and then heads backstage. The backdrop parts. We are in Olga's house.

17. 'The Last to Leave'

The end. Hugo walks out of Olga's door. A spotlight hits him. He tries to scrutinize the darkness, then cries out: "not salvageable" with an indescribable richness that deforms his features into something monstrous. At last, he faces 'his' death, at last he can "look good" on the "stage-scaffolding." Five gunshots ring out. Hugo falls to the ground. He dies. The curtain quickly drops. One of Hugo-Giovanni Visentin's arms pokes through the curtain. Hugo-Giovanni Visentin realizes his mistake, his hand strokes the velour curtain. The arm quickly withdraws and disappears. The house lights go up. The curtain rises and all the actors return to acknowledge the public. The applause begins, but a few whistles are also heard. A fight breaks out in the young audience. We hear insults and slogans: "Provocateurs!" "The truth is revolutionary!" "No compromises with the bourgeoisie!" "Long live national unity!" "No unity with proprietors!" The myth's return is swift, like a spasm. 'Reality' is more vulgar than myth, as well as more tiresome in its opacity and impenetrability. The shadows of adversaries loom in the audience. Onstage, the actors are smiling and congratulating each another. The evening is over. The end is always sad. A light remains in the royal box. We catch sight of the semblance, the shadow, Stalin's ghost. He is the last to leave.

5.
ART CRITIQUE
(1979–1982)

§ 5.1 For Him, We Would Fight [1]

How can one talk about Picasso? I apologize if this sounds rhetorical, but I mean it. Where should we start? Picasso is the viewpoint and spirit of the West. Picasso is painting. He is the natural, biological, childish, and pre-Freudian desire to get our hands actively and instinctively dirty with pure color. But Picasso is also my and our life of ignorant young people, who, faced with his gifts, constructed complex and foggy discourses instead of being silent and thinking.

Should we start from the observation of how Picasso consumed himself in these terrible years of consumption, evacuation, and consumption again of all that is consumable and even in-consumable?

Should we start from the anecdotes about the visits to the first Picasso exhibitions here in Italy, in the postwar years? On those occasions, in those places, and among those people, a comical contentiousness emerged that clouded our vision and paralyzed our intelligence, and since then would prevent us from seeing Picasso as he is. On one side, the eternal philistines with little smirks on their thin stretched mouths and with their scared eyes; on the other, we "children of Picasso," unsure whether to call him Picasso or Picassò, animated by strong emotions, youthful misanthropy, and frenzied misunderstandings. We were ready to reproach but also bang the stubborn heads of the screeching

1. Originally published in *Corriere della Sera* (November 24, 1979). In November 1979, *Corriere della Sera* announced the inauguration of a museum dedicated to Picasso located in an eighteenth-century palace in the Marais area, the Hôtel Salé. Petri's text is a response to this event.

majority that poured in the museum halls, blindfolded and salacious. And on the museum walls Picasso, who looked down at us with irony like a judge from the height of his class, or classicism, and also from the lows of his popular poetry, or quotidianness, all mixed together like saliva with a kiss.

Yet in those years and in those museum halls we were rehearsing the later spectacular relationship of diffidence and incomprehension, and fanaticism, between modern art and its audience, which is to say, between Picasso and us.

At that time, the cult of the 'new' was born, a push to that "moving forward" that Barthes described as the only way to "escape the alienation of present society." Picasso was part of that 'new,' even of the commercial 'new,' with one of his paintings worth a million dollars and perhaps he shrewdly let people believe this while all the time he was peacefully working, hearkening back to antiquity and classicism: cutting out a detail of Jean-Baptiste-Siméon Chardin's *Bénédicité*, painting a few dishes on a white tablecloth, reinventing a few centimeters of painting with his 'new' outlook.

The 'new' is what pushed blind consumption of objects, people, and ideas until annihilation. It is the mourning of the present, the impotence of the future. It is the American 'throwing it all away' and the American 'buying everything.' It is the neurasthenic desire of a metaphysical 'new,' an uncritical rejection of the old that dulls our sensibility to that very limited historical new that seeps through our fingers and in front of our eyes. Despite what it might look like, Picasso was the contrary of all that. However, in those years people started to understand Picasso in a consumerist way, not thinking about his art but rather other aspects.

There was Picasso the spectacle, Picasso the circus. I am not saying that Picasso wasn't also a show. Picasso was *also* spectacular. But his real 'text' was the 'text-tissue' as defined by Roland Barthes, and not the loud sound of a variety show orchestra that sometimes, for the love of irony, he would put up as a façade: it was purely and simply the text of painting.

It is we who disfigured painting into spectacle. Four hundred Picassos, or one hundred Rembrandts, all in one museum hall make for a nauseating Grand-Guignol show.

But how does that relate to Picasso or to Rembrandt?

Picasso is in his studio on Rue Schoelcher studying with his ancient gypsy eyes the relationship between himself and objects, between history and objects. He observes his coffee table, his newspaper that smells like ink, his jug. He is alone among silent twentieth-century objects, like Chardin was alone among eighteenth-century objects. His look demonstrates that he doesn't want to go 'beyond' things, but rather 'inside' things, into their essence. Picasso sits there, researching on our behalf the absolute innocence of color and form, within which, through the perfect taste of naturalness, he can filter all the barbarism of his time and all the history of his profession. In his painting *Maternité*, in that bovine Juno and in the child's terracotta arms, Picasso recalls Raffaello's *Sacra Famiglia*; he looks at it as serenely as an old materialist, with the irony of one who discovered and loved a monster that is first of all a cultural monster, a ghost of unreached and buried values, like that of Beauty, which died a virgin and untouched by the interested commerce of those who desire it.

So, where to start? Jean Cocteau hesitated when describing this great friend of his because "the singular mystery of his beauty, when a writer intrudes and concerns himself with it, threatens to taint with literature the *least* literate of the painters." And he would specify: "I am not going to write the *least* literate."[2]

Indeed. Then we should talk about Picasso's intellectual method (and we should add Stravinsky's as well).

This method can be useful to everyone: intellectuals and non-intellectuals, painters and non-painters, politicians and non-politicians, and to everyone else: educated and ignorant, and even illiterate people, as long as they are animated, like him, by a will to live in the middle of life, in its heart, with eyes wide open.

2. In the mid 30s, Picasso did however experience a crisis, a period during which he ceased painting and devoted himself solely to writing poetry. While he eventually returned to painting, he continued to write and so admirably that he gained the praise of Breton and others, such as Michel Leiris, who compared his writing to Joyce's. See Pablo Picasso, *The Burial of the Count of Orgaz & other poems*, ed. by Jerome Rothenberg & Pierre Joris (Boston: Exact Change, 2004).

Picasso's method consisted in rejecting any prejudice, in the light of the most 'disinterested' and natural irony; and irony is the mark of the true modern man, as well as the ancient one.

It was Picasso in the darkest period of Cubism who said to George Braque, who was showing him one of his paintings: "Too much Cubism!" And in this everyman sentence there is the whole of Picasso, even his unconscious. But most of all, there is his serene mocking of any scheme, of any prejudice, of any dogma. And Picasso's simple words don't only serve as a suggestion for the artistic world.

§ 5.2 The Report of the Onlooker[1]

1. *How should we call* the colors of Claudio Bonichi's painting? First of all, every one of his paintings speaks of Bonichi's clear and transparent tendency to monochromaticism. So we could rephrase the question this way: how should we call the *color* of Bonichi's painting? At this point in his work and in my thoughts, we also cannot say that Bonichi expresses himself through a real monochromaticism. We can, for now, talk about a 'certain' monochromaticism: where 'certain' stands for 'ambiguous' and maybe for 'imprecise.' No: we shouldn't use 'imprecise' for Bonichi's monochromaticism. The aura of the paintings in front of me is defined, essential, and in these paintings, nothing seems technically unexpressed or lazily left to chance and put there to create specious misunderstandings.

2. Bonichi's painting is of the kind that comes to fruition in the acknowledgment of the minimal gesture and every improvement or curtailment in it is equal to a choice that comes from beyond the technical level. Nothing is 'imprecise' in the colors or in the color of Bonichi's painting, then. But can we thus call 'ambiguous' Bonichi's monochromaticism without erring again? Maybe it can be called 'ambiguous.' In fact, it is not authentic monochromaticism, it seems like it, but in reality the colors that form the aura of these paintings are many, and not all of them are that similar.

1. Originally published for an exhibition of Claudio Bonichi's paintings at the gallery Il Gabbiano, Via della Frezza, Roma. The exhibition ran from May 11 to June 12, 1982.

3. Maybe we can comprehend Bonichi's color — or colors? — by taking a better look at these paintings, and noticing that a dialogue 'occurs' in them between a group of colors from which Bonichi almost completely excludes the primary colors: red, yellow, and blue. These big and arrogant protagonists, so prominent in the 'permanent' spectacle of modern art, are confined, in Bonichi's dialogue among colors, to a role as extras, or at most, as special guest appearances.

4. If a thing is yellow, a lemon for example, then let's have yellow, but only to avoid misunderstandings. Only so that the lemon can say: "I am a lemon."

5. With Bonichi, there is no ambiguity or imprecision with the colors red, yellow, or blue. He deliberately dodges their "being primary colors," which can often turn into brutality. He ignores, or pretends to ignore, their arrogance. He leaps over the historical problems connected to their grammar and their syntax. But isn't there hidden in this exclusion a certain vice of Bonichi, of something ill in him? I have to admit this possibility, not as a painter but rather as an 'onlooker,' since I see around me, in Bonichi's study and beyond its windows, many reds, yellows, and blues: all of them are shouting, screeching, and yelling, but 'outside' Bonichi's paintings. I must admit that his systematic exclusion of primary colors already happens in Bonichi's retina.

6. I could say that Bonichi's tendency to monochromaticism seems like color-blindness. What a discovery! All most respectable painters, that is to say, all painters who think with color, are to us simple 'onlookers' sick with color-blindness.

7. I ask Bonichi: "How would you call the color of your paintings?" He answers: "The color of earth." I object: "But there is no painting among all those right in front of us that seems of a truly 'earth' color." Bonichi says: "Maybe you're right." In order to explain himself, Bonichi grabs his painting board and shows it to me. He adds: "Look, these are the colors I use; first of all white, then a bit of black to make grey, natural burnt umber, yellow

ochre, red ochre, English blue for some backgrounds." Bonichi sounds apologetic. He adds, softly: "However, if you were to repeat your question, I would answer again that my paintings are the color of earth." Pointing to the figure of a young woman in the painting entitled *Circo immaginario* I ask him: "And how would you call the color of this girl's body?" Without hesitation, Bonichi answers: "earth color." But I don't give up: "You're telling me that the nipple, or the areola, is also earth color? Honestly, I don't think so." Talking this way I feel like I'm grilling him. Is this a crime? Is it a kidnapping of the colors red, yellow, and blue? Or maybe the under-occupation of three great, hardworking, popular colors, just a bit thuggish.

8. What if it were my own vision that sees too much red, yellow, or blue anywhere, except in Bonichi's paintings? As any other "onlooker" I may be suffering from a particular form of color-blindness, and if I were to start painting, I could provide evidence of that. But that would be a clinical test. Instead, Bonichi's paintings are a poetic test. Bonichi's 'color' comes from an intuition that becomes an idea when encountering things, and I can only see the things that Bonichi represents through the *ideas* they have become.

9. What do I see in Bonichi's paintings? I see in them some representations that have a fictitious quality only found in theater backdrops for example. Such representations happen on two levels, or in two dimensions, whose contiguity is apparent to me, as if all together the paintings formed a single one, one single uninterrupted narration, sliding into one another, the *natures mortes* next to the portraits. But if I say: "that fictitious quality only found in theater backdrops," am I sure that I am expressing what I see? Am I sure that I am making myself clear, even to myself? The word 'theater' is rich with meanings, and it surely can be misleading. And Bonichi's paintings don't exactly make me think of 'theater.' However, if that word came to mind, there must be a reason.

10. In his paintings, Bonichi seems interested in weaving some of his enigmas, which are not at all dark, or threatening, or gruesome. To me, his figurative style does not suggest nightmares (like Surrealism did) that impose on the 'onlooker' only one way of both dreaming and being awake. No. Bonichi's painting tells me: "I am your nightmare," or: "I am the world around you, your *umwelt*." Nor does it try to destructure my reality in the paradoxical way Surrealism did. Bonichi is no visionary, no destroyer.

11. I see in Bonichi's *natures mortes* the care of an old naturalist: dried bugs that almost seem to buzz, little pieces of cork, shriveled grapes, dried flowers, pairs of potatoes immobile in their earthly firmness, a spent match and an old cigarette butt just a few centimeters apart that, in the painting, become an abyss: all these are an analytical list of those dry leftovers of the trash of a garden near the sea, which the wind can playfully take into the house. All of these things cast small perpendicular shadows, meridian shadows, in a not-so-meridian light, on surfaces that become such only through contact with an object, without which they would remain mere color areas.

12. I point out to Bonichi one of the color areas in his *natures mortes*. I ask him: "How would you call this?" Bonichi seems not to understand, or he believes he doesn't understand. He thinks for a while then he answers: "I call it bottom." He pauses, then he adds: "Or, background."

13. I will use "background," too, to indicate the immaterial space that surrounds and illuminates these two potatoes, that becomes a tangible surface only through them, as it happens with memory when, in recalling an object, it thinks that it can become an objective fact itself. But doesn't "background" also recall a theatrical set?

14. These two potatoes could be us, Bonichi & I, while we talk about his trip to Cuba, where two sentinels at the La Havana port played cards with passersby, or about his children, a boy and three girls, who compete to bring him insect carcasses,

or while Bonichi tells me of his passion for theater or for Ingres, or while he tells me about his early years as a painter, with his grandfather, from whom a fresco in a house by the sea had been commissioned. These two potatoes could truly be us, Bonichi and I. Is this related to the understanding of Bonichi's painting?

15. Some bare-breasted young women peer out from other, bigger paintings as if they were at a window. All of their heads have been turned into theatrical masks, except one, the one from *Circo immaginario*, who is not only bare-breasted but also bare faced. Further, she is the only one in the middle of one or even two actions: with her dark-gloved right hand she's taking a panpipe to her lips, and with three fingers of her light-gloved left hand she mimics the movements of a ballerina with a top hat and high heels. So many symbols, everywhere! What about the gloves? They are a symbol of purity and high rank. White gloves in particular are said to allow a beneficial magnetism to be diffused from the tip of the fingers. What about the index finger? It symbolizes life. If a woman shows her bare breast, it is not out of provocation, but a sign of humility and begging. Through a theatrical mask, the universal 'self' finds the most direct way to manifest itself. However, I refuse to think that Bonichi intended, just like a sly creator of puzzles, to stuff his transparent figurations with so many occult meanings. Bonichi's cosmogony emerges as so intimate, humane, and modest, that it can only appear for what it is: a familiar cosmogony. In fact, the question is: are Bonichi's enigmas supposed to be unraveled? And are we sure that Bonichi's paintings really contain any enigma?

16. Here I come up empty-handed. It is difficult to approach an artist's work to try and understand it. But am I completely wrong? I thought I had grasped something: his shifting monochromaticism, for example, or the slight whiff of theatricality, the immateriality of his backgrounds, which become tangible matter when caught in memory, and then? And then, something related to the sea, like a light sea breeze gently blowing on these lemons,

these beach towels, these terraces, and even these young women, who perhaps are feminine epiphanies of a long gone summer at the beach, young women from a shooting gallery by the sea, little beach strollers, acrobats from the small circus on the coast, flea tamers, at times prostitutes who peep out between the shabby cabins, perhaps regular lifeguards. I now want to start this visit all over again: but not in Bonichi's studio. I entered in a windy house by the sea, with big rooms opening onto a sand garden, perhaps abandoned, and surely deserted at this moment. The walls are covered with an uninterrupted fresco, in which a man, unknown to me and to himself, opened and closed glimmers of his childhood in those places, in that house, in that sea breeze, and he was having fun, as if chasing butterflies, while capturing the mythical quality of his first meetings and fantasies. In this way, a lifeguard became Proserpine, her face a mysterious mask, and all the objects must be named, recognized, and listed so that they can become real, even a dying rose, and a butterfly at the end of his life cycle. The air from the sea has put its last veil on the colors of the fresco; it has softened them, so that now the eye sees them as one color. That's how it always is with frescoes, since the wall itself thins down colors, it reduces them to its porosity, to its own color; it tames them. I go from room to room; I follow the itinerary of the 'almost' monochromatic fresco, which unfolds like a theatrical representation. The fresco is also a theater. Memory is also a theater. When I reach the last room, I find the painter's tools left on the ground, in front of an unfinished part of the fresco, the most mysterious: a big naked woman with a small black mask that recalls the black stain of the groin; a grand neoclassical woman with a big belly, perhaps a mother, yet again another glimpse behind the curtains of the theater of memory, a great white body laid on a great bed of white sails, a body exhausted by mysterious feminine languor. Maybe here is the encounter between Bonichi's color with things, here is his idea: in the unwinding of a fresco imagined with the eyes of his childhood, within the big, windy beach house of his puberty.

6.
BRIEF ENCOUNTER

§ 6
Brief Encounter[1]

EXT — STREETS OF ROME — SUNSET

An old movie CAMERA wanders through a crowd of young people who pack Via del Corso,[2] all frantically looking for the famous "Camperos" boots. The CAMERA follows (TRACKING SHOT) a middle-aged man dressed in gray like actor Elisha Cook, Jr. in *The Big Sleep*. The man, whom we will call with his Social Security Number PTRRCL29H29H501C, suddenly turns and stops, as if he senses that he is being followed. Not expecting this abrupt change, the CAMERA keeps TRACKING into an XCU of the man smiling faintly. From the poor state of his teeth, we can guess that PTRRCL — we will shorten his name for practical reasons — must have suffered a lot in his life. On his big head is a wide-brimmed Borsalino, which fills the FRAME, surrounded by the purple light of a dark sunset.

CAMERA (after a short pause)
Are you pretending you don't know me?

PTRRCL turns his back to the CAMERA and slowly starts walking again heading toward Piazza del Popolo. The CAMERA SWIFTLY MOVES AROUND him, as if to block his way; now it PRECEDES him in MCU, while the unaware crowd of "Camperos" fanatics keeps moving around them.

[1]. Originally published in *Nuovi argomenti* (1982).

[2]. Via del Corso is one of the main streets of Rome; it is particularly famous for its highly priced shops.

PTRRCL (suddenly, whispering)
Why don't you leave me alone? We have nothing more to say to each other.

CAMERA
Once, you couldn't live without me.

PTRRCL (gritting his teeth)
Well, I can live without you now. Just look at me.

CAMERA
As usual, you are lying.

PTRRCL
When I was young, everything seemed more natural, even nature itself, even you, the least natural of all things. Can you believe it? Some even thought you were 'reality,' ha, ha, ha…

PTRRCL's bitter laugh echoes the word 'reality.' Then the man suddenly turns gloomy and pensive.

PTRRCL
I realized that I was getting old when I started to go to the movies as a duty. With books, it was the contrary. Perhaps that was another sign of aging? I guess that to make films and watch them one must be young, very young, maybe even a child, and must have the energy to dream.

CAMERA
What about Antonioni? He's no child, yet he continues to think and say that he can't live without me.

PTRRCL
That's because he can't grow up. A wonderful illness, although increasingly rare.

CAMERA

And what about Fellini, huh? What about him?

PTRRCL

He says that he loves you, but he cheats on you with Cinecittà.³ He loves Cinecittà, not you. He secretly sleeps at Cinecittà. The pine trees and the architecture of that place must remind him of the Fascist summer camps organized by the Opera Balilla in Riccione or in Bellaria.⁴ Studio Number 5 in Cinecittà, when the lights are down, is Fellini's only reality: it's his mother, his psychoanalyst, his amniotic liquid.

He pauses.

PTRRCL (CONT'D)

And then, well, they're poets, of course they love you. What do you expect? Bertolucci loves you, too. His films are a long, uninterrupted love letter to you. A flirt-film, worthy of a soap opera.

CAMERA

And what about Rosi?⁵

PTRRCL

A case of rare optimism. He staunchly believes that you can inform the world. Besides, other people even thought that you could lead a revolution, ho, ho, ho…

PTRRCL's sarcastic "ho, ho, ho" seems to echo "revolution."

CAMERA

Why are you laughing? There's nothing to laugh about. Those people really believed that; some still do.

PTRRCL

Really? Where are they now? What are they doing? Are they "entryists" at Fiat commercials?⁶ Did they turn to armed struggle? Do they kill by ZOOMING?

3. Cinecittà (Italian for "Cinema City") is a large film studio in Rome founded in 1937 by Benito Mussolini and his son Vittorio; it is now considered the hub of Italian cinema.

4. Opera Nazionale Balilla (ONB) was an Italian Fascist youth organization functioning, as an addition to school education, between 1926 and 1937.

5. Francesco Rosi (b. 1922 in Naples) is an Italian director, particularly famous for his films of the 1960s and 1970s, which had a strong element of social and political critique.

6. Entryism is a political strategy in which an organization or state encourages its members or supporters to join another, usually larger organization, in an attempt to expand influence and expand their ideas and program. In situations where the organization being 'entered' is hostile to entryism, the entryists may engage in a degree of subterfuge to hide the fact that they are an organization in their own right.

PTRRCL stops. He looks straight into the lens, with irony.

PTRRCL
A director's work is so unrealistic, so superfluous, that if he doesn't believe in something he will never find the energy to shoot a film. In a world so highly specialized as ours, a director's is the most non-specialized profession. A director is not an actor, nor a writer, nor a photographer, nor a dancer, nor a painter, nor an editor: he is nothing. Or, in other words: he is a failed writer, a failed painter, a failed politician, et cetera. So he believes in order to acquire credibility. His specialization is to believe. He believes in an idea, in a school of thought, in an aesthetic principle, or, what do I know, in money; yes, many directors believe in money, though they won't say it. They specialize in money.

The CAMERA SMOOTHLY moves around to FACE the man.

CAMERA
Everybody loves money. Are you telling me you don't?

PTRRCL doesn't answer. The CAMERA insists, with a Lubitsch-like tone,[7] and TRACKS into a CU of PTRRCL, as if it were smothering him.

CAMERA (CONT'D)
Do you like it or not? Are you ashamed to answer?

PTRRCL
You know that I have a soft spot for money. The problem is that I am not good at making money.

He stares into the LENS again.

PTRRCL (CONT'D)
What are you blabbing about, anyway? Don't YOU like money, huh? How much do you cost, per day?

---

[7]. Ernst Lubitsch (1892–1947) was a German-American actor, screenwriter, producer, and film director whose urbane comedies of manners gave him the reputation of being one of Hollywood's most elegant and sophisticated directors. His films were promoted as having "the Lubitsch touch."

CAMERA (without hesitating)
One hundred and fifty thousand lire, not including taxes.[8]

PTRRCL
And what about your accomplice? The one you sometimes 'bite,' the one you mix up with, the one that must be 'virgin' like the Virgin Mary, the one that must always be in the dark or it'll catch on fire, it will be ruined and all the work will be for nothing? How much does that one cost?

CAMERA
Are you talking about film?

PTRRCL
Precisely.

CAMERA
One thousand-one hundred lire, tax included, for 'virgin' film.

PTRRCL takes a small electronic calculator out of a pocket & starts multiplying and adding numbers. The CAMERA TILTS DOWN. CU of the calculator.

PTRRCL (O.S.)
In a ten week-film, working five days per week, you alone cost 7,500,000 lire. If we calculate thirty thousand meters of 'virgin' film, you and your friend together cost already forty million lire.

The CAMERA TILTS UP. CU of PTRRCL's tired face.

PTRRCL (CONT'D)
But you also know that a professional film might last longer than ten weeks and it consumes between fifty and sixty thousand meters of film. Lately a young director went over one hundred

[8]. Lira is the old currency of Italy (now it uses the euro). 150,000 lire roughly equals to $103.

thousand meters: but then he calls himself "The Autocrat," so he must have his reasons.[9] See? You cost too much. A too highly priced deflowering. I can't afford it. That's why I don't love you anymore. And I didn't include development and printing.

CAMERA (with an accusing tone)
In October, I shot a film in three weeks, and the director used only eight thousand-five hundred twenty meters of film; the film came out in November and it made a bunch of money. Just admit that you're not good at it. Don't blame it on others: on the producers' vulgarity, the distributors' illiteracy, the movie theater owners' greediness, the audience's unpreparedness, in short on the whole society. Just say you're not good.

The grin disappears from PTRRCL's face. His lips tremble, his eyes are filled with fear.

PTRRCL (staring in the distance)
Maybe I am not good, that must be it. I am not good. You know me, I am for things done well; and to do things well, one needs the ability to reflect, stubbornness, time, and thus also money.

The CAMERA seems cold, ruthless, Stroheim-like as it cruelly GETS CLOSER AND CLOSER to PTRRCL.[10] XCU of the man's eyes: they seem lost, and they're watery.

CAMERA
Why don't you understand that nobody gives a damn about things done well? And are you sure that you can do things well? Are you sure that you do and have done them well in the past?

PTRRCL (startled)
Well, no, I am not sure. But I do know that I want to do things well. That's how I am. What can I do about it?

9. Here Petri is referring to Italian director Nanni Moretti (b. 1953), whose first film was titled *Io sono un autarchico* (*I am Self Sufficient*, 1976).

10. Erich von Stroheim (1885–1957) was an Austrian-born film star of the silent era, subsequently noted as an auteur for his directorial work. As a director, Stroheim was known to be dictatorial and demanding, often antagonizing his actors.

ELIO PETRI · BRIEF ENCOUNTER

CAMERA
You have to change, this is my advice. Change. Tell a light, funny, tasty, and optimistic story. Maybe add a few bad words and a fart here and there if you want to be sure of success. The formula is always the same. I'll tell you, I know it by heart: "A film should offer the audience a relaxing experience after a hard day at work. It should be pleasant and fun in a simple way, without presenting the torment of complex feelings, but rather alleviating the strains of the day with great optimism, with a happier outlook on life." Aren't those great words?

PTRRCL
Who said that? Willy Hays?

CAMERA
No, it was Senator Luigi Scalfaro, the Undersecretary of Entertainment, at a film press conference. But it could have been the brothers Lumière themselves; these words have always been said and will be repeated forever and ever…

The CAMERA raises his voice, with growing passion.

CAMERA (CONT'D)
… even in a hundred or in a thousand years! That's the formula.

The CAMERA goes silent and the LENS, its only powerful eye, shimmers of its own light, an icy cold, implacable light that is reflected in the tears that roll down its victim's eyes.

PTRRCL (with muffled sobs)
Listen, I am only two years younger than *The Jazz Singer*,[11] you know, the first sound film, with a very young Myrna Loy appearing naked for a brief moment — she was a "chorus girl." Anyhow, the film came out in 1929, that's when I was born, the year of the Great Crisis, twelve years after Caporetto.[12] It was a

---

11. *The Jazz Singer* is a 1927 American musical film. The first feature-length motion picture with synchronized dialogue sequences, its release heralded the commercial ascendance of the "talkies" and the decline of the silent film era.

12. The Battle of Caporetto took place from October 24 to November 19, 1917, near the town of Kobarid (Caporetto in Italian, now in Slovenia), on the Austro-Italian front of World War I. Austro-Hungarian forces, reinforced by German units, were able to break into the Italian front line and defeat the Italian army. After this battle, the term "Caporetto" gained a particular resonance in Italy. It is used to denote a terrible defeat.

very cold winter when I was born, and the world was collapsing, and then it was put back together and it crumbled again, three or four times, and even more if one counts the collapses of entire cultural, ideological, political, & religious underworlds. Among piles of rubble and words, before the Second World War, I saw at least three small preliminary wars, and the harsh and stupid face of Fascism. Then war pretty much never stopped, and now there's talk of a new, definitive one. In the middle of all of this are so many dead people, the longest slaughter in the history of mankind: dead people, shot, hanged, tortured, cremated, massacred… and then friends who change and die, who betray you, whom you betray. It's a continuous metamorphosis of man, and thus of myself too, into something cold, artificial, and unknown, with the only certainty that we are helpless. How can I help it, if all I can only think of are sad & dramatic stories, and dark, black, pessimistic, and even desperate metaphors? In the past, these stories would have been considered dialectic, but today there is no need for dialectics. Now we must hide and conform. Everyone rejects pessimism because we went beyond it, we entered a pure void. Pessimism is too human. Optimism is human too, of course, but it's injected to create euphoria in those who will soon die. Even the political Left hides and conforms. All of this was born, after all, with the crisis of the idea of the Left. We can say that the Left and cinema were synonyms. Do you understand?

CAMERA

What are you… crying? Just stop it. I wasn't being serious. And then, you're not the only one who lived through this mess.

PTRRCL

Who is crying? Not me. Who is listening to you, anyway?

The man blows his nose in his handkerchief, pushed around by the young "Camperos" fanatics. Then he suddenly turns his face, standing still, toward something shimmering to his left.

PTRRCL (CONT'D)
Look over there.

For some reason, the CAMERA hesitates to FOLLOW the direction pointed out by PTRRCL, and doesn't move.

PTRRCL (CONT'D)
Look over there. Turn. Move it, PAN. PAN TO THE LEFT! Come on, do as I say. I am still a director, after all.

Obeying reluctantly, the CAMERA PANS TO THE LEFT to FRAME the window of a photography shop where several cameras and small old movie cameras are on display, like in a small, shimmering zoo. It's now EVENING and the street lights are on. Through the shop window, the small eyes of the cameras and the big eye of the CAMERA stare at each other mysteriously, while the reflection of the street lights shimmers on and through them.

CAMERA
Well?

PTRRCL
That's what you are: an ordinary movie camera. Did you think you were any different? Just a common, little camera. And you thought I would cry for you!

CAMERA (offended)
That's not true, I am a Mitchell, a Lady Mitchell in fact. I cost one hundred and fifty thousand lire per day and if you want to buy me you have to pay one hundred million. Got it?

PTRRCL
You're just an ordinary and violent means of production, like a machine to make shoes, or salami, or Coca-Cola, or…

CAMERA (fuming)

No. I am the Princess of movie cameras, the one used by Gregg Toland, James Wong-Howe, Gianni Di Venanzo, Otello Martelli, Luchino Visconti, and John Ford. Not only technicians, but also poets, philosophers, linguists, semiologists, anthropologists, sociologists, narratologists, theologists, theosophists, orthodox and heretic, wrote about me. And that's because I am ephemeral and cinematic: I dilate and shrink time and space at my will, I empty and then fill them again, I burn and recreate them, and I destroy them, because I am dream, I am the eye of the collective imaginary, I filter straight into the subconscious, I am totality, and I am power...

PTRRCL

Power? What power? That's the new video camera, which works with a film that loses and regains its virginity at will. That is totality, and power. You're like me, you're not electronic or telematic, you're not informatic. You were born in 1895, eight years before my dad and nine years before my mom; you're only seven years older than Zavattini, one year older than Montale, eight years younger than Caldarelli, and just twenty-years younger than Pirandello. End of the century, beauties at the beach, nickelodeon, vaudeville, this is what you were and still are. You are eighty-six years old, but this century burns through means of production at a crazy speed, so you're as obsolete as a woolwinder, or a lithographic stone.

Around PTRRCL and the CAMERA, a small curious crowd has gathered. Some people stand behind PTRRCL's shoulders to enter the CAMERA frame. Some are waving at the LENS. PTRRCL, who has calmed down, leans in toward the CAMERA.

PTRRCL (whispering)

Let's cross the street. I want to see what's playing at the Metropolitan Theater. Come, let's take a look at the posters.

PTRRCL crosses Via del Corso, dodging the "Camperos" fanatics, the taxis, the buses, and the motorcycles, in a cloud of smog. The CAMERA follows him. TRACKING SHOT. Then the camera frames the many young people standing at the movie theater's entrance.

> PTRRCL
> What are they screening?

The CAMERA TRACKS into a CU of the posters exposed in the windows of the Metropolitan Theater. PTRRCL's voice, O.S., reads the title of the film.

> PTRRCL (O.S.)
> *I fi-chis-si-mi.* Did you watch it?

> CAMERA
> I shot *I fichissimi*. So I didn't see it.

> PTRRCL (O.S.)
> What! What about Ford, Visconti, Toland...?

> CAMERA
> I can't go on without working.

The CAMERA PANS toward PTRRCL, who started walking again toward Piazza del Popolo, immersed in his thoughts. Then the CAMERA starts following him.

> PTRRCL
> So... how is *I fichissimi*?

> CAMERA (merry, fake)
> It's pleasant and optimistic. It's young. It offers a relaxing experience after a hard day at work. It is fun in a simple way. It doesn't present complex feelings.

§ 6 · BRIEF ENCOUNTER

PTRRCL
Scalfaro must be happy.

CAMERA
Very happy, in fact. But all the politicians are happy: Tatò, Berlinguer, Longo, Gelli, Martelli, Craxi, and Scoppola.

PTRRCL waits for the CAMERA to get closer and mimics the gesture, a bit absurd, of taking its arm.

PTRRCL
Listen, stop concentrating on me. Look at all those people over there. Focus on them. Look over there at the bus stop, can you see? There is a woman there. I know, there are many, but I am interested in one in particular. Can you see her? Zoom in. There she is. She's crying. Let's follow her.

The CAMERA suddenly turns and WHIP PANS in another direction, where two women are laughing with great cheerfulness.

CAMERA
There are two women laughing over there. I prefer them.

PTRRCL (sighing)
See, that's the thing. If I have to choose between two women, one laughing and the other crying, I would choose the one who is crying.

CAMERA
That's because you're a mannerist. You're all rhetoric. At least do it for your family…

PTRRCL (cutting short the CAMERA's words)
Sure, sure. Now I'm leaving. Don't follow me, there's no point. But I'm going to ask you a favor. Shoot me in CU, but from the

back of my head. Like this. My hat must fill almost the totality of the frame. Now let's pretend that the square is empty. It's empty and in black & white. It's miraculously empty, as it can happen only in a film. A nice and empty square. The pavement is shiny as if it has just rained. We asked Metalli, the fireman of the film industry, to wet it beforehand. Now, look, I'll turn in CU and I'll say — and listen well because I'll whisper: "I love you." Then I'll turn around and leave. And you tilt up into a crane shot, up in the air, don't be afraid, up, up, don't worry. Remember Paul Muni in *I am a Fugitive from a Chain Gang*,[13] when someone in the dark asks him, "Where are you going?" he answers: "I don't know." Well, I am leaving just like him, and good-bye. Then, when I am a tiny point in the frame, that's when the words "THE END" will appear on screen. We'll think about the music later. Got it?

PTRRCL enters the frame. CU of the back of his Elisha Cook, Jr.-style hat, which fills the frame. Suddenly he turns to face the CAMERA and stares at it.

PTRRCL (whispering)
I love you.

He turns around and walks away into the empty square, alone. The CAMERA TILTS UP on a CRANE SHOT. When it stops, the words "THE END" appear on the screen.

---

13. *I am a Fugitive from a Chain Gang*, 1932, by Mervyn LeRoy.

FILMOGRAPHY[1]

1. Elio Petri as Screenwriter & Assistant Director

1952

Roma ore 11 [Rome 11:00]

Director: Giuseppe De Santis

Screenwriters: Cesare Zavattini, Basilio Franchina, Giuseppe De Santis, Rodolfo Sonego, Gianni Puccini, and Elio Petri [not credited]

Cinematographer: Otello Martelli [B/W]

Camera Operator: Roberto Gerardi

Set Designer: Léon Barsacq

Costume Designer: Elio Costanzi

Composer: Mario Nascimbene

Director's Assistant: B. Franchina

Assistant Director: Elio Petri

Editor: Gabriele Varriale

Cast: Lucia Bosè, Carla Del Poggio, Maria Grazia Francia, Delia Scala, Elena Varzi, Lea Padovani, Raf Vallone, Massimo Girotti, Paolo Stoppa, Armando Francioli, Paola Borboni, Irene Galter, Eva Vanicek, Checco Durante, Henri Vilbert, Hélène Vallier, Alberto Farnese, Maria Pia Trepaoli, Michele Riccardini, Fausto Guerzoni. [Elio Petri appears in a frame]

Producers: Léon Wipf, Giorgio Adriani

Executive Producers: Paul Graetz for Transcontinental Film (Roma-Parigi), Titanus

Distributor: Titanus

Première: February 27, 1952

Running Time: 98 minutes

1. The sources listed in the Italian versions are: Roberto Chiti, Roberto Poppi, and Mario Pecorari, *Dizionario del cinema italiano. I film*, vol. 2, 3, and 4 (Rome: Gremese, 1991–1996); Aldo Bernardini, *Archivio del cinema italiano: Il cinema sonoro 1930–1990*, vol. 2 and 3 (Rome: Anica, 1992–1993).

1953

Un marito per Anna Zaccheo [A Husband for Anna]

Director: Giuseppe De Santis

Author: G. De Santis, Alfredo Giannetti, Salvatore Laurani, Cesare Zavattini

Screenwriters: G. De Santis, A. Giannetti, S. Laurani, Elio Petri, Gianni Puccini, C. Zavattini

Cinematographer: Otello Martelli [B/W]

Camera Operator: Roberto Gerardi

Set Designer: Carlo Egidi

Costume Designer: Paolo Ricci

Composer: Rino Da Positano

Director's Assistant: Giulio Petroni

Assistant Directors: E. Petri, Cesare Aldo Trionfo

Editor: Gabriele Varriale

Cast: Silvana Pampanini, Amedeo Bologna, Carletto Sposìto, Enrico Glori, Renato Terra

Producer: Vittorio Musy Glori

Executive Producer: Domenic Forges Davanzati

Distributor: Diana Cinematografica

Première: August 22, 1953

Running Time: 95 minutes

1954

Donne proibite [Angels of Darkness]

Director: Giuseppe Amato

Author: Based on Bruno Paolinelli's play *Vita nuova*

Screenwriters: Giuseppe Mangione, Giuseppe De Santis, Elio Petri, Gianni Puccini, B. Paolinelli, Cesare Zavattini, Siro Angeli, Gigliola Falluto

Cinematographer: Anchise Brizzi [B/W]

Camera Operator: Alberto Fusi

Set Designer: Virgilio Marchi

Set and Costume Designer: Elio Costanzi

Composer: Renzo Rossellini

Songs by: Carletto Concina

Assistant Director: Alberto Cardone

Editor: Gabriele Varriale

Cast: Lirna Darnell, Valentina Cortese, Lea Padovani, Giulietta Masina, Lilla Brignone, Maria Pia Casilio, Lola Braccini, Rossella Falk, Carlo Dapporto, Anthony Quinn, Alberto Farnese, Checco Durante, Roberto Risso, Tino Buazzelli, Aldo Silvani, Antonio Cifariello, Memmo Carotenuto

Producer: Piero Cocco

Executive Producer: Giuseppe Amato

Distributor: Cei-Incom

Première: January 27, 1954

Running Time: 94 minutes

Giorni d'amore [Days of Love]

Director: Giuseppe De Santis

Screenwriter: Libero De Libero, G. De Santis, Elio Petri, Gianni Puccini

Cinematographer: Otello Martelli [Ferrania-color]

Camera Operator: Roberto Gerardi

Set Designer: Carlo Egidi

Set and Costume Designer: Domenico Purificato

Composer: Mario Nascimbene

Director's Assistant: Leopoldo Savona

Assistant Director: E. Petri

Editor: Gabriele Varriale

Cast: Marcello Mastroianni, Marina Vlady, Angelina Longobardi, Dora Scarpetta, Giulio Calì, Fernando Jacovolta, Renato Chiantoni, Pina Gallini, Angelina Chiusano, Lucien Gallas, Franco Avallone, Cosimo Poerio, Santian Tucci, Gildo Bocci, Pietro Tordi, Gabriele Tinti, Olga De Poliakoff

Producer: Mario Silvestri

Executive Producer: Excelsa Film

Distributor: Minerva Film

Première: October 1, 1954

Running Time: 109 minutes

1955

Quando tramonta il sole [Sunset in Naples]

Director: Guido Brignone

Author: Gianni Puccini, Elio Petri, Paolo Ricci

Screenwriters: G. Puccini, Ivo Perilli, E. Petri, G. Brignone

Cinematographer: Gianni Di Venanzo [EASTMANCOLOR]

Camera Operator: Idelmo Simonelli

Set Designer: Ottavio Scotti

Costume Designer: Luciana Angelini

Composer: Salvatore Gambardella, arranged by Michele Cozzoli

Assistant Director: Michele Lupo

Editor: Gabriele Varriale

Cast: Maria Fiore, Abbe Lane, Carlo Giuffré, Mario Carotenuto, Alberto Rabagliati, Franco Caruso, Eduardo Passarelli, Giacomo Rondinella

Producer: Giuseppe Fatigati

Executive Producers: Giovanni Addessi for Trionfalcine

Distributor: Titanus

Première: December 31, 1955

Running Time: 98 minutes

1957

Uomini e lupi [Men and Wolves]

Director: Giuseppe De Santis

Author: Tonino Guerra, G. De Santis, Elio Petri

Screenwriters: G. De Santis, Gianni Puccini, E. Petri, Cesare Zavattini, Tullio Pinelli, Ivo Perilli, Ugo Pirro [not credited]

Cinematographer: Piero Portalupi [EASTMANCOLOR]

Camera Operator: Idelmo Simonelli

Set Designer: Ottavio Scotti

Costume Designer: Graziella Urbinati

Composer: Mario Nascimbene

Director's Assistant: Leopoldo Savona

Assistant Directors: E. Petri, T. Guerra [not credited]

Editor: Gabriele Varriale

Cast: Silvana Mangano, Yves Montand, Pedro Armendáriz, Irene Cefaro, Guido Celano, Giulio Calì, Euro Teodori, Giovanni Matta

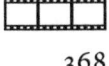

Producer: Alfredo De Laurentiis

Executive Producers: Giovanni Addessi for Trionfalcine, Titanus

Distributor: Titanus

Première: February 2, 1957

Running Time: 95 minutes

1958

Un ettaro di cielo [Piece of the Sky]

Director: Aglauco Casadio

Screenwriters: Aglauco Casadio, in collaboration with Tonino Guerra, Elio Petri, and Ennio Flaiano [not credited]

Cinematographer: Gianni Di Venanzo [B/W]

Camera Operator: Erico Menczer

Set Designer: Gianni Polidori

Composer: Nino Rota

Director's Assistant: Leopoldo Savona

Assistant Directors: Antonio [T.] Guerra, Fabio Rinaudo

Editor: Gabriele Varriale

Cast: Marcello Mastroianni, Rosanna Schiaffino, Silvio Bagolini, Salvatore Cafiero, Luigi De Martino, Carlo Pisacane, Polidor [Ferdinand Guillaume], Felice Minotti, Nino Vingelli

Producer: Nicolò Pomilia

Executive Producers: Franco Cristaldi per Vides Cinematografica, Lux Film, Cinecittà

Distributor: Lux Film

Première: August 16, 1958

Running Time: 102 minutes

1959

Cesta duga godinu dana [La strada lunga un anno — The Year Long Road]

Director: Giuseppe De Santis

Author: G. De Santis, Elio Petri, Gianni Puccini

Screenwriters: G. De Santis, E. Petri, G. Puccini, Maurizio Ferrara, Tonino Guerra, Mario Socrate

Cinematographer: Marco Scarpelli [B/W]

Camera Operators: Pasquale [Pasqualino] De Santis, Branko Blazina

Set Designer: Zlrmir [Zelimir] Zagota

Costume Designers: Oto Reisinger, Jogoda Buic Bonetti

Composer: Vladimir Kraus-Rajteric

Director's Assistant: Leopoldo Savona, Bosko Vucinic

Assistant Director: Franco Giraldi

Editor: Boris Tesija

Cast: Silvana Pampanini, Eleonora Rossi Drago, Massimo Girotti, Bert Sotlar, Milivoje Zivanovic, Gordana Miletic

Executive Producers: Ivo Vrhovec for Jadran Film [Zagabria]

Distributor: Cino Del Duca

Première: April 1959

Running Time: 130 minutes

[Produced in Yugoslavia, the film wasn't widely distributed in Italy — it was screened only in two cities. It was rejected by the Venice Film festival. It was screened at the San Francisco Film Festival in 1959]

Le notti dei Teddy Boys [The Nights of the Teddy Boys]

Director: Leopoldo Savona

Screenwriters: Elio Petri, Franco Giraldi, Tommaso Chiaretti, L. Savona

Cinematographer: Enzo Serafin [B/W]

Camera Operator: Giuseppe Ruzzolin

Set Designer: Ottavio Scotti

Costume Designer: Adriana Monaco

Composer: Armando Trovajoli

Assistant Director: F. Giraldi

Editor: Renato Cinquini

Cast: Geronimo Meynier, Corrado Pani, Enio Girolami, Massimo Girotti, Franca Bettoja, Alessandra Panaro, Luciana Angiolillo, Mario Carotenuto, Ave Ninchi, Andrea Checchi, Gordana Miletic, Giuseppe Porelli, Giulio Paradisi, Carlo Pisacane

Producer: Giuseppe Fatigati

Executive Producers: Gilberto Rossini and Ugo Tucci for Unia Film, ELIBO, Aurelia Film

Distributor: Major Film

Première: October 3, 1959

Running Time: 105 minutes

Vlak bez voznog reda [Train without a Timetable]

Director: Veliko Bulajic

Author: V. Bulajic

Screenwriters: V. Bulajic, Stjepan Perovic, Ivo Braut, Elio Petri

Cinematographer: Kreso Grcevic [B/W]

Set Designer: Dusan Jericevic

Costume Designer: Marko Cerovac

Composer: Vladimir Kraus-Rajteric

Assistant Directors: Pjer Majhrovski, Bero, Orlovic, Radenko Ostojic, Krsto Papic, Krsto Petanjek

Editor: Blazenka Jencik

Cast: Olivera Markovich, Ivica Pajer, Lia Rho-Barbieri, Inge Ilin, Velimir 'Bata' Zivojinovic

Executive Producer: Jadran Film

Première: March 14, 1959

Running Time: 121 minutes

[After studying at the Centro Sperimentale di Cinematografia in Rome, Veliko Bulajic returned to Yugoslavia in 1958 to direct his first film based on a screenplay to which Elio Petri collaborated. The film was never released in Italy.]

1960

L'impiegato [The Employee]

Director: Gianni Puccini

Screenwriters: Elio Petri, Tommaso Chiaretti, Nino Manfredi, G. Puccini

Cinematographer: Carlo Di Palma [b/w]

Camera Operator: Dario Di Palma

Set Designer: Carlo Egidi

Composer: Piero Piccioni

Assistant Directors: Elio Petri, Rinaldo Ricci

Editor: Nino Baragli

Cast: Nino Manfredi, Eleonora Rossi Drago, Andrea Checchi, Gianrico Tedeschi, Gianni Bonagura, Cesare Polacco,

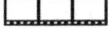

Pietro De Vico, Anna Campori, Arturo Bragaglia, Polidor, Sergio Fantoni, Anna Maria Ferrero [Elio Petri appears in a frame]

Executive Producers: Alessandro Jacovoni and Tonino Cervi for Ajace Compagnia Cinematografica

Distributor: Euro International Film

Première: January 21, 1960

Running Time: 104 minutes

Vento del sud [South Wind]

Director: Enzo Provenzale

Author: Giuseppe Mangione, E. Provenzale

Screenwriters: G. Mangione, Elio Petri, Armando Crispino, E. Provenzale

Cinematographer: Gianni Di Venanzo [B/W]

Camera Operator: Erico Menczer

Set and Costume Designer: Graziella Urbinati

Composer: Gino Marinuzzi Jr.

Assistant Directors: Armando Crispino, Leo Pescarolo

Editor: Ruggero Mastroianni

Cast: Renato Salvatori, Claudia Cardinale, Annibale Ninchi, Laura Adani, Ivo Garrani, Franco Volpi, Rossella Falk

Producer: Gino Millozza

Executive Producers: Franco Cristaldi per Vides, Lux Film, Cinecittà

Distributor: Lux Film

Première: September 1, 1960

Running Time: 98 minutes

Il carro armato dell'8 settembre

Director: Gianni Puccini

Authors: Tonino Guerra, Elio Petri, Rodolfo Sonego, G. Puccini

Screenwriters: Bruno Baratti, Elio Bartolini, Goffredo Parise, Giulio Questi, Pier Paolo Pasolini

Cinematographer: Silvano Ippoliti [B/W]

Set and Costume Designers: Danilo Donati, Mario Bedoni

Composer: Armando Trovajoli

Assistant Director: G. Questi

Editor: Gabriele Varriale

Cast: Jean-Marc Bory, Gabriele Ferzetti, Dorian Gray, Elsa Martinelli, Rossana Martini, Marisa Merlini, Romolo Valli, Catherine Spaak, Yvonne Furneaux, Bice Valori, Tiberio Murgia, Loris Gizzi, Giacomo Furia

Executive Producer: Nino Crisman per Film Napoleon

Distributor: Euro International Film

Première: September 24, 1960

Running Time: 96 minutes

La garçonnière

Director: Giuseppe De Santis

Screenwriters: Tonino Guerra, Elio Petri, G. De Santis, Franco Giraldi, Carlo Bernari, Ugo Pirro

Cinematographer: Roberto Gerardi [B/W]

Camera Operator: Pasqualino De Santis

Set Designer: Ottavio Scotti

Coreographer: Alba Arnova

Composer: Mario Nascimbene

Director's Assistant: Franco Giraldi

Assistant Director: Mario Tota

Editor: Otello Colangeli

Cast: Raf Vallone, Eleonora Rossi Drago, Marisa Merlini, Gordana Miletic, Nino Castelnuovo, Maria Fiore, Clelia Matania, Enio Girolami, Renato Baldini, Franca Marzi

Executive Producer: Roberto Amoroso for Ramo Film

Distributor: Variety Film

Première: October 12, 1960

Running Time: 90 minutes

Il gobbo [The Hunchback of Rome]

Director: Carlo Lizzani

Authors: Luciano Vincenzoni, Elio Petri, Tommaso Chiaretti

Screenwriters: Ugo Pirro, C. Lizzani, Mario Socrate, Vittoriano Petrilli

Cinematographers: Leonida Barboni, Aldo Tonti [B/W]

Camera Operators: Michele Cristiani, Ajace [Aiace] Parolin

Set Designer: Mario Chiari

Costume Designer: Pietro Gherardi

Composer: Piero Piccioni

Assistant Directors: Franco Giraldi, Guido Mazzarella

Editor: Franco Fraticelli

Cast: Gérald Blain, Anna Maria Freccero, Bernard Blier, Ivo Garrani, Pier Paolo Pasolini, Teresa Pellati, Ljuba Bodine, Enzo Cerusico, Nino Castelnuovo, Roy Ciccolini, Franco Balducci, Alex Nicol, Guido Celano, Tino Bianchi

Producer: Domenico Bologna

Executive Producers: Carmine Bologna for Dino De Laurentiis Cinematografica (Rome), Orsay Film (Paris)

Distributor: De Laurentiis

Première: December 1, 1960

Running Time: 103 minutes

1963

I mostri

Director: Dino Risi

Screenwriters: Age [Agenore Incrocci], [Furio] Scalpelli, Elio Petri, D. Risi, Ettore Scola, Ruggero Maccari

Cinematographer: Alfio Contini [b/w]

Camera Operator: Maurizio Scanzani

Set and Costume Designer: Ugo Pericoli

Composer: Armando Trovajoli

Assistant Director: Vana Caruso

Editor: Maurizio Lucidi

Cast: Ugo Tognazzi, Vittorio Gassman, Lando Buzzanca, Marisa Merlini, Ricky Tognazzi, Carlo Bagno, Mario Cecchi Gori, Luisa Rispoli, Michèle Mercier, Marino Masé, Daniele Vargas, Mario Brega, Lucia Modugno

Producer: Pio Angeletti

Executive Producers: Mario Cecchi Gori for Fair Film, Incei Film, Montflour Film (Rome), Dicifrance (Paris)

Distributors: Incei/Titanus

Première: October 26, 1963

Running Time: 118 minutes

2. Elio Petri as Director

1954

Nasce un campione

Director: Elio Petri
Screenwriter: Elio Petri
Cinematographers: Pasqualino De Santis, Arturo Zavattini [b/w]
Producers: Elio Petri, Pasqualino De Santis, Arturo Zavattini
Running Time: 12 minutes

1957

I sette contadini

Director: Elio Petri
Screenwriters: Cesare Zavattini, Luigi Chiarini, Renato Nicolai
Cinematographer: Roberto Gerardi [COLOR]
Composer: Claudio Nizza
Editor: Gabriele Varriale
Cast: Alcide Cervi
Speaker: Renato Cominetti
Producer: Quirino Papi
Executive Producer: A.B. Cinematografica
Running Time: 10 minutes

1961

L'assassino [The Assassin]

Director: Elio Petri

Authors: Tonino Guerra, E. Petri

Screenwriters: Pasquale Festa Campanile, Massimo Franciosa, E. Petri, T. Guerra

Cinematographer: Carlo Di Palma [b/w]

Camera Operator: Dario Di Palma

Set Designer: Carlo Egidi

Architect: Lorenzo Vespignani

Interior Designer: Giovanni Checchi

Costume Designer: Graziella Urbinati

Composer: Piero Piccioni

Songs by: Mina ("Rose" and "Come sinfonia")

Sound Engineer: Giovanni Rossi

Assistant Directors: Giuliano Montaldo, Adolfo Cagnacci, Fabio Rinaudo, Giorgio Trentin

Editor: Ruggero Mastroianni

Cast: Marcello Mastroianni, Micheline Presle, Cristina Gajoni, Salvo Randone, Marco Mariani, Franco Ressel, Giovanna Gagliardo, Paolo Panelli, Toni Ucci, Franco Freda, Carlo Egidi, Francesco Grandjaquet, Max Cartier, Andrea Checchi, Mac Roney, Corrado Zingaro, Ubaldo Mecacci, Loris Bazzocchi, Giuliano Montaldo, Lucia Raggi, Lina Ferri, Silvio Bastonelli

Producer: Gino Millozza

Executive Producers: Franco Cristaldi for Vides Cinematografica, Titanus (Rome), S.G.C. (Paris)

Distributor: Titanus

Première: April 1, 1961

Running Time: 105 minutes

[In the screenplay, the character interpreted by Marcello Mastroianni was called Alfredo Martelli, and the one interpreted by Cristina Gajoni was called Nicoletta.]

1962

I giorni contati [Numbered Days]

Director: Elio Petri

Authors: Tonino Guerra, E. Petri

Screenwriters: T. Guerra, E. Petri, Carlo Romano

Cinematographer: Ennio Guarnieri [B/W]

Camera Operator: Luigi Bernardini

Set Designer: Giovanni Checchi

Costume Designer: Graziella Urbinati

Composer: Ivan Vandor

Musical Director: Pier Luigi Urbini

Sound Engineer: Enzo Silvestri

Assistant Director: Berto Pelosso

Editor: Ruggero Mastroianni

Cast: Salvo Randone, Franco Sportelli, Regina Bianchi, Paolo Ferrari, Vittorio Caprioli, Marcella Valeri, Angela Minervini, Renato Maddalena, Alberto Amato, Giulio Battiferri, Piero Gucaione, Vittorio Bottone, Lando Buzzanca, Aldo Pini, Vittorio Donato, Silvio Silvi, Enrico Salvatore, Egidio Porzia

Producer: Anna Maria Campanile

Executive Producers: Titanus, Metro

Distributor: Titanus

Première: April 5, 1962

Running Time: 102 minutes

[The engravings appearing on screen during the opening titles are by Lorenzo Vespignani.]

1963

Il maestro di Vigevano [The Teacher from Vigevano]

Director: Elio Petri

Author: Based on Lucio Mastronardi's novel *Il maestro di Vigevano*

Screenwriters: Age [Agenore Incrocci], [Furio] Scarpelli, E. Petri

Cinematographer: Otello Martelli [B/W]

Camera Operator: Arturo Zavattini

Set Designer: Gastone Carsetti

Interior Designer: Giovanni Checchi

Costume Designer: Lucilla Mussini

Composer: Nino Rota

Musical Director: Franco Ferrara

Sound Engineer: Luigi Salvi

Assistant Directors: Vana Stefani Caruso [Vana Caruso], Berto Pelosso

Editor: Ruggero Mastroianni

Cast: Alberto Sordi, Claire Bloom, Vito De Taranto, Ya Doucheskaya, Guido Spadea, Eva Magni, Piero Mazzarella, Lilla Ferrante, Enzo Sancrotti, Anna Carena, Gustavo

D'Arpe, Ignazio Gibilisco, Bruno De Cerce, Adriano Tocchio, Tullio Scavazzi, Egidio Casolari, Aniello Coastabile, Lorenzo Logli, Enzo Savone, Olivo Mondin, Gaetano Fusari, Joris Muzio, Franco Moraldi, Umberto Rocco, Nando Angelini, Carlo Montini, Franco Tuminelli

Producer: Alfredo De Laurentiis

Executive Producer: Dino De Laurentiis Cinematografica

Distributor: De Laurentiis

Première: December 24, 1963

Running Time: 100 minutes

[Claire Bloom was dubbed by Adriana Asti.]

1964

Alta infedeltà — Episode: Peccato nel pomeriggio [High Infidelity: Sin in the Afternoon]

Director: Elio Petri

Screenwriters: Age [Agenore Incrocci], [Furio] Scarpelli, Ruggero Maccari, E. Petri

Cinematographer: Ennio Guarnieri [B/W]

Camera Operators: Danilo Desideri, Pasquale [Pasqualino De Santis]

Set Designer: Pietro Gherardi

Interior Designers: Giovanni Checchi, Ferdinando Giovannoni

Costume Designer: Lucia Mirisola

Composer: Armando Trovajoli

Sound Engineer: Luigi Salvi

Assistant Director: Berto Pelosso

Editor: Ruggero Mastroianni

Cast: Charles Aznavour, Claire Bloom

Producer: Fausto Saraceni

Executive Producers: Gianni Hecht Lucari for Documento Film (Rome), S.P.C.E. (Paris)

Distributor: De Laurentiis

Première: January 22, 1964

Running Time: 35 minutes

[The other episodes of *Alta infedeltà* include: *Gente Moderna* by Mario Monicelli, *Scandaloso* by Franco Rossi, *La sospirosa* by Luciano Salce.]

Nudi per vivere

Director: Elio Montesti [Elio Petri, Giuliano Montaldo, Giulio Questi]

Cinematographer: Ennio Guarnieri, Giuseppe De Mitri [EASTMANCOLOR]

Set Designer: Giuseppe Ranieri

Composer: Ivan Vandor

Editor: Elio Montesti

Cast: Negro African Dance Company, Club Drout, Chet Baker, Dupont and Pondu, Nancy Holloway, Marianette Regens, Patrick Maurandi, Les Oscar's, Lana Purua, Françoise Soleville, Rapha Temporel, Roger Stefani's Can-Can Dance Company, Michaeli

Speaker: Giancarlo Fusco

Producer: Carmet Bajot

Executive Producers: Lorenzo Pegoraro for P3 G2 Cinematografica

Distributor: Dear Film/Fox

Première: February 28, 1964

Running Time: 90 minutes

[The film is signed with a nickname composed of parts of the names of the three directors, with the goal of helping a producer facing a difficult time, Lorenzo Pegoraro, who was Elio Petri's father-in-law.]

1965

La decima vittima [The Tenth Victim]

Director: Elio Petri

Author: Based on Robert Sheckley's short story "The 7th Victim"

Screenwriters: Tonino Guerra, Giorgio Salvioni, Ennio Flaiano, E. Petri

Consultant for English Dialogue: Mickey Knox

Cinematographer: Gianni Di Venanzo [Technicolor]

Camera Operator: Pasqualino De Santis

Set Designer: Piero Poletto

Interior Designer: Giovanni Checchi, Dario Micheli

Costume Designer: Giulio Coltellacci

Composer: Piero Piccioni

Songs by: Mina ["Spiral Waltz"]

Sound Engineers: Ennio Sensi, Emilio Rosa

Choreographer: Gino Landi

Assistant Director: Berto Pelosso

Editor: Ruggero Mastroianni

Cast: Marcello Mastroianni, Ursula Andress, Elsa Martinelli, Salvo Randone, Massimo Serato, Milo Quesada, Luce Bonifassy, George Wang, Evi Rigano, Walter Williams, Richard Armstrong, Anita Sanders, Mickey Knox, Antonio Ciani

Producer: Jone Tuzi

Executive Producers: Carlo Ponti for Compagnia Cinematografica Champion (Rome), Les Films Concordia (Paris)

Distributor: Interfilm

Première: December 1, 1965

Running Time: 90 minutes

1967

A ciascuno il suo [We Still Kill the Old Way]

Director: Elio Petri

Author: Based on Leonardo Sciascia's novel *A ciascuno il suo*

Screenwriter: E. Petri, Ugo Pirro

Cinematographer: Luigi Kuveiller [Technicolor]

Camera Operator: Danilo Desideri

Set Designer: Sergio Canevari

Interior Designer: Giuliana Serano

Costume Designer: Luciana Marinucci

Composer: Luis Enríquez Bacalov

Musical Director: Bruno Nicolai

Songs by: L. E. Bacalov [music], Arthur Rimbaud [lyrics], "Pour rêver l'hiver"

Sound Engineer: Mario Bramonti

Assistant Director: Marcello Crescenzi

Editor: Ruggero Mastroianni

Cast: Gian Maria Volontè, Irene Papas, Gabriele Ferzetti, Salvo Randone, Laura Nucci, Mario Scaccia, Luigi Pistilli, Leopoldo Trieste, Giovanni Pallavicino, Franco Tranchina,

Anna Rivero, Luciana Scalise, Orio Cannarozzo, Carmelo Oliviero, Carlo Ferro, Tanina Zappalà, Michele Vannucci

Producer: Felice D'Alisera, Luigi Millozza

Executive Producer: Giuseppe Zaccariello for Cemofilm

Distributor: Panta Cinematografica

Première: February 22, 1967

Running Time: 99 minutes

Awards: Prize for Best Adapted Screenplay at the 1967 Cannes Film Festival; 1968 Nastro d'Argento prize for Best Direction, Best Actor (Gian Maria Volontè) and Best Actor in a Supporting Role (Gabriele Ferzetti)

1968

Un tranquillo posto di campagna [A Quiet Place in the Country]

Director: Elio Petri

Authors: Tonino Guerra, E. Petri

Screenwriters: E. Petri, Luciano Vincenzoni

Cinematographer: Luigi Kuveiller [Technicolor]

Camera Operator: Ubaldo Terzano

Set Designer: Sergio Canevari

Costume Designers: Franco Carretti, Giulio Coltellacci [Vanessa Redgrave's costumes]

Composer: Ennio Morricone [played by the experimental group "Nuova Consonanza," with Edda Dell'Orso's voice]

Sound Engineer: Mario Bramonti

Assistant Director: Mario Chiari

Editor: Ruggero Mastroianni

Cast: Franco Nero, Vanessa Redgrave, Georges Géret, Gabriella Grimaldi, Madeleine Damien, Rita Calderoni, Renato Menegatto, David Mansell, John Francis Lane, Valerio Ruggeri, Arnaldo Momo, Costantino De Luca, Marino Biagiola, Piero De Franceschi, Camillo Besenzon, Renato Lupi, Umberto Di Grazia, Giuseppe Bello, Bruna Simionato, Graziella Simionato, Giulia Menin, Snoopy the dog

Producer: Gino Millozza

Executive Producers: Alberto Grimaldi for P.E.A. (Rome), Productions Artistes Associés (Paris)

Distributor: PEA / United Artists

Première: November 14, 1968

Running Time: 105 minutes

[The paintings of Franco Nero's character are made by painter Jim Dine.]

1970

Indagine su un cittadino al di sopra di ogni sospetto [Investigation of a Citizen Above Suspicion]

Director: Elio Petri

Screenwriters: E. Petri, Ugo Pirro

Cinematographer: Luigi Kuveiller [Technicolor]

Camera Operator: Ubaldo Terzano

Set Designer: Carlo Egidi

Costume Designer: Angela Sammaciccia

Composer: Ennio Morricone

Musical Director: Bruno Nicolai

Sound Engineer: Mario Bramonti

Assistant Directors: Antonio Gabrielli, Lorenzo Magnolia

Editor: Ruggero Mastroianni

Cast: Gian Maria Volontè, Florinda Bolkan, Gianni Santuccio, Orazio Orlando, Sergio Tramonti, Salvo Randone, Arturo Dominici, Aleka Paizi, Vittorio Duse, Also Rendine, Pino Patti, Giuseppe Licastro, Filippo De Gara, Massimo Foschi, Vincenzo Falanga, Ugo Adinolfi, Gino Usai, Fulvio Grimaldi, Franco Marletta, Giacomo Bellini, Giuseppe Terranova, Roberto Bonanni, Guido Buzzelli

Producer: Romano Cardarelli

Executive Producers: Daniele Senatore for Vera Film and Marina Cicogna for Euro International Film

Distributor: Euro International Film

Première: February 9, 1970

Running Time: 115 minutes

Awards: Special Grand Prize of the Jury at the 1970 Cannes Film Festival; Academy Award for Best Foreign Film in 1971.

1970

Documenti su Pinelli (alternate title: Dedicato a Pinelli) Episodio: Ipotesi

Director: Elio Petri

Cinematographer: Luigi Kuveiller [B/W]

Director's Assistant: Ugo Pirro

Editor: Raimondo Crociati

Cast: Gian Maria Volontè, Luigi Diberti, Renzo Montagnani

Executive Producers: Comitato Cineasti against the Repression

Running Time: 12 minutes

[The film is divided in two parts: in the first, director Nelo Risi interviews the people who knew anarchist Giuseppe Pinelli; in the second, Elio Petri reenacts the different accounts given by the police about the defenestration of anarchist Pinelli, which happened on December 15, 1969 at Police Headquarters in Milan. As a sign of solidarity, the film was signed by many Italian directors, and it was distributed through an alternative circulation network.]

1971

La classe operaia va in paradiso [Lulu the Tool, or The Working Class Goes to Heaven]

Director: Elio Petri

Screenwriters: E. Petri, Ugo Pirro

Consultant for the Union: Mario Bartolini

Cinematographer: Luigi Kuveiller [EASTMANCOLOR]

Camera Operator: Ubaldo Terzano

Set Designer: Dante Ferretti

Interior Designer: Carlo Gervasi

Costume Designer: Franco Carretti

Composer: Ennio Morricone

Musical Director: Bruno Nicolai in collaboration with Alessandro Alessandroni's Cantori Moderni

Sound Engineer: Mario Bramonti

Assistant Directors: Antonio Gabrielli, Franco Longo

Editor: Ruggero Mastroianni

Cast: Gian Maria Volontè, Mariangela Melato, Salvo Randone, Gino Pernice, Mietta Albertini, Luigi Diberti, Renata Zamengo, Donato Castellaneta, Federico Scrobogna,

Giuseppe Fortis, Adriano Amidei Migliano, Ezio Marano, Flavio Bucci, Luigi Uzzo, Corrado Solari, Carla Mancini, Guerrino Crivello, Antonio Mangano, Lorenzo Magnolia, Giovanni [Nino] Bignamini, Eugenio Fatti, Renzo Varallo, Marina Rossi, Orazio Stracuzzi, Alberto Fogliani

Producers: Mario Cotone, Stefano Pegoraro

Executive Producer: Ugo Tucci for Euro International Film

Distributor: Euro International Film

Première: September 17, 1971

Running Time: 111 minutes

Awards: Grand Prix at the 1972 Cannes Film Festival [ex-aequo with Francesco Rosi's *The Mattei Affair*].

1973

La proprietà non è più un furto [Property Is No Longer Theft]

Director: Elio Petri

Screenwriters: E. Petri, Ugo Pirro

Cinematographer: Luigi Kuveiller [EASTMANCOLOR]

Camera Operator: Ubaldo Terzano

Set and Costume Designers: Gianni Polidori, Carlo Palazzi [Ugo Tognazzi's costumes]

Interior Designer: Massimo Tavazzi

Composer: Ennio Morricone

Musical Director: Bruno Nicolai

Sound Engineer: Mario Bramonti

Assistant Director: Rinaldo Ricci

Editor: Ruggero Mastroianni

Cast: Ugo Tognazzi, Flavio Bucci, Daria Nicolodi, Salvo Randone, Mario Scaccia, Orazio Orlando, Julien Guiomar, Cecilia Polizzi, Jacques Herlin, Gino Milli, Ettore Garofalo, Luigi [Gigi] Proietti, Ada Pometti, Luigi Antonio Guerra, Pier Luigi D'Orazio

Producer: Franco Committeri

Executive Producers: Claudio Mancini for Quasars Film Company (Rome), Labrador Film (Paris)

Distributor: Titanus

Première: October 3, 1973

Running Time: 125 minutes

[A painting by Renzo Vespignani serves as the backdrop to the opening titles.]

1976

Todo modo

Director: Elio Petri

Author: Based on Leonardo Sciascia's novel *Todo modo*

Screenwriters: E. Petri, in collaboration with Berto Pelosso

Consultant: Marco Ferronato

Cinematographer: Luigi Kuveiller [EASTMANCOLOR]

Camera Operator: Ubaldo Terzano

Set Designer: Dante Ferretti

Costume Designer: Franco Carretti

Composer: Ennio Morricone

Assistant Director: Umberto Angelucci

Editor: Ruggero Mastroianni

Cast: Gian Maria Volontè, Marcello Mastroianni, Mariangela

Melato, Michel Piccoli, Ciccio Ingrassia, Franco Citti, Renato Salvatori, Cesare Gelli, Tino Scotti, Adriano Amidei Migliano, Giancarlo Badessi, Mario Bartoli, Luigi Uzzo, Loris Pereira Lopez, Nino Costa, Guerrino Crivello, Marcello Di Falco, Giulio Donnini, Aldo Farina, Giuseppe Leone, Renato Malavasi, Riccardo Mangano, Piero Mazzinghi, Lino Murolo, Piero Nuti, Riccardo Satta, Luigi Zerbinati

Producer: Stefano Pegoraro

Executive Producer: Daniele Senatore for Cinevera

Associate Producers: Francesco Genesi, Giorgio Cardelli

Distributor: PIC

Première: April 30, 1976

Running Time: 130 minutes

1978

Le mani sporche [tv series] [Dirty Hands]

Director: Elio Petri

Author: Based on Jean-Paul Sartre's play *Les Mains sales*

Screenwriter: E. Petri [also translator]

Cinematographers: Alberto Savi, Nando Forni [EASTMANCOLOR]

Camera Operators: Gianni Bonaldi, Lorenzo Villa, Renzo Ratti

Set Designer: Filippo Corrado Cervi

Set Coordinator: Alberto Pizzarelli

Interior Designer: Letizia Amadei

Costume Designer: Barbara Mastroianni

Artistic Consultant: Lorenzo Vespignani

Composer: Ennio Morricone

Assistant Directors: Maria Teresa Manara, Enzo Di Francesco

Editor: Gianni Lari

Cast: Marcello Mastroianni, Giovanni Visentin, Anna Maria Gherardi, Giuliana De Sio, Omero Antonutti, Massimo Foschi, Pietro Biondi, Giorgio Trestini, Bruno Pagni, Umberto Verdone, Ferruccio Cainero, Giovanni De Lucia, Ezio Sancrotti, Bruno Rasia

Producer: Nazareno Marinoni

Executive Producer: Radiotelevisione Italiana – Rai Uno

Première: Rai Uno channel broadcasted the series in three episodes on November 14, 15, and 19, 1978

Running Time: 234 minutes

1979

Buone Notizie [Good News]

Director: Elio Petri

Screenwriter: E. Petri

Cinematographer: Tonino Nardi [EASTMANCOLOR]

Camera Operator: Ubaldo Terzano

Set Designers: Amedeo Fago, Franco Velchi Pellecchia [Franco Velchi]

Costume Designer: Barbara Mastroianni

Composer: Ennio Morricone

Sound Engineer: Giuseppe Muratori

Assistant Directors: Gianni Arduini, Fabio Terzetti

Editor: Ruggero Mastroianni

Cast: Giancarlo Giannini, Angela Molina, Aurore Clément, Paolo Bonacelli, Ombretta Colli, Ninetto Davoli, Ritza

Brown, Franco Javarone, Filippo De Gara, Giovanni [Gianni] Baghino

Producers: Stefano Pegoraro

Executive Producers: E. Petri & G. Giannini for Medusa Distribuzione

Distributor: Medusa Distribuzione

Première: November 22, 1979

Running Time: 107 minutes

[The previous title for the film was *La personalità della vittima*. Berto Pelosso filmed the sequences shown in various televisions throughout the film.]

3. Elio Petri as Theater Director

L'orologio Americano [The American Clock]

Arthur Miller's *The American Clock* was translated into Italian by Gerardo Guerrieri

Director: Elio Petri

Set Designer: Dante Ferretti

Costume Designer: Barbara Mastroianni

Composer: Piero Piccioni

Cast: Eros Pagni, Lino Capolicchio, Enrico Ardizzone, Ferruccio De Ceresa, Marzia Ubaldi, Franco Carli, Rachele Gersi, Claudio Gora, Ugo Maria Morosi, Camillo Milli, Giorgio Gallione, Carla Signoris, Massimo Olcese, Luca Dal Fabbro, Fulvia Bardelli, Linda Lippi, Marcello Cesena, Benedetta Buccellato

Première: The show debuted on Broadway in 1980. In January & March–April 1981, it was at the Teatro Duse in Genoa.

BIBLIOGRAPHY

ELIO PETRI: BOOKS

Roma ore 11 (Rome & Milan: Sellerio Editore Palermo, 1956; 2004).

L'assassino (Milan: Zibetti, 1962). With Tonino Guerra.

Indagine su un cittadino al di sopra ogni sospetto (Rome: Tindalo, 1970). With Ugo Pirro.

La proprietà non è più un furto (Milan: Bompiani, 1973). With Ugo Pirro.

Scritti di cinema e di vita, ed. by Jean A. Gili (Rome: Bulzoni Editore, 2007).

ELIO PETRI: INTERVIEWS

Joan Mellen, "Cinema is Not for an Elite but for the Masses," *Cinéaste*, Vol. 6, N° 1 (1973) 8–13.

Gaston Haustrate, "Le cinéma italien des années soixante," *Cinéma 74*, N° 190–191 (September/October 1974).

Jean A. Gili, "*Todo modo*," *Ecran*, Vol. 74, N° 31 (January 1977) 54–56.

Aldo Tassone, "Elio Petri," *Parla il cinema italiano* (Milan: Edizioni il Formichiere, 1979) 223–284.

Andree Tournès & Aldo Tassone, "L'Enfer selon Petri: Bonnes nouvelles," *Jeune Cinéma* (September/October 1980) 1–3.

ON PETRI: MONOGRAPHS

Elio Petri, ed. by Jean A. Gili (Nice: Faculté des Lettres Sciences Humaines Section d'Histoire, 1974).

Alfredo Rossi, *Elio Petri: Il Castoro cinema* (Florence: La Nuova Italia, 1979).

Jean A. Gili, *Elio Petri & Le Cinéma Italien* (Bassac: Rencontres du Cinéma Italian d'Annecy, 1996).

Felice Laudadio, *Rediscovering the Cinema of Elio Petri* (Rome: Cinecittà Holding, 2001).

Lucia Cardone, *Elio Petri, Impolitico: La decima vittima* (Pisa: Edizioni ETS, 2005).

Lucidita inquietà: Il cinema di Elio Petri, curated by Paola Pegoraro (Turin: Museo Nazionale del Cinema, 2007).

Claudio Bisoni, *Elio Petri: Indagine su un cittadino al di sopra di ogni sospetto* (Turin: Lindau, 2011).

L'ultima trovata: Trent'anni di cinema senza Elio Petri, ed. by Diego Mondella (Bologna: Pendragon, 2013).

ON PETRI: ARTICLES & BOOK CHAPTERS

James Roy MacBean, "The Working Class Goes Directly to Heaven, without Passing Go: Or, the Name of the Game Is Still Monopoly," *Film Quarterly* 26.3 (1973) 52–58.

Lino Miccicchè, "Le contraddizioni di Elio Petri," *Il cinema italiano degli anni '60* (Venice: Marsilio, 1975) 145–150.

Sandro Zambetti, "*Todo modo*: Ogni mezzo va bene per cercare di battere il regime DC," *Cineforum* 154 (May 1976) 245–52.

Roberto Alemanno, "Da Rosi a Petri: *Todo modo* dentro il contesto," *Cinema Nuovo* (July/August 1976) 266–75.

Raymond Lefèvre, "*Todo modo*: La classe bourgeoise va en enfer," *Cinéma* (March 1977) 91–92.

"Pour mieux connaître Elio Petri," *Jeune Cinéma* (December 1983/January 1984).

Millicent Marcus, "Petri's *Investigation of a Citizen above Suspicion*: Power as Pathology," *Italian Film in the Light of Neorealism* (Princeton, NJ: Princeton University Press, 1986) 263–282.

John Michalczyk, "Elio Petri: A Kafkaesque Moralist (Often) above Suspicion," *The Italian Political Filmmakers* (New Jersey: Associated University Presses, 1986) 210–234.

John J. Michalczyk, "The Political Adaptation: Rosi and Petri Film Sciascia," *Film and Literature* 6 (1988) 220–230.

Franz Everschor, "Faszination mit Gewalt und Tod," *Film-Dienst*, Vol. 47, № 20 (December 1994).

Maurizio Grande, "L'antro e il camerino," *Eros e politica: sul cinema di Bellocchio, Ferreri, Petri, Bertolucci, P. e V. Taviani* (Siena: Protagon Editori Toscani, 1995) 67–88.

Roberto De Gaetano, "Le maschere del politico (Petri)," *Il corpo e la maschera: il grottesco nel cinema italiano* (Rome: Bulzoni Editore, 1999) 87–98.

Ugo Pirro, *Il cinema della nostra vita* (Turin: Lindau, 2001).

Richard Drake, "The Aldo Moro Case in Retrospect," *Journal of Cold War Studies*, Vol. 8, № 2 (spring 2006) 114–125.

Ennio Morricone, "A Composer Behind the Film Camera," *Music, Sound, and the Moving Image*, Vol. 1, № 1 (June 2007) 95–105.

Larry Portis, "The Director Who Must (Not?) Be Forgotten: Elio Petri and the Legacy of Italian Political Cinema," *Film International* 44, Vol. 8, № 2 (2010) 17–29.

Daniela Bini, "The Failure of the Intellectual: Elio Petri's Filming of Leonardo Sciascia's *To Each His Own*," *Mafia Movies: A Reader*, ed. Dana Renga (Toronto, Canada: University of Toronto Press, 2011) 243–251.

Andrea Minuz, "Il doppio stato e le convergenze parallele. *Indagine su un cittadino al di sopra di ogni sospetto* e Piazza Fontana," *Strane storie: il cinema e i misteri d'Italia*, ed. by Christian Uva (Soveria Mannelli: Rubbettino Editore, 2011).

OTHER: with mention of Petri or his films

Carlo Lizzani, *Storia del cinema italiano, 1895–1961* (Florence: Parenti Editore, 1961).

Goffredo Fofi, *Cinema italiano: Servi e padroni* (Milan: Feltrinelli Editore, 1971).

Mino Argenteri, *La censura nel cinema italiano* (Rome: Editori Riuniti, 1974).

Lino Miccichè (ed.), *Il cinema italiano degli anni '60* (Venice: Marsilio, 1975).

Franca Faldini & Goffredo Fofi, *L'avventurosa storia del cinema italiano, raccontata dai suoi protagonisti (1935–1959)* (Milan: Feltrinelli Editore, 1979).

Franca Faldini & Goffredo Fofi, *L'avventurosa storia del cinema italiano, raccontata dai suoi protagonisti (1960–1969)* (Milan: Feltrinelli Editore, 1979).

Aldo Tassone, *Parla il cinema* (Milan: Edizioni il Formichiere, 1979).

Giorgio Tinazzi, *Il Cinema italiano degli anni '50* (Venice: Marsilio, 1979).

Lorenzo Quaglietti, *Storia economico-politica del cinema italiano, 1945–1980* (Rome: Editori Riuniti, 1980).

Lino Miccichè (ed.), *Il cinema italiano degli anni '70: cronache 1969–1978* (Venice: Marsilio, 1980).

Roberto Alemanno, *Itinerari della violenza: Il filme negli anni della restaurazione (1970–1980)* (Bari: Edizioni Dedalo, 1982)

Franca Faldini & Goffredo Fofi, *Il cinema italiano d'oggi (1970–1984), raccontato dai suoi protagonisti* (Milan: Mondadori Editore, 1984).

Mira Liehm, *Passion and Defiance: Film in Italy from 1942 to the Present* (Berkeley: University of California Press, 1984).

Vittorio Spinazzola, *Cinema e pubblico: Lo spettacolo filmico in Italia 1945–1965* (Rome: Bulzoni Editore, 1985).

Antonio Vitti, *Giuseppe De Santis and Postwar Italian Cinema* (Toronto, Canada: University of Toronto Press, 1996).

Angelo Restivo, *The Cinema of Economic Miracles* (Durham & London: Duke University Press, 2002).

Maurizio Fantoni Minnella, *Non riconciliati: Politica e società nel cinema italiano dal neorealismo a oggi* (Turin: UTET, 2004).

Maggie Gunsberg, *Italian Cinema: Gender and Genre* (New York: Palgrave MacMillan, 2005).

Mary Wood, *Italian Cinema* (New York: Berg, 2005).

Gian Piero Brunetta, *Il cinema italiano contemporaneo. Da "La dolce vita" a "Centochiodi"* (Bari: Editori Laterza, 2007).

Christian Uva, *Schermi di Piombo: il terrorismo nel cinema italiano* (Soveria Mannelli: Rubbettino Editore, 2007).

Peter Bondanella, *Italian Cinema from Neorealism to the Present* (New York: Continuum, 2008).

Claudio Bisoni, *Gli anni affollati. La cultura cinematografica italiana (1970–1979)* (Rome: Carocci Editore, 2009).

Alan O'Leary, *Tragedia all'italiana: Italian Cinema and Italian Terrorisms, 1970–2010* (New York: Peter Lang, 2011)

Ruth Glynn, Giancarlo Lombardi & Alan O'Leary, eds, *Terrorism, Italian Style: Representations of Political Violence in Contemporary Italian Cinema* (London: IGRS Books, 2012)

DISSERTATIONS

Lorenza Macciò, *Critica sociale, crisi individuale: Il cinema politico di Elio Petri negli anni della collaborazione con Ugo Pirro* (Pisa: Università degli Studi di Pisa, 2008–2009).

Laura Cusmà Piccione, *La frequentazione delle idee: Elio Petri e l'arte contemporanea* (Milan: Università degli Studi di Milano, 2008–2009).

DOCUMENTARY

Federico Baci, Nicola Guarneri, and Stefano Leone, *Elio Petri: appunti su un autore* (Milan: Feltrinelli, 2005).

WEBSITE

www.eliopetri.net

COLOPHON

WRITINGS ON CINEMA & LIFE was typeset in InDesign 5.0.
The text & page numbers are set in *Adobe Jenson Pro*.
The titles are set in *Berliner Grotesk & Schneid Handwriting Pro*.
The notes are set in *Duru Sans*, courtesy of Onur Yazıcıgil.
Photos courtesy of the Archives of the National Cinema Museum,
Torino & the Paola Petri Archive; digital editing by A. Segalini.

Book design & typesetting: Alessandro Segalini
Cover design: Alessandro Segalini

WRITINGS ON CINEMA & LIFE
is published by Contra Mundum Press
and printed by Lightning Source, which has received Chain of
Custody certification from: The Forest Stewardship Council,
The Programme for the Endorsement of Forest Certification,
and The Sustainable Forestry Initiative.

CONTRA MUNDUM PRESS

Contra Mundum Press is dedicated to the value & the indispensable importance of the individual voice.

Contra Mundum Press will be publishing titles from all the fields in which the genius of the age traditionally produces the most challenging and innovative work: poetry, novels, theatre, philosophy — including philosophy of science & of mathematics — criticism, and essays. Upcoming volumes include Richard Foreman's *Plays with Films,* Friedrich Nietzsche's *Greek Music Drama,* & *Selected Poems of Emilio Villa.*

For the complete list of forthcoming publications, please visit our website. To be added to our mailing list, send your name and email address to: info@contramundum.net

Contra Mundum Press
P.O. Box 1326
New York, NY 10276
USA
http://contramundum.net

OTHER CONTRA MUNDUM PRESS TITLES

Gilgamesh
Ghérasim Luca, *Self-Shadowing Prey*
Rainer J. Hanshe, *The Abdication*
Walter Jackson Bate, *Negative Capability*
Miklós Szentkuthy, *Marginalia on Casanova*
Fernando Pessoa, *Philosophical Essays*
Elio Petri, *Writings on Cinema & Life*

SOME FORTHCOMING TITLES

Richard Foreman, *Plays with Films*
Miklós Szentkuthy, *Towards the One & Only Metaphor*
William Wordsworth, *The Sublime & the Beautiful*
Friedrich Nietzsche, *Greek Music Drama*
Louis Auguste Blanqui, *Eternity by the Stars*
Emilio Villa, *The Selected Poems of Emilio Villa*
Robert Kelly, *A Voice Full of Cities: Collected Essays*
Jean-Jacques Rousseau, *Narcissus*

www.ingramcontent.com/pod-product-compliance
Lightning Source LLC
Chambersburg PA
CBHW080538230426
43663CB00015B/2637